Bus.

FUNDAMENTALS OF CORPORATE GOVERNANCE

A Guide for Directors and Corporate Counsel

Gregory V. Varallo
Daniel A. Dreisbach

SECTION OF BUSINESS LAW
AMERICAN BAR ASSOCIATION

01 00 99 98 97   5 4 3 2 1

Varallo, Gregory V., 1959–
        Corporate governance in the 1990s : new challenges and evolving
    standards / Gregory V. Varallo, Daniel A. Dreisbach.
            p.   cm.
        Includes bibliographic references.
        ISBN 1-57073-271-X (pbk.)
            1. Corporate governance—Law and legislation—United States.
    2. Directors of corporations—Legal status, laws, etc.—United
    States.   I. Dreisbach, Daniel A., 1956– .   II. Title.
    KF1422.V37   1996
    346.73 ' 0664-dc20
    [347.306664]   95-51336
                                                        CIP

Discounts are available for books ordered in bulk. Special consideration is given to state bars, CLE programs, and other bar-related organizations. Inquire at Publications Planning & Marketing, American Bar Association, 750 North Lake Shore Drive, Chicago, IL 60611.

CONTENTS

FOREWORD

> Corporate governance in the United States is not working the
> way it should. The problem . . . is the failure by too many
> boards of directors to make the system work. . . .[1]

This was the central theme of the widely debated paper by Martin
Lipton and Jay W. Lorsch entitled "A Modest Proposal for Improved Corporate Governance," which appeared in late 1992. Perhaps even more than they imagined, as Lipton and his coauthor
Harvard Business School Professor Lorsch prepared their Proposal,
corporate governance practitioners and board members were
witnessing the beginning of a sea change in that area. Because of
the evolution of a fiercely competitive global market, corporate
governance issues increasingly have been the focus of newly active
institutional shareholders, most notably the large public pension
funds.[2] During the first half of the 1990s, these investors have become more vocal in their demands for change, sponsoring formal
resolutions for stockholder consideration and openly criticizing
management practices.

The agenda of many large institutional investors also has
evolved from concerns related to defensive measures taken by corporations to corporate performance and related issues. For example,
in both 1993 and 1994 CalPERS, the nation's largest pension fund
with $91 billion in assets, selected its targets on the basis of "poor
long-term performance" with industry peers. One commentator
has described this new institutional focus on corporate performance as "militant monitoring."[3] This new "market" of perfor-

mance and accountability also appears to demand that the directors who manage the companies in which the institutions have large stakes are not merely independent of management, but, in fact, *act* independently of management.

Either coincidentally or as a reaction to the new era of "militant monitoring," the early 1990s also saw the beginning of a revitalization of the role of independent, outside directors. Courts, commentators, and activist stockholders all have expressed the realization that without active and functioning outside directors, the system is not likely to work. As independent directors again found their voices in the governance process, a trend appeared to develop in which outside directors stepped forward to exert their influence and to insist on change.[4]

In a much publicized example of this apparent trend, the board of directors of General Motors Corporation removed the company's chief executive officer as chairman of the executive committee of the board, replacing him with an outside director and, only months later, forced the resignation of the same executive, placing the chairmanship of the board in the hands of an outside director.[5] Not long after, the same board set the agenda for further institutional activism by adopting a comprehensive statement of governance principles calling for a more active and energized role for the company's outside directors.[6] No sooner had the GM board adopted its "Principles" than CalPERS wrote to every one of the top 200 Standard & Poor's companies urging them to adopt those principles.[7] Although by late 1995 the GM board turned the chairmanship of the board back to the new chief executive officer it had installed in 1992,[8] its Principles remain intact and continue to be a focal point for discussion several years later. Indeed, CalPERS itself, after years of urging others to adopt the GM Principles, recently adopted its own set of corporate governance principles for its thirteen-member board.[9]

Likewise, at Chrysler Corporation, an outsider-dominated board of directors was reported to have declined to extend the retirement date for its popular chairman and chief executive officer, despite his request that the board do so.

At IBM, the company first announced that the salary of its chairman and chief executive officer would be cut almost 40% amid widespread reexamination of executive compensation practices led by institutional shareholders. Only months later, IBM announced the CEO's retirement after months of persistent pressure from large shareholders.

Finally, at American Express, a "very public" debate ensued about a chairman/CEO who had met with the disfavor of certain influential stockholders in light of corporate performance. Following press reports that indicated that the chairman/CEO would retain several important roles, that same individual resigned, apparently after a breakfast meeting with representatives of several large institutions at which the stockholders registered their complaints. The American Express board then split the roles of chairman and CEO.[10]

In light of the emergence of institutional investors who perceive a role for themselves and their beneficiaries in corporate governance and the apparent revitalization of the role of independent outside directors, the 1990s likely will be a turbulent time for corporate governance and the individuals called upon to make the difficult decisions that are required in leading any large institution.[11] Whether or not Lipton and Lorsch were right that our system of governance was not working in the early 1990s, it appears that the forces exerted by institutional investors and the emerging global marketplace "for good or ill . . . will powerfully exert transformative pressure on corporate governance structures."[12] That process is upon us and is here to stay, focusing new and perhaps overdue attention on an emerging discipline: corporate governance.[13]

As practitioners of that discipline, we have attempted to distill practical advice for counsel, advising directors and board members themselves. We trust that the reader will understand that what follows is intended to serve only as a brief overview of the subjects covered, many of which are treated in significantly greater depth elsewhere in the literature.

Notes

1. Martin Lipton & Jay W. Lorsch, *A Modest Proposal for Improved Corporate Governance*, 48 Bus. Law. 59, 59 (Nov. 1992).

2. William T. Allen, *Defining the Role of Outside Directors in an Age of Global Competition*, 16 Director's Monthly (National Ass'n of Corporate Directors), Nov. 1992, at 1, 4 [hereinafter, "Outside Directors"].

3. James M. Tobin, *The Squeeze on Directors—Inside Is Out*, 49 Bus. Law. 1707, 1721, 1731 (Aug. 1994).

4. Ira M. Millstein, *The Evolution of the Certifying Board*, 48 Bus. Law. 1485, 1490 (Aug. 1993).

5. *See* Paul Ingrassia, *Board Reform Replaces the LBO*, Wall St. J., Oct. 30, 1992, at A14; Joann S. Lublin, *Management: Other Concerns Are Likely to Follow GM in Splitting Posts of Chairman and CEO*, Wall St. J., Nov. 4, 1992, at B1.

6. *GM Guidelines Embracing Lead Director Idea, Meetings of Outside Directors Praised by Investor Representatives,* Corp. Couns. Wkly. (BNA), Apr. 6, 1994, at 8.

7. James M. Tobin, *The Squeeze on Directors—Inside Is Out,* 49 BUS. LAW. 1707, 1733 (Aug. 1994).

8. Robert L. Simison & Rebecca Blumenstein, *GM Decides One Head Is Better Than Two,* WALL ST. J., Dec. 5, 1995, at B1.

9. *Heal Thyself,* CORP. CONTROL ALERT, Nov. 1995, 8.

10. Ira M. Millstein, *The Evolution of the Certifying Board,* 48 BUS. LAW. 1485, 1489 (Aug. 1993).

11. Joann S. Lublin, *Recent Wave of Activism in Boardroom Will Gain Momentum, Survey Suggests,* WALL ST. J., Dec. 9, 1992, at A5 (reporting on results of survey of board members commissioned by CalPERS); *and see* Korn/Ferry International, *Board of Directors Nineteenth Annual Study 1992* 14 (June 1992) (majority of chief executive officers surveyed anticipate increase in institutional investor involvement in governance).

12. *Outside Directors, supra* note 2, 16 DIRECTOR'S MONTHLY 1, 4.

13. E. Norman Veasey, *The Emergence of Corporate Governance as a New Legal Discipline,* 48 BUS. LAW. 1267 (Aug. 1993).

CHAPTER 1

Overview: The Role of the Board in Corporate Governance

When addressing the role of the board of directors in the governance of modern corporations, it is helpful to discuss two questions at the outset: the duties owed by a director (and collectively by the board as a body) and to whom those duties are owed. By generally addressing these issues at the outset, a more specific analysis of the role of the board in corporate governance becomes meaningful.

What Duties Does a Director Owe?

It often is said that directors owe duties of care and loyalty.[1] Directors of a Delaware corporation[2] also are held to a duty to disclose fully and fairly all material information when seeking stockholder action.[3] The various formulations of the duties of loyalty, care, and full disclosure are, however, merely descriptive of the *way* in which directors are required to carry out their most fundamental duty: the duty to manage the corporate enterprise.[4] This "duty to manage" also has been expressed as a duty of oversight,[5] and is central to everything a director does. Delaware, as do many states, imposes the duty by statute: The "business and affairs of every [Delaware] corporation . . . shall be managed by or under the direction of a board of directors. . . ."[6] This statutory mandate contemplates either direct "hands on" management ("shall be managed *by*") or delegation to full-time professional managers who report to the board ("managed . . . *under the direction of* a board . . .").[7] The Model Business Corporation Act contains a similar statement of the duty but makes it clear that the corporation is managed generally "under

1

the direction of," rather than by, its board.[8] The *Corporate Director's Guidebook* follows the same formulation.[9] Indeed, the Delaware Supreme Court has recognized that "[t]he realities of modern corporate life are such that directors cannot be expected to manage the day-to-day activities of a company."[10] Obviously, most boards choose to delegate daily management of the company to a carefully chosen chief executive and professional staff.

As one might expect, the specific steps any board of directors takes to fulfill its duty to manage or oversee the management of an enterprise are not easily cataloged. Practically, and most broadly, discharging the duty of oversight in a large company involves giving careful attention to the selection of competent senior management, establishment of institutional norms and procedures, review and input into management-formulated strategy (or, in appropriate cases, actual formulation of strategy), and a careful and continuous monitoring of the performance of senior management and the enterprise itself.[11]

Perhaps reflecting the renewed emphasis on independent action by outside directors (rather than merely independence in appearance), the 1994 edition of the *Guidebook* deals with some of the board's oversight responsibilities more pointedly than typically seen in the literature. For example, the *Guidebook* now expressly suggests that the board's duty to evaluate the performance of the corporation and senior management includes "removal, when warranted" of senior management.[12] Likewise, reflecting the recent trend toward board self-examination evident in the General Motors Governance Principles, the *Guidebook* also suggests that the directors' oversight responsibility includes the responsibility to evaluate the "overall effectiveness of the board."[13]

The Delaware chancellor has suggested that the "monitoring" function of the board should be a key responsibility of outside directors and should take place not only in crisis situations but continually. The directors, writes the chancellor, "should have an active role in the formulation of the long-term strategic, financial and organizational goals of the corporation and should approve plans to achieve those goals; they should as well engage in a periodic review of short- and long-term performance according to plan and be prepared for correction when in their judgment there is a need."[14] Lipton and Lorsch go further, suggesting that the board's agenda be structured around an annual monitoring schedule that regularly includes a review of issues such as strategic planning and goal formulation, capital and manpower allocation and planning, and performance appraisals.[15]

In light of the fundamental obligation of oversight, classic formulations of the duties of care, loyalty, and disclosure serve to "flesh out" how the duty to manage must be discharged. Under Delaware law the duty of care is said to require directors to appraise themselves of all reasonably available material information before taking action,[16] i.e., to act in a fully informed manner after the exercise of that due diligence that is appropriate under the circumstances. Similarly, the duty of loyalty requires directors to discharge their duties unselfishly, in a manner designed to benefit only the enterprise and not the directors personally.[17]

Finally, the duty of full and fair disclosure, imposed under Delaware law, usually arises in the context of a board submitting matters to stockholders for a vote. In that context, the duty of full disclosure requires directors "to disclose fully and fairly all material information within the board's control when it seeks stockholder action."[18] Similarly, if directors volunteer information to stockholders, "the information must be stated truthfully and candidly."[19] Whether or not information is "material" to a particular decision is measured by the same test used under federal disclosure law.[20]

To Whom Does a Director Owe Duties?

Having set forth in a broad way the duties owed by a director, the next question is: To whom are those duties owed? At the outset, it may be helpful to address a common misconception on this point often found among directors elected or appointed by a special constituency, for example, a large stockholder. Such a director does not owe any special duties to the constituency that caused his or her election. As the *Guidebook* correctly states, the director is required to exercise independent judgment "for the overall benefit of the corporation and all of its shareholders, even if elected at the request of a controlling shareholder, a union, a creditor, or an institutional shareholder or pursuant to contractual rights."[21]

The simple answer to the question "to whom are duties owed?" is that directors owe their duties to the shareholder-owners of the enterprise that the directors manage. This sensible answer finds its roots in the very reason for the existence of a director's duties. Directors owe duties of a fiduciary nature because the property they manage is not their own, a necessary result of the separation of ownership and control that has characterized the development of the corporate form. It has been said, then, that because it was the shareholders' property that directors controlled, it was to the owners of that property that "fiduciary" duties flowed.[22]

Notwithstanding the soundness of the logic apparent in this view, the law has developed significantly since this rule of law was first announced. Today, one could argue that both the precise nature of the duties owed and the group to whom those duties run shifts based upon the economic condition of the firm and related external factors. Under this model, a director's duties (and those to whom the duties are owed) can be imagined to fall along a continuum, influenced importantly by forces outside the control of the enterprise.

At one end of this continuum is the case of the solvent corporation, the sale of which is "inevitable." Directors of that corporation owe duties to one group and one group only—the shareholder-owners of the enterprise. In this context, the duties of the directors come to this: to act in a fully informed manner to maximize the return to shareholders from the sale.[23]

At the other end of the continuum is the company that is not for sale but is "clearly" insolvent. Directors of this corporation are said to owe duties to creditors of the enterprise,[24] although there is no unanimous view whether such duties are owed *to the exclusion* of the directors' duties to shareholders or others. In New York, at least, directors of such a "clearly" insolvent firm are said to act as "trustees" for the company's creditors and to have a duty to husband remaining corporate assets for eventual dissolution or bankruptcy.[25]

Between these two poles is where the great majority of boards will operate. Directors of companies not clearly "for sale" and not "clearly insolvent" owe duties to the company's shareholders and to the corporation itself.[26] To say as much, however, raises more questions than it answers. What is "the corporation" and, if it is something more than merely the sum of its shareholders, how do the directors reconcile conflicts between duties to shareholders and duties to the corporation?

The Traditional Model and the Focus on Other Constituencies

The traditional model of corporate governance provided a complete answer to the questions raised previously: A corporation was nothing more or less than the sum of its owners' aggregate interests and the object of the enterprise was solely value maximization.[27] Two important assumptions underlying this model seem to have been that the interests of shareholders would always be consistent and would always coincide with the interests of the entity itself.

Neither assumption has survived recent developments unscathed. There are clearly times when the interests of shareholders themselves fail to coincide. For example, the short-term orientation of the professional arbitrageur often has been contrasted with the longer-term view of the "investor."[28] It follows, therefore, that if shareholders themselves cannot be said to share common interests in all cases, any governance model that views shareholders as monolithic and identical to the corporate enterprise itself is outmoded.

Moreover, the view of the enterprise itself has expanded dramatically. No longer is the corporate entity viewed as simply a collection of shareholders. Instead, some modern legal theorists view the corporate enterprise as a varied collection of stakeholders: employees, creditors, suppliers, community groups, etc.[29] Modern corporate legal theory is, however, less than satisfactory in answering the directors' practical dilemma: When faced with conflicts between the interests of corporate stakeholders and stockholders, how should the conflicts be resolved?

In all but the most extreme circumstances, it still appears that the director of a solvent corporation may safely resolve conflicts between stockholder and stakeholder interests in favor of stockholders. All but one of the state corporate statutes that address the subject *permit*, but do not *require*, that a director, when considering the "best interests of the corporation," take into account the effects of the action upon nonstockholder constituents, including the corporation's suppliers and customers and the communities in which the enterprise has offices.[30] Only Connecticut *requires* directors of corporations chartered there to take such factors into consideration in change-of-control situations.[31]

Delaware has no such statute, but several important decisions of the Delaware Supreme Court have sanctioned (but not required) consideration of nonstockholder interests in decision making at least in connection with a board's assessment of, and response to, a takeover proposal. In *Unocal Corp. v. Mesa Petroleum Co.*,[32] the court examined a defensive measure taken by the Unocal board of directors when faced with a hostile bid. In the now-classic formulation of the review that a Delaware court will give to defensive measures taken by the board of a company under attack, the court crafted a two-part test. A defensive measure would be upheld by the court if the directors reasonably perceived a threat to corporate policy and effectiveness, and the response crafted by the board was reasonable in relation to the threat posed.

In connection with the second part of this test, i.e., the reasonableness of the board's response to the threat posed, the court expressly stated that the board's analysis in this regard entailed "an analysis . . . of the nature of the takeover bid and its effect on the corporate enterprise." In analyzing the effect of the bid on the corporate enterprise and its shareholders, the court stated that directors' concerns could legitimately include factors such as "the impact on 'constituencies' other than shareholders (creditors, customers, employees, and perhaps even the community generally). . . ."[33]

It was in this context that the Delaware Supreme Court first gave express recognition to a role for nonshareholder constituencies in corporate governance.[34] Several years later, in the seminal decision in *Paramount Communications, Inc. v. Time Inc.*,[35] the Delaware Supreme Court expanded the scope of permissible analysis of nonshareholder constituency interests.

Time, like *Unocal*, arose in the context of a board of directors defending against an unwanted takeover bid. Unlike the Unocal board, however, the Time directors were not only fending off an unwanted suitor, they also were attempting to preserve their carefully chosen and long-negotiated merger with Warner Communications Inc., which the boards of both companies had concluded was threatened by the unsolicited Paramount bid for Time. In upholding the lower court's refusal to enjoin Time's defensive maneuvers to ward off Paramount, the Supreme Court expressly stated that the board's analysis of the impact of an unwanted offer on "'constituencies' other than shareholders" could extend to the board's analysis of whether a threat existed to corporate policy and effectiveness.[36] *Time* appears to allow the directors of a Delaware corporation the flexibility to take into account the effect of an unwanted takeover bid on constituencies other than shareholders at each step in its analysis of and response to such an offer. The board's consideration may include the interests of "creditors, customers, employees, and perhaps even the community generally. . . ."[37]

Although *Unocal* and *Time*, taken collectively, only address the "other constituencies" issue in the context of a hostile acquisition offer, with the exception of the case where the sale or breakup of the company is "inevitable," no principled basis appears for suggesting that directors of a Delaware corporation could not consider the impact of *any* decision on constituencies other than shareholders. If, as *Time* appears to confirm, directors may take into account such factors when under the enhanced scrutiny mandated by *Unocal*, it follows that without the specter of self-interest implicated by the presence of a hostile takeover attempt, directors also may take into account factors other than purely shareholder interests.[38]

Time also appears to place some emphasis on the directors' duties to the corporation qua corporation, as distinct from the directors' duties to the shareholders of the corporation. Although this approach has been criticized,[39] some commentators have attempted to integrate the emerging recognition of corporate and stakeholder interests with the more classic governance model. Professor A.A. Sommer argues, for example, that long-term value maximization must necessarily include consideration of stakeholder or nonstockholder constituency interests, and that without such consideration a corporation is not likely to be able to achieve long-term value.[40]

Any discussion of the Delaware approach to the issue is, however, incomplete without an analysis of the Supreme Court's decision in *Revlon, Inc. v. MacAndrews & Forbes Holdings, Inc.*,[41] a case decided after *Unocal* but before *Time*. *Revlon* reaffirmed generally that in responding to most takeover situations, a board could consider nonshareholder constituencies, but qualified the emerging doctrine by providing that consideration of nonstockholder constituencies was appropriate "provided there are rationally related benefits accruing to the stockholders."[42] This is an important limitation on the board's discretion to take into account nonshareholder interests, and tends to harmonize the Delaware approach to the issue with the more traditional model of corporate governance.

In *Revlon*, the board was faced with several constituencies, including an active group of noteholders who had threatened the board with litigation to recover for the loss in value of their notes as a result of board action that caused the value of the notes to fall precipitously. Although the breakup and sale of the company had become "inevitable," the board ended the auction by giving a lockup option to one of two competing bidders on the grounds that the favored bidder's proposal protected *noteholder* value. In doing so, the Revlon board expressly relied upon the Supreme Court's earlier holding in *Unocal*, which on its face appeared to authorize board consideration of constituencies other than shareholders in responding to a takeover. The directors argued that *Unocal* empowered them to take a suboptimal price for shareholders because they were protecting the interests of another important (and possibly litigious) constituency.

The Supreme Court disagreed. Addressing the directors' "constituency" argument, Justice Andrew G.T. Moore (who had authored the earlier *Unocal* opinion) wrote for the court:

> Although such considerations may be permissible, there are fundamental limitations upon that prerogative. A board may have regard for various constituencies in discharging its responsibilities, provided there are rationally related benefits accruing to the stockholders. *Unocal*, 493 A.2d at 955. However, such concern for nonstockholder interests is inappropriate when an auction among active bidders is in progress, and the object no longer is to protect or maintain the corporate enterprise but to sell it to the highest bidder.[43]

It appears, then, that the answer to the practical question about how to resolve conflicting interests of stakeholders and stockholders may turn on the context in which the conflict arises. As demonstrated previously, Delaware law may recognize as a special case the context in which directors are charged solely with maximizing value for shareholders. *Unocal* and *Time* appear to recognize a second "special" context: that of a board faced with a hostile acquisition offer. *Unocal's* recognition of a director's duty to analyze a response to a hostile takeover in connection with its effect upon the corporate enterprise, including nonshareholder interests, suggests, and analysis of the *Time* decision leads to the conclusion, that a board may prefer the interests of the enterprise to the interests of the shareholder-owners of the enterprise in responding to an unwanted acquisition offer, provided there are rationally related benefits accruing to the stockholders, or to the enterprise itself.

As to the great number of decisions that fall outside these two "special" cases, however, the answer is less clear. In states that have adopted statutes such as those found in Indiana, Iowa, and Pennsylvania, all of which permit the board, in considering the interests of other constituencies, not to treat the interests of any one constituency (such as shareholders) as dominant, one could argue that directors could make decisions that benefit *only* stakeholders. While this conclusion is not clear, outside of these few states the common law counsels that directors who act in preference for stakeholder interests *at the expense of* stockholders' interests do so at their own peril without a powerful case that preferring stakeholders' interests is clearly in the long-term best interests of the enterprise (and, therefore, indirectly consistent with long-term shareholder value maximization) or directly in the long-term best interests of shareholders.[44]

The Closely Held Corporation

Having reviewed elemental principles of corporate governance, we now turn briefly to note those special statutory provisions applicable to the governance of the closely held corporation, as well as some of the practical aspects of acting as a director of such a corporation.

At the outset, it may be helpful to define a "closely held" corporation, a term that has different meanings in federal tax law, state corporation law, and common usage. Although as a matter of common usage a "close corporation" is one that is not widely held, under Delaware law, as under the corporation statutes of several states, a close corporation has a meaning defined by statute.

A Delaware close corporation is one that includes in its certificate of incorporation requirements that: (1) Share ownership is evidenced only by certificated securities held by no more then thirty holders of record; (2) All of the stock of the company is subject to some restriction on transfer; and (3) No public offering of the shares of the company is permitted.[45]

Governance of a statutory close corporation may differ significantly from governance of other corporate entities. For example, under the Delaware statutes, stockholders of a close corporation holding a majority of the stock of the company can, in certain circumstances, agree in writing to restrict the discretion or power of the board of directors of the company to manage the "business and affairs" of the enterprise,[46] and such an agreement is not invalid simply because it restricts directorial discretion, even if it addresses the division of the firm's profits or the payment of dividends,[47] traditionally matters relegated solely to directorial discretion.

In the presence of such a contract, the directors of the close corporation are statutorily relieved of liability "for managerial acts or omissions . . . to the extent and so long as the discretion or powers of the board in its management of corporate affairs is controlled by such agreement."[48]

Likewise, the Delaware statute permits the certificate of incorporation of a close corporation to provide that the "business of the corporation shall be managed by the stockholders . . . rather than by a board of directors,"[49] effectively supplanting the role of the board in corporate management. In the event the charter contains such a provision, stockholders are "deemed" to be directors and are "subject to all liabilities of directors."[50]

In short, the Delaware close corporation statute allows owners of a close corporation to vary the ordinary role of directors in corporate governance and, in one type of arrangement, to abolish altogether the board of directors. Clearly, an individual invited to become a director of such an enterprise will want to examine carefully the certificate and bylaws of the entity, as well as all pertinent agreements by stockholders of the company relating to governance before accepting a directorship, to understand fully the role of the director in the company, as well as the scope of the responsibility that he or she is being asked to undertake.

Notes

Portions of this chapter and others in this book have appeared previously in the Corporate Practice Series (BNA), No. 63, *The Board of Directors* (1993), and have been used herein with permission.

1. Guth v. Loft, Inc., 5 A.2d 503 (Del. 1939); Smith v. Van Gorkom, 488 A.2d 858 (Del. 1985).

2. While the authors have attempted to provide the reader with different points of view on the issues presented, many of the authorities relied on are decisions of Delaware courts or articles commenting on Delaware law. The wealth of Delaware corporate case law makes this approach almost unavoidable.

3. Stroud v. Grace, 606 A.2d 75, 84 (Del. 1992); Lynch v. Vickers Energy Corp., 383 A.2d 278 (Del. 1977). The duty of full and fair disclosure also extends to directors when they voluntarily make disclosures to shareholders. Marhart, Inc. v. Calmat Co., C.A. No. 11820, slip op. at 5 (Del. Ch. Apr. 22, 1992).

4. Paramount Communications Inc. v. Time Inc., C.A. No. 10866, slip op. at 77–78 (Del. Ch. July 14, 1989), *aff'd*, 571 A.2d 1140 (Del. 1990).

5. *See, e.g.*, Graham v. Allis-Chalmers Mfg. Co., 188 A.2d 125 (Del. 1963). Writing in the Balotti & Finkelstein treatise, Chief Justice E. Norman Veasey of the Delaware Supreme Court has suggested that the two principal functions of directors are decision making and oversight. 1 R. FRANKLIN BALOTTI & JESSE A. FINKELSTEIN, THE DELAWARE LAW OF CORPORATIONS AND BUSINESS ORGANIZATIONS § 4.8, at 4-196 (2d ed. Supp. 1995) [hereinafter "BALOTTI & FINKELSTEIN § ___"].

6. 8 DEL. CODE ANN. § 141(a).

7. We agree with Lipton & Lorsch when they argue that "directors simply cannot and should not try to manage the daily affairs of the business," *id.* at 67, at least in a large public company.

8. 2 MODEL BUSINESS CORP. ACT ANN. § 8.01(b) (3d ed. 1994) [hereinafter "MODEL ACT § ___"].

9. ABA COMM. ON CORP. LAWS, CORPORATE DIRECTOR'S GUIDEBOOK (Section of Business Law, 2d ed. 1994), *reprinted in* 49 BUS. LAW. 1243, 1249 (1994) [hereinafter "GUIDEBOOK at ___"].

10. Rosenblatt v. Getty Oil Co., 493 A.2d 929, 943 (Del. 1985).

11. *See* GUIDEBOOK at 1249; *see also Corporate Governance and American Competitiveness March, 1990: Statement of the Business Roundtable,* 46 BUS. LAW. 241, 246 (1990) [hereinafter *"Roundtable* at ___"] (specifying "five primary functions" of the board).

12. GUIDEBOOK at 1249. *See also* GUIDEBOOK at 1250 (director should be sufficiently knowledgeable of corporate business to allow the director "to join with other directors to support, challenge, and reward management as warranted.").

13. GUIDEBOOK at 1249; and *cf. GM Board Guidelines on Significant Corporate Governance Issues,* No. 21 (Feb. 1994), *reprinted in* GREGORY V. VARALLO & DANIEL A. DREISBACH, THE BOARD OF DIRECTORS, C.P.S. (BNA) No. 63 (1994).

14. William T. Allen, *Defining the Role of Outside Directors in an Age of Global Competition,* 16 DIRECTOR'S MONTHLY (National Ass'n of Corporate Directors), Nov. 1992, at 1, 4 (hereinafter *"Outside Directors* at ___").

15. Martin Lipton & Jay W. Lorsch, *A Modest Proposal for Improved Corporate Governance,* 48 BUS. LAW. 70 (Nov. 1992).

16. Aronson v. Lewis, 473 A.2d 805, 812 (Del. 1984). Chapter III treats the duties of care, loyalty, and disclosure in depth.

17. Guth v. Loft Inc., 5 A.2d 503 (Del. 1939). Special circumstances and conflicted transactions are addressed in more detail in Chapter 3.

18. Stroud v. Grace, 606 A.2d 75, 84 (Del. 1992); Lynch v. Vickers Energy Corp., 383 A.2d 278 (Del. 1977).

19. Marhart, Inc. v. Calmat Co., C.A. No. 11820, slip op. at 6 (Del. Ch. Apr. 22, 1992) (citing Freedman v. Restaurant Assocs. Indus., Inc., C.A. No. 9212 (Del. Ch. Sept. 19, 1990, revised Sept. 21, 1990)).

20. Stroud v. Grace, 606 A.2d at 84; *see* Rosenblatt v. Getty Oil Co., 493 A.2d 929, 944 (Del. 1985).

21. GUIDEBOOK at 1250; and *cf.* Phillips v. Insituform of N. Am., Inc., C.A. No. 9173 (Del. Ch. Aug. 27, 1987), *reprinted in* 13 DEL. J. CORP. L. 774, 790 (1988).

22. *In re* USACafes, L.P. Litig., 600 A.2d 43, 49 (Del. Ch. 1991).

23. Revlon, Inc. v. MacAndrews & Forbes Holdings, Inc., 506 A.2d 173 (Del. 1986); and *see* Paramount Communications Inc. v. QVC Network Inc., 637 A.2d 34 (Del. 1994). Much has been written about a director's duties in the so-called *Revlon* mode. This topic is explored at greater length in Chapter 3.

24. This topic is covered in detail in Chapter 6.

25. *See* New York Credit Men's Adjustment Bureau, Inc. v. Weiss, 110 N.E.2d 397 (N.Y. Ct. App. 1953).

26. Of course, this view is not unanimous. Under Pennsylvania statutory law, for example, the director is required to "stand in a fiduciary relation *to the corporation.*" 15 PA. CONS. STAT. ANN. § 1712(a) (emphasis supplied).

27. *See, e.g.,* Adolf A. Berle, Jr., *For Whom Corporate Managers Are Trustees: A Note,* 45 HARV. L. REV. 1365 (1932); William T. Allen, *Corporate Takeovers and Our Schizophrenic Conception of the Business Corporation* at 5–10 (Dec. 3, 1991) (Univ. of Pa. Institute of Law and Economics) [hereafter *"Corporate Conception* at ___"] (citing Dodge v. Ford Motor Co., 204 Mich. 459, 170 N.W. 668 (1919)), which the author refers to as "as pure an example as exists" of this model of the corporation; and *cf. Roundtable, supra* note 11, at 243 ("A corporation has as its prime purpose the long term optimization of economic outcomes.").

28. *See, e.g.,* Shamrock Holdings, Inc. v. Polaroid Corp., 559 A.2d 278 (Del. Ch. 1989), where the company justified issuing a large block of stock to a so-called "white knight" during a proxy contest on grounds that, *inter alia,* such issuance would tend to neutralize the block of shares then believed to be held by short-term speculators and arbitrageurs. *Cf.* ABA Committee on Corporate Laws, *Other Constituencies Statutes: Potential for Confusion,* 45 BUS. LAW. 2253, 2268 (1990) ("Often the shareholder's interest in the corporation is transitory, frequently a matter of days or weeks. . . ."); James J. Hanks, Jr., *Playing With Fire: Nonshareholder Constituency Statutes in the 1990s,* 21 STETSON L. REV. 97 (1991).

29. *See, e.g.,* A.A. Sommer Jr., *Whom Should The Corporation Serve? The Berle-Dodd Debate Revisited Sixty Years Later,* 16 DEL. J. CORP. L. 33 (1991); and *see Corporate Conception* at 10–11.

30. The first such statute was adopted by Pennsylvania in 1983. 42 PA. CONS. STAT. ANN. § 8363(b) (Purdon Supp. 1982). Eighteen of the twenty-four statutes that track this model apply to all board decisions and six are limited solely to change-of-control situations. Ohio allows the board to go further and consider how its actions affect the economy of Ohio and the United States and related societal considerations. OHIO REV. CODE ANN. § 1701.59(E)(2)–(4) (Anderson Supp. 1990). These so-called "other constituency statutes" have been roundly criticized. *See, e.g.,* James J. Hanks, Jr., *Non-Stockholder Constituency Statutes: An Idea Whose Time Should Never Have Come,* 3 INSIGHTS, Dec. 1989, at 20.

31. The statutory mandate in Connecticut reaches only corporations registered under the Securities Exchange Act of 1934. CONN. GEN. STAT. ANN. §§ 33-313(e)(3), (4) (West Supp. 1990).

32. 493 A.2d 946 (Del. 1985).

33. Unocal Corp. v. Mesa Petroleum Co., 493 A.2d at 955. To be sure, the first prong of this test had been explored in the takeover arena twenty years before *Unocal. See* Cheff v. Mathes, 199 A.2d 548 (Del. 1964). *Unocal's* restatement and revival of the test received particular attention and application during the 1980s when the Delaware courts were routinely called upon to decide takeover cases.

34. Prior Delaware case law had recognized that directors could, in certain circumstances, take action that protected nonstockholder groups. *See* Kors v. Carey, 158 A.2d 136 (Del. Ch. 1960); Cheff v. Mathes, 199 A.2d 548 (Del. Ch. 1964); *and cf.* TW Servs., Inc. v. SWT Acquisition Corp., C.A. No. 10427 (Del. Ch. Mar. 2, 1989). *Unocal* is, however, the first Delaware case to address the issue directly.

35. 571 A.2d 1140 (Del. 1990).

36. Paramount Communications Inc. v. Time Inc., 571 A.2d at 1153.

37. *Unocal, supra* note 33 (cited in *Paramount, supra* note 36, at 1153).

38. Although there is no Delaware case that has directly addressed this issue outside the takeover context, commentators appear to agree that the precedents apply outside of the takeover context. *See, e.g.,* Charles Hansen, *Other Constituency Statutes: A Search for Perspective,* 46 BUS. LAW. 1355 (1991); *cf. supra* note 27, *Corporate Conception* at 14.

39. *See* Trevor S. Norwitz, *"The Metaphysics of Time": A Radical Corporate Vision,* 46 BUS. LAW. 377 (1991).

40. *See* A.A. Sommer Jr., *Whom Should The Corporation Serve?, supra* note 29, at 53. *Cf.* TW Servs., Inc. v. SWT Acquisition Corp., *supra* note 34, at 18 ("the interests of the shareholders as a class are seen as congruent with those of the corporation *in the long run*") (emphasis supplied). The Business Roundtable takes a similar approach. *Roundtable* at 244 (stakeholders are "vital to the long term successful economic performance of the corporation"). Sommers' helpful approach appears to be at odds with *Time,* which expressly rejects that portion of the trial court's analysis distinguishing between short- and long-term interests of the company and its shareholders. *See Time,* 571 A.2d at 1154.

41. 506 A.2d 173 (Del. 1986).

42. *Revlon,* 506 A.2d at 182. Interestingly, the court cited *Unocal* for this proposition, notwithstanding that the case never qualifies the directors' ability to take into account nonstockholder interests. *Cf.* Mills Acquisition Co. v. Macmillan, Inc., 559 A.2d 1261, 1282 n.29 (Del. 1989) (Court reiterated that board may consider the impact of hostile bid on nonshareholder constituencies "provided that it bears some reasonable relationship to general shareholder interests.").

43. *Revlon,* 506 A.2d at 182.

44. Reviewing the seminal Delaware decisions outlined previously, the American Bar Association (ABA) Committee on Corporate Laws concluded in 1990 that with respect to the "other constituency" debate, "the Delaware courts have stated the prevailing corporate common law in this country. . . ." ABA Committee on Corporate Laws, *Other Constituencies Statutes: Potential for Confusion, supra* note 28, at 2261. The Committee also concludes that, without clearly defined legislative intent, the various constituency statutes "should be interpreted in a manner consistent with the existing common law. . . ." *Id.* at 2254.

45. 8 DEL. CODE ANN. § 342. In addition, Section 343 of the statute requires that the heading of the company's certificate of incorporation state that it is a close corporation.

46. 8 DEL. CODE ANN. § 350.

47. *Id.* at § 354.

48. *Id.* at § 350.

49. *Id.* at § 351.

50. *Id.* at § 351.

CHAPTER 2

Structure of the Board

Much of the public scrutiny of corporate governance issues over the past decade has focused on structural issues: questions related to board size and makeup; the splitting of the chairman and CEO posts; issues concerning the composition and function of board committees; and, finally, new efforts to create structures in which independent outside board members can most readily assert their actual independence from corporate management.

Even the courts, which largely focus on director decision making rather than structural issues, have found their voice in the public debate concerning board structure, stating concerns over the composition and functioning of certain types of board committees. This section briefly addresses structural issues: the size of the board and its composition; the role of several oversight committees of the board; and, finally, an examination of the General Motors Corporation (GM) corporate governance "Principles" and the direction they suggest for corporate governance in this decade.

Size of the Board and the Terms of Its Members

State law has little to say about the size of a board of directors. Although some states still impose a minimum number of directors, Delaware does not, and a company could well be run by a one-person board. Most state statutory schemes leave the size of the board to be set in the certificate of incorporation or the bylaws of the company. Common practice is to define the minimum and maximum number of directors that can constitute the board in the company's certificate of incorporation, and provide that the exact number is to be set in the bylaws, or by resolution of the board.[1]

As a practical matter, most substantial corporations work with a board that reflects a diversity of viewpoints and talents, but is still not so large as to frustrate the accomplishment of business at meetings. The Business Roundtable estimates that, on average, large, publicly held companies are likely to have a board composed of thirteen members.[2] Of course the optimal size of any board depends upon the nature of the business of the company and the personalities of the members of the board.

Lipton and Lorsch argue that the size of a board should be limited to a maximum of ten members, stating a preference for boards of eight or nine members.[3] The *Guidebook* suggests that there is "emerging consensus" that smaller boards (defined as those with twelve or fewer members) function more effectively than larger boards.[4] Similarly, other commentators suggest that smaller boards are likely to behave more cohesively. Small board size may allow more interchange between directors who might not otherwise have an opportunity to explain their views in detail in a larger group given the limited time available for board meetings. In considering the appropriate size for the public company board, it also is advisable to include a sufficient number of independent directors to staff the "oversight" committees of the board, which will be discussed later in this chapter.

Under most state corporation statutes, the members of a board of directors ordinarily are elected to one-year terms of office. Similarly, every state except California provides the option to institute a "staggered" board of directors, whose members are ordinarily divided into three separate classes,[5] each class serving a three-year term. Typically, a nine-member staggered board will have three directors up for election each year. Staggered boards have been widely used to repel hostile takeovers and to discourage proxy contests, largely because most statutes that allow the device protect staggered directors by providing that they may be removed only for "cause."[6] Staggered boards also tend to promote stability in corporate affairs, because they make a precipitous change in the majority of the membership of the board less likely.

Board Composition

Who should be asked to serve on the board? Not long ago, most commentators would have suggested that the board be comprised of representatives of senior management, the company's principal outside legal counsel, its banker, and perhaps a representative from the community where the company has its headquarters. Although this may describe the composition of many boards, powerful tides in the professional community and in society itself appear to be at work changing the composition of a "typical" board. For example, lawyers, who frequently would be asked to serve on the boards of important clients, are carefully reexamining the wisdom of such service in light of emerging views of ethical obligations and a desire to serve their clients without some of the conflicts that board service could entail.[7]

The goal of the selection process for board membership has not fundamentally changed, however. It should be to bring to the service of the corporation a broad spectrum of thoughtful men and women with wide experience in the business world and diverse problem-solving talents.

A more hotly debated topic is who should serve as the chairman of the board, and whether the chairman's position should be held by the company's chief executive officer. One recent study reports that 20 percent of companies studied divide the two roles; others have estimated that no more than 5 percent of major U.S. companies have outside directors in the chairman's spot.[8] Nonetheless, the issue promises to merit continued debate as large institutional investors continue to press to accomplish this change. In a recent study commissioned by CalPERS, 35 percent of the 600 board members responding were reported to favor this change.[9]

In our view, dividing the posts of chairman and CEO may add importantly to the ability of the board to monitor senior management, especially where the chairman is an outside director.[10] Clearly, however, such a structure might not work in all cases, nor need it. As most chairmen serve at the pleasure of the board and usually are reappointed by that body annually, the outsider-dominated board run by a chairman/CEO always has the option of replacing the chairman at its pleasure.

Much attention also has been focused recently on the number of "outside" or "independent" directors who make up the board. The *Guidebook* recommends that at least a majority of the members of public company boards should be independent.[11] For their part, Lipton and Lorsch argue that the board should include at least two outsiders for each "inside" or management director.[12]

Even in light of an emerging consensus that outsider-dominated boards are preferable for public companies, not all of the courts and commentators share a common definition of the "outside" director. Several large corporations have attempted to define "outside" directors in their bylaws. For example, the GM and Chrysler bylaws both define an "outside" director as one who has not been employed by the corporation for five years; is not a "significant" adviser or consultant; is not affiliated with a "significant" customer or supplier; does not have a "significant" personal services contract with the company; and is not affiliated with a tax-exempt entity that receives "significant" contributions from the company.[13] Lipton and Lorsch add to the list the executive of a different company "on the board of which an executive of the company serves."[14]

In short, to qualify as "independent," a director should have no material ties to the corporation. While there certainly is no prohibition on service by individuals who fail to meet the test of "independence," the need to encourage an environment of "independence in fact" on the board, as well as the benefits of being perceived as an outsider-dominated board, counsel a balancing of the board in favor of outside, independent members.

Committees

Although no particular committee structure is mandated by state law,[15] New York Stock Exchange (NYSE) listed companies, American Stock Exchange (ASE) companies, and National Association of Securities Dealers Automated Quotations (NASDAQ) National Market System (NMS) companies are typically required to have an Audit Committee.[16] Boards of many large enterprises have several committees, as the work of the board of a large corporation often is best addressed in the first instance by small, working committees, comprised of board members with special talents or expertise in a particular area. In addition to an Audit Committee, many boards also will have a Compensation Committee and often a Nominating Committee, among others.[17] In addition, larger boards also may find an Executive Committee helpful, to allow a smaller group of directors to guide the company between meetings of the full board.

Under Delaware law, a committee may be comprised of one or more directors. About half of the states require that a committee be comprised of at least two directors,[18] and New York and Ohio require no less than three directors to constitute a quorum.[19] Following, we list limitations on the scope of committee activities imposed by state law and briefly address the roles of the most commonly encountered "oversight" committees.

Permissible Scope of Committee Activity

Every state corporation statute authorizes the use of board commit-tees. Many state corporation law statutes, and notably that of Dela-ware, place certain restrictions on the scope of the activities that may be conducted by a committee of less than the entire board. Un-der Delaware law, a duly appointed committee may exercise all those powers delegated to it by the full board of directors (or pro-vided for in the bylaws or certificate of incorporation) except that no committee has the authority to recommend that shareholders act to amend the certificate of incorporation of the company; adopt a merger agreement; recommend that shareholders approve the sale of all or substantially all of the corporation's assets; advise shareholders to vote to dissolve the corporation (or revoke its dis-solution) or amend the bylaws of the corporation.[20] Further, a com-mittee will have the power only to declare a dividend, authorize the issuance of stock, or approve a "short-form" merger if these powers are expressly delegated to the committee. Apart from these limitations on significant corporate action, a committee of the board of directors may take any action that could be taken by the full board under Delaware law.[21]

The Audit Committee

As noted previously, every company listed on the NYSE, the ASE, and every NASDAQ NMS company is required to have an Audit Committee, and recent studies show that the vast majority of large companies include such a committee in their board structure.[22] Here we address both the composition of the Audit Committee and the role of that committee in corporate governance.

The NYSE regulation requiring an Audit Committee for listed companies also prescribes the composition of that committee. The regulation states that the Audit Committee must be comprised "solely of directors independent of management and free from any relationship that . . . would interfere with the exercise of indepen-dent judgment as a committee member."[23] Although this regulation applies to NYSE-listed companies, and the *Guidebook* recommends that the committee be composed solely of independent directors,[24] other sources have suggested that a majority of outside directors may be sufficient. For example, the American Bar Association (ABA) Report of the Committee on Corporate Law Departments, which critiqued the 1976 version of the *Guidebook,* states: "Having audit and compensation committees staffed by a majority of outsiders . . ., may be a legal safeguard, but there is no legal reason why the range of choices available to a well governed corporation should not include providing for a minority of management directors on those committees."[25] It is clearly the consensus that at least a majority of audit committee members should be independent of management.[26] In light of the ASE and NASDAQ NMS requirements to this effect, few large companies are likely to arrange the composition of the Audit Committee differently. Obviously, the number of members of the Audit Committee, and the clear preference for at least a majority of outsiders on the committee, also will affect the number of outside directors sitting on the board itself.

Regardless of how salutary an independent Audit Committee might be in principle, a committee that does not meet regularly may be of little use. The authors had occasion to act as counsel in one matter challenging certain questionable accounting practices of a listed company where the defendant corporation's Audit Committee had not met in more than a full year. Moreover, the company's outside auditors' comment letter to the committee was not issued (or requested) for almost a full year after an important annual audit, even though the auditors subsequently concluded that certain accounts needed to be restated. Although there is no prescribed minimum number of meetings an Audit Committee must hold annually, many well-run committees meet at least quarterly, and occasionally more often at year-end.

There is no clear consensus on the precise function of the Audit Committee. Recognizing as much, some commentators have suggested that the company or the committee itself prepare and disclose a written "charter" for the committee so that committee members clearly understand the scope of the duties expected from them as members of the committee and so that stockholders are aware of the role played by the Audit Committee of that particular company.[27] While some commentators stress the role of the committee as the "direct line" of communication between the company's outside auditors and its nonmanagement directors, and others stress the committee's function as the body primarily charged with "review and oversight of management's performance with respect to its financial responsibilities and disclosure,"[28] one need not choose between the two views, for a description of the role of the Audit Committee appears readily to accommodate both views.

There is some degree of consensus regarding the core functions of the "typical" Audit Committee. Most practitioners agree that the role of the committee should include, at a minimum:

1. making recommendations regarding the engagement or termination of the company's outside auditors, including a review of the compensation and independence of such auditors;
2. examining the overall audit plan to determine whether the plan is appropriate and/or to recommend improvements in the plan;
3. studying the external audit;
4. reviewing the internal audit; and
5. discussing internal financial controls.[29]

Within these broad parameters, commentators have suggested that the Audit Committee also should review carefully issues relating to changes in accounting principles[30] and, depending upon the needs of the corporation, involve itself in such additional tasks as establishing and/or monitoring corporate codes of conduct, reviewing conflicts of interest, and examining "irregular" or "sensitive" payments.[31]

Regardless of how involved an Audit Committee becomes in the foregoing (or other) functions, federal law suggests certain minimum functions of the committee. Specifically, the Foreign Corrupt Practices Act imposes upon companies with registered securities the obligation to "devise and maintain a system of internal accounting controls sufficient to provide reasonable assurances" that:

- transactions are executed in accordance with management authorization;
- transactions are recorded to permit preparation of financial statements in accordance with generally accepted accounting practices (GAAP) and to maintain accountability for assets;
- access to assets is permitted only in accordance with authorization; and
- recorded assets are compared with existing assets at "reasonable intervals" and appropriate action is taken with respect to differences.[32]

In light of the foregoing legal requirements, the prudent member of an Audit Committee of a listed company will want to assure that the company's system of internal accounting controls meets at least the foregoing criteria.

It also has been suggested that members of the Audit Committee of a financially distressed corporation may have special duties, or at least be expected to play a more active role in corporate governance. One commentator has written that in the "troubled" company, "it might be appropriate . . . for the audit committee to discuss with management and with the auditors the status of any defaults on debt and the accuracy of public disclosure as to such defaults; [and] to review carefully with management and with auditors the management discussion and analysis of financial results. . . ."[33] Whether or not the duties of directors serving on an Audit Committee expand in times of corporate financial difficulty, appropriate practice would be for the Audit Committee to become active, even aggressive, in discharging its role in such circumstances.

The Compensation Committee

The Compensation Committee is likely second only to the Audit Committee in its prevalence, and the primary purpose of the committee is not in dispute. Most commentators and practitioners agree that the Compensation Committee should have responsibility for approving or disapproving (or recommending approval or disapproval to the full board) of the compensation arrangements for senior management of the corporation, and often the committee also addresses issues concerning the compensation of the board itself.[34]

Although the *Corporate Director's Guidebook* suggests that the Compensation Committee be comprised entirely of nonmanagement directors, neither state nor federal law mandates that only nonmanagement directors may serve on this committee.[35]

The work of the Compensation Committee recently has been the subject of intense public scrutiny by activist institutional investors. A February, 1993, survey identified eighty proposals related to executive pay in the 1993 proxy season, including thirty-three that sought restrictions on executive pay and twenty-eight seeking additional disclosure regarding executive pay.[36]

In late 1992, the Securities and Exchange Commission (SEC) amended its rules to require particular disclosure of certain relationships of members of the Compensation Committee and for the first time imposed specific disclosure requirements on the Compensation Committees of public companies. Companies that are registered under the Securities Exchange Act of 1934 other than so-called "small business issuers" are subject to the new regulations.

The regulation requiring disclosure of certain relationships does not require that the Compensation Committee be comprised entirely of independent directors, but does require disclosure of any committee member who was, at any time during the preceding fiscal year, an officer or director of the company or any of its subsidiaries, formerly an officer of the company or its subsidiaries, or who had certain transactional relationships with the company.[37] The regulations also require disclosure of other so-called "interlocks," i.e., where an executive officer of one company serves on the Compensation Committee of another company that has an executive officer serving on the first company's board.

The SEC also has imposed on the Compensation Committee of public companies the duty to issue, in connection with the annual proxy statement relating to the annual meeting at which directors are elected, a report, "made over" the names of each member of the committee, that discusses: (1) the committee's compensation policies applicable to all of the company's executive officers; (2) the committee's bases for determining the CEO's compensation for the most recently completed fiscal year, including the factors and criteria upon which the compensation was based; and (3) the relationship of executive and CEO compensation to company performance for the most recently completed fiscal year.[38] Finally, if executive officers' stock options or stock appreciation rights were repriced during the most recently completed fiscal year, the committee is required to explain the basis for such repricing.[39]

In the release proposing these regulations, the SEC explained that these regulations were designed to "bring shareholders into the Compensation Committee or board meeting room and permit them to see and understand the specific decisions made through the eyes of the directors."[40] A year after first instituting the foregoing requirements, the SEC issued a release calling for a greater degree of detail throughout the Compensation Committee report.[41] The Commission made it clear that it would not accept generalized statements regarding compensation, and put the corporate community on notice that it will require a much higher standard of disclosure than provided in many early committee reports.[42]

Practically, the authors believe that the new regulations are intended to impact the way the Compensation Committee functions. For example, the relationship disclosures appear to be designed to drive reporting companies toward entirely independent Compensation Committees (thus avoiding the need to disclose potentially embarrassing relationships). Similarly, the very specific requirements of the new committee report appear designed to energize the work of the Compensation Committee and to force it to focus (to the extent it is not already doing so) upon the methodology it employs in compensating senior executives and particularly the extent to which compensation is performance-driven. Indeed, the specific focus of the regulations on the extent to which the Compensation Committee rewards actual performance appears designed to encourage more Compensation Committees to move toward pay-for-performance criteria in executive compensation. In addition, the new requirement that the committee disclose the basis for repricing stock option and stock appreciation rights (SAR) grants and the specific disclosure requirements imposed on the Compensation Committee in connection with such repricing appear designed to require the committee to explain the bases for its decision to take such steps with some degree of particularity.

Although the Commission lacks authority to mandate the way in which directors discharge their duties as members of the Compensation Committee, it is likely that these disclosure requirements will impact upon director conduct. In addition, another likely practical result of the SEC's new regulations is to drive the retention of compensation consultants to assist the work of the committee, even at smaller public firms.

Both these disclosure requirements and the significant focus on compensation practices brought to bear by institutional investors are likely to make the work of the Compensation Committee more challenging—and public— than ever before.

The Nominating Committee

The basic functions of the Nominating Committee are to recommend nominees for election to the board, to recommend candidates for membership on the various committees of the board, and, in the event of a vacancy in the office of the CEO of the company, to recommend a successor to the full board.

As with the other board committees, there has been a fair amount of debate regarding the appropriate composition of the Nominating Committee. The *ALI Principles* and the *Guidebook* recommend that the committee be comprised exclusively of outside directors. The American Law Institute (ALI) excepts from its recommendation companies in which a single person owns a majority of the voting securities, or situations where a family or control group owns a majority of such securities.[43]

The practice of including the CEO of a company on the Nominating Committee, once widespread, appears to be changing rapidly. One recent survey showed that 30 percent of the large public companies surveyed barred insider membership on the Nominating Committee, up from 16 percent of companies who responded to a similar survey conducted two years earlier.[44]

Recently, three major institutional investors, CalPERS, the New York State Retirement Fund, and the Connecticut State Treasurer, wrote to approximately 300 corporations in which they held stock, suggesting that future directors be nominated by Nominating Committees composed solely of outside board members. As of June, 1992, more than twenty-five of these companies agreed to do so.[45]

Regardless of whether or not the Nominating Committee is composed solely of independent directors or only a majority of such directors, the most critical aspects of the work of the committee involve the active and disinterested judgment of its members. Like the other oversight committees of the board, the functioning Nominating Committee can enhance both the perception and reality of an independent board.

The GM Board Guidelines and Board Structure

In February, 1994, the directors of GM issued guidelines on significant corporate governance issues, which, in part, served to define the role of the outside directors of the company in monitoring management. These guidelines have received widespread attention and were warmly received by institutional shareholders.

While it is too early to tell the extent to which the Guidelines will impact corporate governance in this country, the authors believe that the broad institutional support for the Guidelines virtually guarantees that they will be carefully considered and in many cases adopted in whole or in part at major corporations across the United States. In response to a recent study conducted by CalPERS, for example, forty-five of the largest 200 U.S. industrial companies indicated that they had adopted corporate governance guidelines, and twenty-eight others were reviewing the issue.[46]

The Role of Outside Directors under the Guidelines

The Guidelines suggest that outside directors play a significant role in corporate governance. As noted previously, the GM bylaws require that a majority of the board be made up of outside directors. The Guidelines go further and endorse the concept of a "lead director." This director is chosen by the outside directors only and has the responsibility for chairing meetings of outside directors, in addition to other functions that the outside directors may delegate.

The Guidelines also mandate that the outside members of the board meet in executive session at least three times each year. While the Guidelines expressly state that the format of these meetings will include a "discussion" with the CEO on each occasion, the meetings appear designed to establish a regular schedule on which outside directors will be able to discuss company business and to interact outside of the presence of management.

The Role of Committees

The Guidelines endorse the current six GM committees: Audit, Capital Stock, Director Affairs, Finance, Incentive and Compensation, and Public Policy. The Guidelines also suggest that committee memberships be rotated periodically at approximately five-year intervals, although the Guidelines make clear that there may be reasons why an individual director should continue as a member of a particular committee for longer. Finally, the Guidelines mandate that each committee is to prepare an agenda of subjects to be discussed at the beginning of each year (to the extent possible) and share this agenda with the entire board.

Term Limits and Retirement

The Guidelines expressly reject the notion of term limits for directors. Nonetheless, they do acknowledge that the GM Committee on Director Affairs, in consultation with the CEO and chairman of the board, will review each director's continuation on the board every five years. The Guidelines also reaffirm GM's current board retirement age of seventy.

While these and the related innovations of the Guidelines do not break startling new ground, they do begin to create the structures in which the board has an opportunity to enhance the perception and reality of independence in the governance of one of the world's largest companies. While not every innovation in the Guidelines will necessarily be appropriate for every company, the Guidelines appear to reflect a significant trend in modern corporate governance.

Notes

1. It bears noting that failing to maintain board size parameters in the certificate of incorporation could enable a hostile acquiror to expand the size of even a so-called classified board and elect a majority of the board, without ever having to remove the duly elected board. Thus, protecting board size in the certificate of incorporation is a prudent practice.

2. *Corporate Governance and American Competitiveness, March 1990: Statement of the Business Roundtable,* 46 Bus. Law. 241, 248 (1990) [hereinafter *"Roundtable* at ___"].

3. Martin Lipton & Jay W. Lorsch, *A Modest Proposal for Improved Corporate Governance,* 48 Bus. Law. 67 (Nov. 1992) [hereinafter "Lipton & Lorsch at ___"].

4. ABA Comm. on Corp. Laws, Corporate Director's Guidebook 1259 (Section of Business Law, 2d ed. 1994) [hereinafter "Guidebook at ___"].

5. The New York Stock Exchange Listed Company Manual states that the Exchange "will refuse to authorize listing where the board of directors is divided into more than three classes." New York Stock Exchange Listed Company Manual § 304.00 (1983).

6. *See* 8 Del. Code Ann. § 141(k). Note that the Model Act does not *automatically* protect such directors from removal. Model Business Corp. Act Ann. § 8.08(a) (3d ed. 1994) [hereinafter "Model Act"].

7. *See, e.g., Lawyers Manual on Professional Conduct* (ABA/BNA) Ethics Opinion 86-14, at 901:3004 (May 13, 1987); D. Block, et al., *Lawyers Serving on the Boards of Directors of Clients: A Survey of Problems,* 7 Insights, Apr. 1993, at 3.

8. *Other Concerns Are Likely to Follow GM in Splitting Posts of Chairman and CEO,* Wall St. J., Nov. 4, 1992, at B1.

9. *Recent Wave of Activism in Boardroom Will Gain Momentum, Survey Suggests,* Wall St. J., Dec. 9, 1992, at A5.

10. *Compare* Ira M. Millstein, *The Evolution of the Certifying Board,* 48 Bus. Law. 1485, 1495 (1993) (splitting roles enhances credibility of the CEO and the board) *with* Lipton & Lorsch (declining to endorse such a structure on grounds that it is "strongly resisted by top management in most U.S. companies "), Lipton & Lorsch at 70.

11. Guidebook, *supra* note 4, at 1257. This suggestion is said to "encourage an environment likely to nurture independence in fact and to communicate the appearance of independence. . . ." *Id.*

12. Lipton & Lorsch, *supra* note 3, at 67.

13. GM Bylaws § 2.12; Chrysler Bylaws, Art. II, § 7. Chrysler avoids using the "significance" test by tying its definition of a disqualifying interest to Securities and Exchange Commission (SEC) disclosure rules.

14. Lipton & Lorsch, *supra* note 3, at 67–68.

15. Connecticut is an exception. Connecticut law requires that the boards of certain corporations incorporated there have an Audit Committee. *See* Samuel S. Cross, Connecticut Corporation Law & Practice § 5.4 (1992).

16. New York Stock Exchange Listed Company Manual § 303.00; NAS-DAQ National Market System Listing Agreement ¶ 1(c) (1987).

17. The Business Roundtable estimates that the average board of a large, publicly held corporation has five committees. *Roundtable, supra* note 2, at 249. The 1992 Korn/Ferry Study demonstrates that of the companies studied, 98 percent have Audit Committees, 95 percent have Compensation Committees, and 67 percent have Nominating Committees. Korn/Ferry International, *Board of Directors Nineteenth Annual Study 1992,* 9 (June 1992) [hereinafter "1992 Korn/Ferry Study"].

18. Model Act, *supra* note 6, § 8.25 commentary at 918.

19. *Id.*

20. 8 Del. Code Ann. § 141(c).

21. The Model Act similarly restricts the permissible activity of a committee. For example, under the Model Act, a committee may not authorize dividend distributions, fill vacancies in its own number, amend the bylaws or the certificate, or approve a plan of merger.

22. 1992 Korn/Ferry Study at 9.

23. New York Stock Exchange Listed Company Manual § 303.00 (1983). The ASE and NASDAQ NMS require that at least a majority of the members of the Audit Committee be independent directors.

24. Guidebook, *supra* note 4, at 1264. Other commentators also have favored an entirely nonmanagement Audit Committee. *See, e.g.,* Edward F. Greene & Bernard B. Falk, *The Audit Committee—A Measured Contribution to Corporate Governance: A Realistic Appraisal of Its Objectives and Functions,* 34 Bus. Law. 1229, 1239 (1979) [hereinafter "Greene & Falk at ___"]; *Roundtable, supra* note 2, at 249; and *see* R. Franklin Balotti & Jesse A. Finkelstein, The Delaware Law of Corporations and Business Organizations, § 4.3, at 4-20 (2d ed. Supp. 1995) [hereinafter "Balotti & Finkelstein § ___"] (it has become "customary" for most public companies to have Audit Committees comprised of only outside directors); Lipton & Lorsch, *supra* note 3, at 69 (Audit Committee should be composed solely of outside directors); *ALI Principles of Corporate Governance: Analysis and Recommendations* §§ 3.05 and 3A.02 (1994) [hereinafter "*ALI Principles* § ___"] suggesting that the Audit Committees of public companies should be composed "exclusively of directors who are neither employed by the corporation nor were so employed within the two preceding years, including at least a majority of members who have no significant relationship with the corporation's senior executives."

25. Report of the Committee on Corporate Law Departments on Corporate Director's Guidebook.

26. Daniel J. McCauley Jr., & John C. Burton, *Audit Committees,* C.P.S. (BNA) No. 49, at A-18 (1986) [hereinafter "C.P.S. No. 49"].

27. Greene & Falk, *supra* note 24, at 1239.

28. *Cf.* Richard J. Farrell, *The Audit Committee—A Lawyer's View,* 28 Bus. Law. 1089, 1091 (1973); and C.P.S. No. 49, at A-23; and *see* Greene & Falk, *supra* note 24, at 1240 ("The primary objective of the Audit Committee should be to

ascertain that various processes, controls and procedures confirming or reviewing financial . . . information relating to the company are conducted by the designated persons in an adequate and appropriate manner.").

29. *See* C.P.S. No. 49, *supra* note 26, at A-23-28; GUIDEBOOK at 1265; Greene & Falk, *supra* note 24, at 1241–44; *and see Roundtable, supra* note 2, at 249–50; *see also ALI Principles* § 3A.03.

30. GUIDEBOOK, *supra* note 4, at 1267.

31. *Id.;* C.P.S. No. 49, *supra* note 26, at A-31. Some Audit Committees have taken a broad view of their roles, acting as aggressive adversaries in combating perceived management excess. At Todd Shipyards Corporation, for example, the entire Audit Committee resigned from membership on the board of directors of the company, publicly citing the view of the committee that the executive officers of the corporation had become "entrench[ed]" and that various matters were not presented to the company's board in an appropriate manner. *See* Todd Shipyards Corporation Form 8-K, filed June 9, 1992 (attaching resignation letter). Although this is an admittedly extreme example, it underlines the importance of open communication between management and the Audit Committee.

32. 15 U.S.C. § 78m(b)(2). Federal law also prohibits the knowing failure to implement a system of accounting controls, 15 U.S.C. § 78m(b)(4), and the knowing falsification of any book, record, or account, 15 U.S.C. § 78m(b)(5).

33. Meredith M. Brown, *When the Corporation Is Financially Troubled, Director's Role Changes,* 13 NAT'L L.J. S10, S13 (1991).

34. GUIDEBOOK, *supra* note 4, at 1269; *Roundtable, supra* note 2, at 250.

35. GUIDEBOOK, *supra* note 4, at 1268; *accord* Lipton & Lorsch, *supra* note 3, at 69; *cf.* BALOTTI & FINKELSTEIN, *supra* note 24, § 4.3, at 4–20; *Roundtable, supra* note 2, at 249.

36. *Shareholder Activism at Home, Abroad to See Rise in 1993 as Executive Pay, Board Reform Top Governance Issues List,* Corp. Couns. Wkly. (BNA), Feb. 17, 1993, at 8.

37. *See* Securities Exchange Act Release No. 31327 (Oct. 16, 1992), Regulation S-K Item 402(j) [hereinafter Regulation S-K Item ___].

38. Regulation S-K Item 402(k), *supra* note 37. As originally proposed, the regulation required each member of the Compensation Committee to sign the report. After considering comments made to this proposed requirement, the SEC relaxed its position and required merely that the report be "made over" the names of the committee members. Emanuel D. Strauss, *The Compensation Committee Report on Executive Compensation,* 6 INSIGHTS, Dec. 1992, at 11, 12. In the event there is no Compensation Committee, either the full board or the committee that performs the functions of the Compensation Committee is required to prepare the report.

39. Regulation S-K Item 402(i), *supra* note 37.

40. 57 Fed. Reg. 29594.

41. Securities Exchange Act Release No. 33-7009 (Aug. 6, 1993), 58 Fed. Reg. 42882.

42. *See* Emanuel D. Strauss, *The Honeymoon Is Over for Compensation Committee Reports*, 7 INSIGHTS, Oct. 1993, at 2.

43. *ALI Principles, supra* note 24, § 3A.04; GUIDEBOOK, *supra* note 4, at 1271.

44. Stuart Mieher, *Firms Restrict CEOs in Picking Board Members*, WALL ST. J., Mar. 15, 1993, at B1.

45. John Pound, *After Takeovers, Quiet Diplomacy*, WALL ST. J., June 8, 1992, at A10.

46. *CalPERS Pleased with High Number of Responses to Governance Survey*, Corp. Couns. Wkly. (BNA), Nov. 9, 1994, at 1.

CHAPTER 3

Duties and Liabilities of Individual Board Members

Duties of Board Members

As discussed briefly in Chapter 1, common law imposes fiduciary obligations of loyalty and care on directors. In addition, Delaware law imposes a duty of full and fair disclosure. Here, we explore each of these duties in detail and examine how they shift in circumstances such as when the board is confronted with an unwanted takeover offer.

Duty of Loyalty and "Interested" Transactions

Duty of Loyalty

The duty of loyalty requires that a director make decisions based on the best interests of the corporation and not on any personal interest. The duty of loyalty is said to prohibit "self-dealing" by directors. As the Chancellor of the Delaware Court of Chancery has stated:

> Without intending to necessarily cover every case, it is possible to say broadly that the duty of loyalty is transgressed when a corporate fiduciary, whether director, officer or controlling shareholder, uses his or her corporate office . . . to promote, advance or effectuate a transaction between the corporation and such person (or an entity in which the fiduciary has a substantial economic interest, directly or indirectly) and that transaction is not substantively fair to the corporation. That is, breach of loyalty cases inevitably involve conflicting economic or other interests. . . .[1]

Questions regarding the director's duty of loyalty may arise in any number of contexts, and they frequently do arise in the context of sales to or purchases by the corporation from directors or related entities; dealings by a parent corporation with a subsidiary; insider trading and other misuse of corporate information; financing of an undercapitalized company by a director; and usurpation of corporate opportunities.

"Interested" Transactions

Under common law, self-dealing transactions are considered "voidable." Many states have adopted so-called "safe harbor" statutes,[2] however, that generally provide that a conflict transaction is not voidable "solely" because it is between the corporation and directors and officers if: (1) It is approved by either informed, disinterested directors or stockholders, or (2) The transaction is shown to be fair to the corporation.[3] Critical to the operation of the Delaware safe-harbor statute (and all those based on the Delaware model) is the concept of full disclosure of all facts material to the transaction. While directors or shareholders may approve an otherwise conflicted transaction, their approval has no legal effect without full disclosure.

An "interested" transaction also may be upheld if it is "fair."[4] Delaware law requires that the proponents of an interested transaction demonstrate the "entire" fairness of the transaction, which entails a showing of both "fair dealing" and "fair price."[5] "Fair dealing" involves "questions of when the transaction was timed; how it was initiated, structured, negotiated, disclosed to the directors; and how the approvals of the directors and the stockholders were obtained."[6] The fair price inquiry "relates to the economic and financial consideration[s]" to be paid in the proposed transaction. The test of fairness is not bifurcated, and "[a]ll aspects of the issue must be examined as a whole. . . ."[7]

The notion of "fair dealing" may present the director with interesting practical dilemmas. The series of decisions in *Rabkin v. Philip A. Hunt Chemical Corp.*[8] illustrate the point. In *Rabkin*, shareholders challenged the merger of Hunt Chemical Corporation (Hunt) into Olin Corporation (Olin). Olin originally had acquired 63.4 percent of the stock of Hunt and in the stock purchase agreement had agreed that any cash-out merger of the minority stockholders of Hunt accomplished within one year from its purchase would take place at no less than the $25/share price paid by Olin for its original block. Olin did not seek to merge out the Hunt minority during the one year-time period, but did so soon after the period had expired, at $20/share, a price $5/share below that provided for in the then-expired contract. Stockholders sued, challenging the price and the timing of the merger. The trial court dismissed the action, relegating plaintiffs to a statutory appraisal remedy.

On appeal, the Delaware Supreme Court reversed, holding that the trial court should not have dismissed plaintiffs' "fair dealing" claims in light of the allegations in the case concerning the timing of the merger.[9] Although Olin eventually prevailed at the final trial of the case, it did so by showing that the $20/share merger price was entirely fair.[10]

"Entire fairness" also has been explored outside the merger context. Where a 50 percent stockholder made loans to his corporation that were challenged by the other 50 percent stockholder, the court found that the loans were fair to the corporation where the terms of the loans were identical to those available to the company from an outside lender and the company needed the funds for ordinary business operations.[11]

Use of Independent Committees in Conflict Transactions

When addressing conflict transactions, the Delaware courts also have emphasized the use of committees of the board comprised of independent, outside directors. In the context of parent-subsidiary mergers, for example, the Delaware Supreme Court has indicated on several occasions that the use of a properly functioning independent negotiating committee provides "strong evidence" of fairness.[12] Importantly, the courts appear less willing to defer to committees, even committees made up of purely independent, outside directors, where the evidence demonstrates that the committee failed to negotiate forcefully, or where it was poorly informed.[13] In its decision after trial in the *Rabkin* case, the court identified two factors that it would look for to determine whether an independent committee will be entitled to invoke special judicial deference in the merger context: First, the majority or controlling shareholder (if any) must not have dictated the terms of the merger, and second, the committee must have "real bargaining power," which it exercised in true arm's length negotiations.[14]

Likewise, in *Kahn v. Lynch Communication Systems, Inc.*, the court was critical of a facially independent committee's failure to exercise its "power to say no," even in the face of a threat by the controlling stockholder to commence a hostile offer at a price substantially lower than the negotiated price. Expounding on the "power to say no," which belongs to every truly independent committee, the court wrote:

The power to say no is a significant power. It is the duty of directors serving on [an independent] committee to approve only a transaction that is in the best interests of the public shareholders, to say no to any transaction that is not fair to those shareholders and is not the best transaction available. It is not sufficient for such directors to achieve the best price that a fiduciary will pay if that price is not a fair price.[15]

The *Lynch* court's focus on the power of an independent committee to "say no" to a transaction provides an important touchstone for directors serving on such committees. While the committee may be charged with investigating and negotiating an offer, the duty of the committee is not invariably to conclude a transaction. As *Lynch* teaches, this is so even where a controlling stockholder threatens the minority with a plainly inadequate bid if the negotiated price is not approved.

Other cases and commentators provide further practical guidance.[16] The case law indicates that both the process of selection of committee members and the composition of the committee are likely to be the subject of scrutiny. Neither the controlling or interested shareholder nor his or her representatives (if there are such) should dictate the composition of the committee or its advisers.[17] Similarly, the committee should be comprised of truly outside independent directors, who have absolutely no ties whatsoever to the transaction at issue or to the people involved.[18] If it is necessary to add outsiders to the board to achieve this goal, it may be advisable to do so.

Moreover, the properly constituted committee should have access to sufficient information to make an informed judgment. When considering a change-of-control transaction such as a management buy-out proposal, for example, it has become customary for the committee to retain its own legal and financial advisers. Should the committee determine to retain advisers, it should select them itself, without interference from management or others. In the end, however, the committee should never lose sight of its "power to say no" and should be prepared to exercise that power in appropriate circumstances.

Duty of Care and Reliance upon "Experts"

Duty of Care

Directors owe a duty of care in connection with the discharge of their responsibilities. One commentator has characterized this duty as a "duty of attention."[19] Under Delaware law, directors are obliged, before acting, to inform themselves of "all material information reasonably available" to them. Having become so informed, they then must act with requisite care in the discharge of their duties.[20] The Delaware courts have determined that directors will be held liable for breach of the duty of care if they act in a "grossly negligent" fashion, that is, with "reckless indifference to or a deliberate disregard of the whole body of stockholders," or when their actions can be said to be "without the bounds of reason."[21]

The Delaware courts have made clear that the standard outlined in their decisions does not require perfection, and directors certainly are not required to know everything about a topic that they are asked to consider. Under Delaware law it has been held that the directors' choice of which material to study and which to ignore is itself a decision to which a reviewing court should defer.[22]

Implicit in the due-care analysis is the notion that directors have, in fact, acted. Delaware law draws a distinction between claims that a director acted without due care (discussed previously) and claims that a director failed to act. Where a plaintiff is able to prove that a director neglected to act, the standard of care in such a "neglect" claim is that "which 'ordinarily careful and prudent men' would use in similar circumstances," which, in this context, appears to be an "ordinary negligence" standard.[23]

On the other hand, the "oversight" responsibility of the director also has its reasonable limits. Without some notice, the director of a large multinational corporation should not be held responsible for "neglect" for failing to discover corporate wrongdoing at a low operational level of a remote corporate division. Recognizing this practical dilemma, the law has developed a "red flag" test in the oversight area. Under this test, a director may be liable for ignoring "obvious danger signs of employee wrongdoing" or recklessly "repos[ing] confidence in an obviously untrustworthy employee," but need not go further than to apply "that amount of care that ordinarily careful and prudent men would use in similar circumstances."[24]

There have been several cases decided in Delaware and elsewhere in which directors have been found to be liable for a breach of the duty of care in the decision-making (as opposed to oversight) area, most notably the TransUnion case, *Smith v. Van Gorkom*.[25] More recently, the board of directors of Paramount Communications saw its preferred merger with Viacom Inc. imperiled when a reviewing court found that the directors gave "insufficient attention" to the potential consequences of the defensive aspects of their proposed combination.[26]

The commentators have distilled the case law into several practical guidelines:[27]

First: Take your time. Avoid haste in decision making, as well as the appearance of haste in decision making. Although the courts have recognized that there may be circumstances beyond the control of the board that dictate an accelerated timetable in making a decision (such as a deadline imposed by a bona fide bidder),[28] more likely than not a reviewing court will ask: What was the hurry? Prudent practice suggests that major decisions be made only after directors have had a full opportunity to digest all available material information. Practically, this may mean introducing a subject at one board meeting, presenting an overview of the proposed action, and then tabling consideration for the following meeting, to allow board members to reflect upon the matter in a mature way. If pressed by circumstances beyond the control of the board to act promptly, the chairman may want to consider advising board members in advance of a meeting of the pressing business that the board will be called upon to consider to allow board members the opportunity to begin to focus on the subject prior to the meeting itself. If time permits, advance dissemination of data and other materials will enhance the opportunity of the directors to inform themselves adequately prior to acting. Finally, if a subject needs extended debate, every member of the board should be concerned that the matter is fully aired before action is taken, so that all members may benefit from the views of their colleagues.

Second: Prepare. The courts have been particularly critical of directors who acted without having acquainted themselves with available material information. A good chairman will assure that pertinent information is provided to the board as far in advance as possible. A board member should consider materials provided before a meeting, together with any other reasonably available information before acting. Should a board member desire the input of inside[29] or outside experts on a topic, he or she should request that input sufficiently far in advance of a meeting to allow the company to arrange for appropriate presentations.

Third: Ask questions. Individual board members should take an active interest in every decision that they are called upon to make. The courts have encouraged activity on the part of directors, often focusing on whether individual members of the board asked questions of management or outside consultants. The unifying theme in the various decisions that address this point appears to be that a director should not merely accept information presented to him or her, but instead should probe and test that information to be able to form a judgment about its reliability and accuracy, as well as to understand it fully.

Fourth: Make a record. Assure that the proceedings of the board are faithfully recorded. The lack of a contemporaneously prepared set of minutes of a meeting may trouble a reviewing court. Although this is admittedly less important in small, privately held companies, it is extremely important in publicly held corporations, which may find themselves the subject of shareholder scrutiny.

Fifth: Review all materials. Avoid acting on matters that should be documented without a prior review of the relevant documents. Although it is not required that a director approve only the "final" draft of a document, directors who give approval to a transaction without having reviewed its material terms may find themselves subject to judicial criticism. If the documents are available, they should be presented to the board for review prior to the meeting. If they are not available until the meeting itself, prudent practice suggests that counsel or other experts review with the board each and every material provision, and allow members an opportunity to ask questions and to become familiar with the documents they are being asked to approve.

Reliance on Experts

Recognizing that directors cannot be expected to be experts in all fields of endeavor, most state corporation statutes expressly allow directors to rely upon reports submitted to them by experts, provided the experts are chosen with reasonable care, the director acts in good faith in relying upon the report, and no "red flag" exists that would suggest to a prudent person that the report should not be entitled to weight. Although states differ on whether meeting these criteria unconditionally protects a director's reliance on such a report, the debate in this regard may be more esoteric than practical. As in most areas of the law of corporate governance, the director is expected to exercise common sense and, having done so, he or she is not likely to be subject to liability in the event the report upon which he or she relied eventually is proven incorrect.

The decision of the Pennsylvania Supreme Court in *Cornell v. Seddinger*[30] provides a helpful case study. There, directors authorized a dividend payment apparently believing that it could be made without impairing capital. They were wrong. The dividend actually paid was paid from capital. When the dividend declaration was challenged, the outside directors argued that they should be protected from liability because they had relied upon the report of the company's treasurer to the effect that the company had legally available funds from which a dividend could be declared. The trial court found for the outside directors. On appeal, the Pennsylvania Supreme Court reversed. The Supreme Court found extremely persuasive the context in which the directors made their decision. The company was under contract to build ships for the U.S. Navy and was incurring heavy losses in doing so. At the same meeting at which the dividend was declared, the directors also discussed the shortage of working capital facing the company and the necessity of borrowing money to keep the company afloat. In this context, was it reasonable for directors to declare a dividend without carefully examining the report upon which they relied? The court thought not.

Moreover, the report itself showed the company's "work in process" (i.e., its shipbuilding for the Navy) as an asset, on the theory that the "fair value" of the ships exceeded the contract price and therefore the report should reflect "fair value" (and thus a profit) rather than the significant loss guaranteed under the contracts. The court found particularly important that no director asked any questions of the treasurer about this report, although all the directors clearly knew that the company would realize a significant loss upon completion of the company's "work in process." The court concluded, therefore, that the report was untrustworthy on its face, and anyone who examined it in any detail would have discovered as much.

Most of the statutory reliance provisions differ very little from the law of the *Cornell* case. Almost all require directors to assure themselves that appropriate diligence was exercised in selecting the expert who prepared the report and to have a reasonable basis upon which to conclude that the report is worthy of credence.

In deciding whether to rely on a report, directors might ask the following questions:

- Does the person presenting the report appear knowledgeable with respect to its contents?
- Is the presenting person recognized in the field or from a reputable firm?

- Does he or she answer questions in a sensible way?
- Do circumstances exist that make the result reached in the report one that is counterintuitive or unusual?
- Are the assumptions made in the report realistic?
- Is the technique underlying the report generally accepted?
- Does the report make sense?

If a director is satisfied with the answers to these questions, his or her judgment that a report is reliable will likely be entitled to deference by a court.

An interesting example of proper and protected reliance on an expert's report is illustrated by a merger case, *Rosenblatt v. Getty Oil Co.*[31] In *Rosenblatt*, the Getty Oil Company decided to merge with its majority-owned subsidiary, Skelly. Both Getty and Skelly established independent negotiating teams that engaged in hard-fought, arm's length negotiations on the appropriate merger ratio. A critical aspect of the deal was the value of each company's oil, gas, and minerals in the ground (so-called "subsurface assets"). Unable to agree on the value of each other's subsurface assets, both companies retained DeGolyer and MacNaughton (D&M), a firm of expert petroleum engineers, to assist in the valuation. The two companies used the reports prepared by D&M to negotiate a final merger ratio. Finding that D&M had "the requisite reputation and experience to assist Getty and Skelly" and that D&M acted independently of the influence of either party in carrying out its work, the Delaware Supreme Court affirmed that the directors acted properly in relying on D&M's report.

As *Rosenblatt* and *Cornell* make clear, directors may expect to be protected from liability if they rely on rational expert advice that they reasonably believe to be worthy of reliance. A board can increase the chance that its reliance on expert advice will be protected by assuring that the person or firm advising the board in fact has recognized expertise in the subject the board is considering and by carefully examining the advice received so that it is in a position to determine that the advice may be relied on.

Duties in Exceptional Circumstances

The "rules of the road" of director conduct change in certain extraordinary circumstances. Following, we examine a director's duties in the face of a takeover proposal (including adoption of defensive measures); in connection with the sale of the company; and during a proxy or written consent contest.

Duties in the Face of a Takeover Proposal

The takeover activity of the 1980s spawned the development and refinement of a large body of law regarding the duties of a board of directors faced with unwanted takeover bids. The Delaware courts led the development of this area of the law, and many jurisdictions eventually adopted the Delaware approach.[32] Under Delaware law, directors are required to show that before taking action to impede an unwanted takeover attempt, they: (a) reasonably perceived a "danger to corporate policy and effectiveness" and (b) that the action taken was "reasonable in relation to the threat posed."[33] A board that is able to demonstrate that it reasonably perceived a threat and took action that was proportional to the threat posed is entitled to the highly deferential "business judgment rule" type of review by the courts.

DOES THE BID PRESENT A "DANGER TO CORPORATE POLICY AND EFFECTIVENESS"?

Determining whether a particular offer poses a danger to corporate policy and effectiveness "requires directorial analysis of the nature of the takeover bid and its effect on the corporate enterprise."[34] In performing this analysis, directors may wish to consider the following factors, all of which are drawn from Delaware case law:[35]

a. the "inadequacy" (or adequacy) of the bid in financial terms;
b. the "nature and timing of the offer";
c. whether the bid complies with state and federal law, or poses antitrust or other regulatory obstacles;
d. "the impact on constituencies other than shareholders";[36]
e. the "risk of nonconsummation";
f. the "basic stockholder interests at stake," including the "past actions of the bidder and its affiliates in other takeover contests"; and
g. an analysis of the "bidder's responsibility," including factors such as the proposed or actual financing for the offer, and the "consequences" of the financing.[37]

The foregoing list of factors is not intended to be exclusive.[38] In general, the court seeks to determine whether the board has acted in "good faith" and upon "reasonable investigation." Directors will want to consider taking both financial and legal advice in determining whether a "threat" exists and in deciding upon an appropriate response to that "threat."

The courts have struggled with the question whether a bid for all shares of the company that offers all cash to all tendering shareholders could present a threat other than inadequate value. The early holdings in Delaware reflect an economic analysis of the issue and suggest that the only cognizable threat from a fairly timed, all-cash, all-shares tender offer could be inadequate value.[39] The Delaware Supreme Court, however, appears to have definitively settled the issue in its decision in *Paramount Communications Inc. v. Time Inc.,* by rejecting the notion that the only threat from such an offer is inadequate value. Instead, the court stated that an all-cash, all-shares offer could present other types of threats to "corporate policy and effectiveness," including the threat that shareholders might tender into the unwanted offer "in ignorance or a mistaken belief of the . . . benefit" of the offer and the possibility that the conditions attached to the offer might obfuscate or skew a reasonable analysis of the offer.[40]

Finally, the requirement to show that the board reasonably investigated a threat has led some to suggest that the board's duty should include a duty to conduct negotiations with the bidder. If a board is able to gather reliable information about the bid and the bidder, however, a refusal to negotiate could be upheld as reasonable, depending upon the circumstances. Although it is clear that a board faced with a hostile takeover bid must inform itself in the same way it does before making any other decision, the Delaware courts have nonetheless held that the board is under no "duty" to negotiate before deciding to reject a bid.[41]

IS THE BOARD'S RESPONSE
"REASONABLE IN RELATION TO THE THREAT POSED"?

If after a good faith investigation, the board concludes that the bid it faces is a "threat," it has a "fundamental duty and obligation" to oppose the offer.[42] This duty flows from the duty of loyalty the director owes the corporation, which "embodies . . . an affirmative duty to protect the interests of the corporation."[43] Although the board need not oppose a bid it determines does not threaten "corporate policy and effectiveness," it never may be a mere "passive instrumentality" when faced with a threat to the company or its stockholders.[44]

In discharging its duty to defend, the board is required to design a response to the "threat" that is "proportional," i.e., "reasonable in relation to the threat posed."[45] Restructurings, adoption of stockholder rights plans (also known as "poison pills"), selective repurchase offers, defensive acquisitions, stock placements, lockup options, and defensive tenders all have been upheld as reasonable in particular circumstances.[46] Of course, these responses were upheld under the unique facts of each case, and no director should assume that the foregoing list constitutes a catalog of responses that would be approved by a court on different facts.

In fashioning a response, a board may not use any "draconian" measure available to it. The court will review the response chosen to determine whether it is in some sense proportional to the identified threat. While some corporate restructurings have been approved, others have been struck down as disproportionate; the refusal to redeem a poison pill has been disapproved in certain circumstances; employee stock option plan (ESOP) transactions have been enjoined; and stock placement and repurchase transactions occasionally have met with judicial disfavor.[47] Although it is difficult to generalize, it may be assumed that the notion of proportionality implies that the board should review the range of responses available to it and attempt to select the response that least intrudes on the ordinary functioning of the entity and least disrupts the balance between directors and shareholders, while at the same time also promises to be effective in neutralizing the identified threat. This is not actually a "least-restrictive-alternative" test in the sense that a court would not be likely to penalize a board that chose to implement a more disruptive defense rather than the least disruptive defense if the directors could show they adopted the defense in good faith and in the reasonable belief that it best neutralized the threat they faced. In *Unitrin, Inc. v. American General Corp.*, the Delaware Supreme Court rejected the motion that a defensive response was subject to challenge under *Unocal* on grounds that it was "unnecessary" under the circumstances. Instead, the court directed that in applying the proportionality review mandated by *Unocal*, the reviewing court must focus first on whether the board's response to a threat was draconian, which the Supreme Court defined to mean either preclusive or coercive, and if not draconian, whether the response was "within a range of reasonable responses" to the identified threat.[48]

In short, this is yet another area where the board is called upon to exercise its informed judgment (and ordinary common sense) in determining the appropriate response to an identified threat. A board that is able to demonstrate that it carefully reviewed its alternatives and made a rational judgment about the appropriate alternative to choose is likely to survive challenge under this analysis, provided the court did not conclude that the chosen response was an abuse of power.

Duties in Connection with the Sale of the Company

A director is presented with a unique set of business problems when the board considers the sale of a company. The director still owes duties of care and loyalty in connection with the sale, but because the object of the exercise is limited to maximizing the price received in the sale, the permissible scope of considerations that may enter into directorial decision making become far more limited. For example, as noted previously, the directors' ability to consider the welfare of constituencies other than shareholders disappears in the context of a sale, unless such considerations are likely to lead to increased value for stockholders.

Here, we address three practical issues: (1) What are the special duties that arise in connection with the sale of the company? (2) How should the director attempt to discharge these duties? and (3) When, other than in the sale context, might these duties also be implicated?

THE DIRECTORS' DUTIES IN THE SALE OF CONTROL

The first significant judicial decision to address this issue directly was the Delaware Supreme Court's decision in *Revlon, Inc. v. MacAndrews & Forbes Holdings, Inc.*[49] *Revlon* addressed a board's use of defensive devices in the context of an "auction" for control of a company. There, the board, faced with what it considered an unfairly low bid by an unwelcome suitor, Pantry Pride, found a second firm, Forstmann Little, willing to make a higher bid. The emergence of the second bidder led to an "auction" between the two firms. The board ended the auction by granting Forstmann a "lockup" option on certain important assets of Revlon, even though Pantry Pride had announced its intention to top any bid made by Forstmann.

In light of the board's use of defensive devices to stop the auction process, apparently before its "natural" conclusion in the marketplace, the trial court granted an injunction to halt the Revlon-Forstmann deal. On appeal, the Delaware Supreme Court affirmed. Assessing the board's conduct, that court stated:

> [W]hen Pantry Pride increased its offer . . . it became apparent to all that the break-up of the company was inevitable. . . . The duty of the board has thus changed from the preservation of Revlon as a corporate entity to the maximization of the company's value at a sale for the stockholders' benefit. This significantly altered the board's responsibilities under the *Unocal* standards. It no longer faced threats to corporate policy and ef-

fectiveness, or to the stockholders' interests, from a grossly inadequate bid. The whole question of defensive measures became moot. The directors' role changed from defenders of the corporate bastion to auctioneers charged with getting the best price for the stockholders at a sale of the company.[50]

The colorful language of the *Revlon* decision raised numerous questions and misconceptions among corporate governance practitioners and academics. Perhaps the most common misconception following *Revlon* was the notion that the case imposed a "duty to auction" in connection with every change of control.

Subsequently, the Delaware Supreme Court has made clear that *Revlon* does not impose a "duty to auction." Instead, the duty imposed in connection with the sale of control of the corporation is the duty to maximize the shareholders' return. This is said to be the "sole responsibility" of the board in this context.[51] In discharging the duty of value maximization in connection with the sale of the enterprise, the board must be fully informed, and each director must act free from any disabling personal interest.

In the *Macmillan* case, the Delaware Supreme Court confronted an auction process that had impermissibly favored a bidder preferred by management at the expense of an outside bidder. This favoritism culminated in a "tip" to the favored bidder in the last round of bidding, informing it of the terms of the rival bid. In deciding that the auction had been impermissibly skewed toward management's favored bidder, the Supreme Court was harsh in its criticism of the other members of the board. Calling for "intense scrutiny and participation" in the sale process by the independent members of the board, the court made clear that the duty of oversight was heightened at this critical juncture in corporate existence. The outside directors' failure to become actively involved in the design and oversight of the sale process was characterized by the court as the "virtual abandonment of [the directors'] oversight functions" constituting "a breach of [the board's] fundamental duties of loyalty and care in the conduct of this auction."[52]

Finally, in *Paramount Communications Inc. v. QVC Network Inc.*, the Supreme Court again revisited the duties of directors in a sale of control. Where two companies were engaged actively in attempting to purchase control of Paramount, the court described the directors' "one primary objective" as "secur[ing] the transaction offering the best value reasonably available for the stockholders. . . ."[53] Consistent with earlier cases addressing directors' duties in this context, the *Paramount* court stressed that directors will be expected to have actually exercised their duties in connection with the sale of control. Again, the court stressed the need for directors to be adequately informed in connection with negotiating a sale of control, describing the need for information in this context as "central" to the evaluation the board is called upon to make.[54] The court summarized the board's duties under the facts of the *Paramount* case as follows:

> the Paramount directors had the obligation: (a) to be diligent and vigilant in examining critically the Paramount-Viacom transaction and the QVC tender offers; (b) to act in good faith; (c) to obtain, and act with due care on, all material information reasonably available, including information necessary to compare the two offers to determine which of these transactions, or an alternative course of action, would provide the best value reasonably available to the stockholders; and (d) to negotiate actively and in good faith with both Viacom and QVC to that end.[55]

Three principles can be deduced from *Revlon* and its progeny. First, if called upon to make decisions regarding the sale of the corporation, the sole object of the directors' activities should and must be geared toward generating the highest possible return to shareholders. Second, in a sale of the enterprise, the directors' duty of oversight is heightened. Delaware law appears to encourage, if not require, the board to be actively involved in the design and execution of the sale. The board should not be content merely to delegate the conduct of the sale to others and receive periodic reports. Instead, the board should be prepared to give "intense scrutiny" to the process and, where appropriate, to participate in its execution. Third, except as they may enhance the value ultimately received by shareholders (and that special case is dealt with in the following section), defensive devices are likely to be subject to close scrutiny in connection with the sale of the company.

THE DISCHARGE OF THE DIRECTORS' DUTIES
WHEN THE SALE OF THE COMPANY IS INEVITABLE

Delaware law makes clear that in maximizing stockholder value in a sale of the company, "there is no single blueprint that a board must follow to fulfill its duties."[56] In several recent decisions, the courts have provided helpful guidance to a board seeking to discharge its duties in this context.

Two patterns of transactions have emerged: the classic "auction," in which several bidders are actively competing for the same company, and the sale of control not preceded by an active auction, by far the more common type of transaction. Perhaps because of the intense notoriety surrounding several of the control auctions, the law in this area has received a great deal of attention by the commentators. The case law also addresses the second transactional pattern, however, and provides useful guidance to the structuring of a sale of control outside the "auction" context.

THE "AUCTION" CONTEXT   In the auction context, directors may want to focus on the issues such as whether the auction is open to all potential bidders likely to make a responsible bid; the rules of the auction; and when and how to end the auction.

Is the auction open to all potential bidders likely to be able to make a responsible bid? Few firms set out to sell themselves at an unrestrained, all-comers "auction." The disruption attendant to such an uncontrolled process often is enormous, with potential damage to employees, customers, suppliers, and other vital constituencies. In fact, almost all of the cases dealing with such auctions arise where the company finds itself the subject of several committed and not always welcome bidders. In recent years, therefore, counsel and other advisers have developed the notion of a "controlled" auction, i.e., an auction open only to a select group of invited bidders. The benefits of such a process flow from the fact that such an auction may be conducted outside the spotlight, resulting in far less disruption to the firm and its constituencies. Similarly, a properly designed "controlled" auction may minimize the risk of a "fire sale" or the perception that the company on the auction block has put itself in that position because it is somehow distressed.

Using a "controlled" auction process places special burdens on the board. If the auction is conducted quietly, the board must be convinced that an appropriate group of firms has been invited to submit bids. Because a "controlled" auction by definition does not contemplate the participation of every firm with any interest in the company to be auctioned, the directors should be convinced that the group selected to participate truly does represent the universe of most likely responsible bidders best able to complete a transaction. Put in the language of the cases, the selection of discrete bidders is likely to be respected by the reviewing court—at least when the challenge comes from a shareholder plaintiff rather than an overlooked bona fide bidder—provided the directors make a good faith, informed judgment that this approach to an "auction" is designed to return maximum value to stockholders by avoiding the direct and indirect costs attendant to the free-for-all auction scenario.

The directors also will want to consider how uninvited firms who express a desire to participate in the auction will be treated. Finally, while the use of an investment banker is not required by law, directors are well-advised to assure that a recognized investment bank is retained to assist the board in fulfilling its duties. The banker chosen to solicit bids should be one with appropriate experience and contacts, and if the firm has a presence abroad, solicitation of international buyers should be considered.

The auction's rules. Directors also will want to give careful attention to the rules and procedures established for bidding. What are potential bidders being told? Are all bidders being given access to the same information? With how much nonpublic information are they being provided? Are confidentiality agreements required, and, if so, do the agreements contain "standstill" provisions that might inhibit the emergence of a bid? How much "due diligence" is being permitted to interested potential bidders? How are direct competitors treated? Are they included in the process at all? If they are not invited to participate but express an interest in doing so, how are they to be dealt with?

The courts have made clear that the goal of the design of the auction is not some sense of abstract "fairness" to bidders, but instead value maximization for stockholders.[57] Although equal treatment of all bidders usually is the norm, should the circumstances suggest that different treatment for a particular bidder could enhance the ultimate result, such an approach may be acceptable. In the *Macmillan* case, the Delaware Supreme Court held that the reviewing court would consider the following factors in cases of "disparate treatment" among bidders: First, the court will examine "whether the directors properly perceived that shareholders' interests were enhanced" by the disparate treatment, and second, the disparate treatment must be "reasonable in relation to the advantage sought to be achieved. . . ."[58]

Ending the auction: "lockup" and "no-shop" provisions. Perhaps the most critical part of any auction, controlled or otherwise, is the decision to end the process. Certainly, in this regard, the director will want to consider whether the auction has been structured in advance to end at a "final" round of bidding, and, if so, whether further bidding is likely to bring forth a higher price. The auction cases have been extremely critical of director decisions to end an auction. Surely, directors will want to assure themselves that the auction process has run its course before calling an end to bidding. Similarly, directors will want to assure that the timing of the "final" bidding round (if one is planned) is such that all interested and responsible bidders have sufficient time to make their best and final offers.

Some auctions have ended with the grant of lockup options or no-shop agreements. In *Revlon*, the board determined to end the auction by granting its white knight bidder the right to purchase a "crown jewel" asset at a fixed price, regardless of whether the hostile bidder raised its price or not. Other auctions have ended when the successful bidder demands and receives a "no-shop" clause, in a form that prohibits the corporation from making further attempts to sell the company.[59] Such potentially auction ending devices have received intense scrutiny in the courts.

With respect to asset option agreements, the Delaware courts have repeatedly held that such agreements, while not illegal per se, must "confer a substantial benefit upon the stockholders in order to withstand exacting scrutiny by the courts."[60] If such an agreement is not absolutely necessary to draw bidders into an auction and does not materially enhance the final price received in the process, directors should be particularly careful about agreeing to it. Although no case explicitly so holds, the analysis of the lockup option is one that approaches a "strict liability" analysis, primarily because it often is conducted with the benefit of hindsight. Unless a bid is so clearly preemptive and is highly likely to be materially more than any other bidder can afford to pay, directors are well advised to avoid the grant of auction-ending lockup agreements.

As for the auction-ending no-shop clause, the courts have held that the use of such a clause is "even more limited than a lockup agreement." The standard enunciated by the courts is that "[a]bsent a material advantage to the stockholders from the terms or structure of a bid that is contingent on a no-shop clause, a successful bidder imposing such a condition must be prepared to survive the careful scrutiny which that concession demands."[61]

In the *Paramount* case, the court narrowly circumscribed the ability of a board to utilize lockup and no-shop provisions. As for the no-shop provision, the court held that to the extent such a provision purports to require a board to act in a way that limits its exercise of fiduciary duties, "it is invalid and unenforceable."[62] Similarly, a lockup option that allowed the option holder to "put" the option back to the issuer, requiring the issuer to pay the holder the difference between the option strike price and then-current value, was held to be sufficiently "draconian" as to be unenforceable, at least where combined with several other unusual features and likely to lead to a payment of almost one half billion dollars if not enjoined.

While the court left open the possibility that both no-shop provisions and options could be held valid in other circumstances, the court reiterated its observation that absent a reasonable basis upon which to judge the adequacy of a particular transaction, a no-shop restriction "gives rise to the inference that the board seeks to forestall competing bids."[63]

In its examination of the various defensive measures that were part of the Paramount transaction, the court wrote that the provisions "necessarily implicated various issues," including whether or not the provisions, separately or in the aggregate:

a. adversely affected the value to be received by stockholders;
b. inhibited or encouraged alternative bids;
c. were enforceable; and
d. "in the end would advance or retard the Paramount directors' obligation to secure for the Paramount stockholders the best value reasonably available under the circumstances."[64]

SELLING CONTROL OUTSIDE THE "AUCTION" CONTEXT. Several of the issues outlined previously also arise in the nonauction context. The negotiated sale of control to a single buyer presents special issues in this regard. For example, the courts have recognized that an unimpeded auction is likely to yield the best possible information regarding the real value of the company. Without an opportunity to "price" the company in the marketplace for control, directors must confront a practical dilemma: how to be sure that the price at which the company is sold is the best value that could be achieved for stockholders? In this regard, the courts have concluded that an investment banker's opinion is a "pale" substitute for the type of reliable value information that could be generated in an auction.[65]

The answer to the dilemma that has evolved over the past several years is the "market check." In recent years, negotiated acquisitions have included various forms of market-check provisions.[66]

The market check is used principally as a mechanism to canvass the market to determine whether a better deal is available and therefore is typically used where a seller has a firm deal in hand.

An effective market check possesses certain characteristics. First, it establishes a "floor price" for the company in light of the fact that a signed deal exists. Second, in one form or another, it allows the seller to provide information to those who learn of the potential sale. Third, the market-check period is open for a long enough time to allow other potential bidders the opportunity to analyze the relevant data and to formulate a proposal.[67] Fourth, the signed deal typically does not include structural impediments that would discourage a second bidder from emerging.[68] Finally, the press release announcing the original deal must be sufficient in distribution and content to put other potential bidders on notice of the possibility of receiving information and making a bid. Although no court has required a particular form of press release, logic suggests that, at the least, the press release should not actively discourage other bidders from coming forward.

The effective use of a well-structured market check is likely not only to enhance the information available to directors in connection with the sale of the company, but also to affect favorably a reviewing court's analysis of other features of the merger or sale agreement, such as a no-shop clause. In *Amsted Industries,* for example, the Delaware Supreme Court held that the use of a no-shop provision in the nonauction setting "gives rise to the inference that the board seeks to forestall competing bids."[69] The court expressly held, however, that the use of a market check would tend to rebut such an inference "since it would have made it clear beyond question [at least in the context of the facts presented in *Amsted*] that the board was acting to protect the shareholders' interests." Similarly, the Delaware court has held that a board's failure to conduct a market check in the face of a hostile offer (among other things) rendered the directors' refusal to redeem a rights plan "unreasonable" and not in good faith.[70]

In selling control outside the auction context, therefore, directors may want to consider the judicious use of a properly structured market check. Of course, the market check is not the only way a board may fulfill its duties, but because it has received widespread judicial recognition, such an approach may be more likely to receive judicial deference than other, less widely examined approaches.

Duties during the Conduct of a Proxy Fight
or Written Consent Contest

The corporation law of most jurisdictions historically has given special solicitude to the shareholders' right of corporate suffrage. Because the ability to vote (especially on the question of who will make up the board) is the factor that legitimates the directors' control over property that is not their own, corporate actions that are designed to, or have the effect of, thwarting the free exercise of the stockholders' franchise, although not per se illegal, are subject to close scrutiny in the courts.[71] Where an incumbent board takes action to frustrate the franchise rights of an insurgent minority, for example, the board may be required to show a "compelling justification" for its actions.[72]

The board of directors of a public corporation is most likely to face the issues that arise in this area when confronted by a proxy contest or, where available, a shareholder challenge employing written consents. Because a reviewing court is likely to examine both the purpose and the effect of a board's actions during the pendency of a proxy or consent challenge, the board must be careful in this setting not to take action that, while arguably noble in purpose, has some inequitable effect. In one case, for example, well-intended directors expanded the size of the board to frustrate an insurgent shareholder's attempt to take control of a majority of the board and were held to have committed an "unintended" breach of the duty of loyalty.[73]

The directors' duty to avoid action that might have an inequitable impact on the franchise during the pendency of a proxy or consent fight becomes more problematic when a proxy or consent fight is coupled with a tender offer. As demonstrated previously, at least in Delaware, directors have a duty to defend against offers they reasonably perceive to be harmful. Although not yet entirely clear, it may be that the special solicitude for the franchise yields to the directors' duty to defend the enterprise. Actions that could otherwise affect the vote in a proxy contest might be viewed with a less critical eye if the directors can make a good-faith showing that their action was designed to deflect the parallel tender offer and not the proxy fight.

The issue was raised in *Shamrock Holdings, Inc. v. Polaroid Corp.*[74] There, Shamrock, which had outstanding a tender offer to buy Polaroid, also announced its intention to conduct a proxy fight at the upcoming annual meeting of the company. When Polaroid sold a significant block of its shares to Corporate Partners, a white squire fund, Shamrock challenged the sale and asserted that the board acted with the purpose of thwarting Shamrock's announced intention to wage a proxy fight. Finding that the defendants' primary purpose was not to interfere with the electoral process and further that the Polaroid board had met its burden under *Unocal* in reasonably responding to a threat to corporate policy and effectiveness, the court declined to enjoin the transaction.

The same issues were raised anew in *Stahl v. Apple Bancorp, Inc.*[75] There, the plaintiff had acquired 30 percent of the stock of the company, commenced a tender offer, and announced his intention to conduct a proxy contest. The board adopted a shareholder rights plan (colloquially known as a "poison pill") that contained certain prohibitions against a 15 percent shareholder entering into binding agreements with other large shareholders regarding the voting of their Apple shares and related matters. Stahl argued that these provisions of the rights plan inequitably interfered with his ability to conduct a proxy contest. The court noted that the special scrutiny reserved for franchise cases was implicated "when board action appears directed primarily towards interfering with the fair exercise of the franchise. . . ."[76] Finding that the rights plan was not adopted primarily to interfere with the right of shareholders to elect directors, the court declined to consider Stahl's challenges under the strict scrutiny reserved for "franchise" cases, using instead the so-called *Unocal* analysis. In light of the tender offer, which the board had determined to oppose, and the "minimal" impact of the rights plan on proxy contests, the court declined to order that the rights plan be redeemed or modified.

In *Stroud v. Grace,*[77] the Delaware Supreme Court addressed this issue, stating that a reviewing court was bound to apply the *Unocal* analysis "where the board 'adopts any defensive measure taken in response to some threat to corporate policy and effectiveness which touches upon issues of control.'"[78] The court went on to note, however, that its mandate did not render the special scrutiny applied to franchise cases "meaningless." The court explained:

> In certain circumstances, a court must recognize the special import of protecting the shareholders' franchise within *Unocal's* requirement that any defensive measure be proportionate and "reasonable. . . ." A board's unilateral decision to adopt a defensive measure touching "upon issues of control" that pur-

posefully disenfranchises its shareholders is strongly suspect under *Unocal*, and cannot be sustained without a "compelling justification."[79]

Thus, although the courts appear reluctant to allow an acquiror who couples a proxy fight with a tender offer to make offensive use of the strict scrutiny implicated in franchise cases, such scrutiny may be appropriate in light of the factual context of future cases. In short, while the existence of a proxy or consent fight does not ameliorate the board's duty to defend the corporate enterprise from a tender offer the board reasonably concludes is a "threat," in designing its response the board must be especially aware of the law's special concern for the shareholder franchise and should attempt to minimize the impact of its response on the franchise.

Duties to Preferred Shareholders

In addressing directors' duties, most sources refer to duties to stockholders generally without distinguishing between duties to different classes of stockholders. Under Delaware law, however, the duties a board owes to preferred stockholders may be different in certain respects from those owed to common stockholders.

Preferred stock, like common stock, is a creature of statute and its terms are delineated in the certificate of incorporation. Preferred stock is so named because it provides the holders with special rights not possessed by holders of common stock. For example, additional rights of preferred stock could include special voting, dividend, dissolution, and liquidation rights. In addition to these special rights vis-à-vis the common stock, holders of preferred stock also have a special relationship with the board of directors.

Unlike a board's duties to common stockholders, the board's duties to preferred holders may be limited by the preferred stock contract itself. Under Delaware law, for example, preferred stockholders appear to be owed duties of a fiduciary nature when their contract does not address an issue, but solely contractual duties when it does. It follows, therefore, that the relationship between a board of directors and holders of preferred stock is not capable of ready generalization. On the one hand, the elements that distinguish preferred stock from common stock are spelled out in the contract between the corporation and the holders of preferred stock—the certificate of incorporation. These special rights held by the preferred shareholders are afforded protection by the express terms of the contract. On the other hand, preferred stock represents an equity interest in the corporation. In this respect, holders of preferred stock are entitled to the same fiduciary duties that members of the board of directors owe to all stockholders.

The Delaware Court of Chancery addressed the equity-contract dichotomy of preferred stock as follows:

> with respect to matters relating to preferences or limitations that distinguish preferred stock from common, the duty of the corporation and its directors is essentially contractual and the scope of the duty is appropriately defined by reference to the specific words evidencing that contract; where however the right asserted is not to a preference as against the common stock but rather a right shared equally with the common, the existence of such right and the scope of the correlative duty may be measured by equitable as well as legal standards.[80]

Accordingly, even though the rights and obligations of preferred shareholders are "essentially contractual," a board of directors owes preferred shareholders the fiduciary duties of care, loyalty, and good faith where the contract is silent.[81] Holders of preferred stock thus stand in a unique position compared to debt and other equity securities. Preferred stock is not pure equity like common stock, nor is it pure debt. Rather, it is a unique blend with rights and obligations of each type of security.

An expansion and a clarification of the idea that "[r]ights of preferred stock are primarily but not exclusively contractual in nature" is found in *HB Korenvaes Inv. v. Marriott Corp.*[82] There, the preferred shareholders of Marriott Corporation ("Marriott") claimed that the distribution of a special dividend to the common stockholders violated the fiduciary duty of loyalty owed to them by the board of directors. The distribution of the special dividend was to be accomplished through a transaction that would effectively result in the splitting of Marriott into two separate companies. One of the resulting entities, Marriott International, Inc. ("International"), would hold Marriott's lodging, food services and facilities management, and senior living services operations, while the other company, Marriott Host Corporation ("Host"), would retain real estate, stadium, and toll-road concessions. The plan then proposed to distribute, as a special dividend to Marriott common stockholders, all of the stock of International. The preferred shareholders viewed the restructuring plan and the subsequent special dividend as an attempt to transfer wealth from the preferred shareholders to the holders of Marriott's common stock, in violation of the duty of loyalty owed to them by the board. The preferred shareholders also claimed that the proposed transaction violated the terms of the certificate of designation that delineated their rights.

After analyzing the terms of the certificate of designation, the court found that the rights of the preferred shareholders with respect to the proposed special dividend transaction were contractual in nature. Because that governing document expressly provided for special dividends and corresponding contractual protections, the court determined that the question of the liability of the directors was to be determined solely by contractual principles in reference to the certificate. Because equitable principles were not implicated, the court held that the preferred stockholders could not maintain a claim of breach of the fiduciary duty of loyalty against the Marriott directors. Accordingly, where the dispute is centered on the terms of the contract, the fiduciary duties of directors are not implicated.[83] In other words, directors do not owe fiduciary duties to holders of preferred stock when the certificate of incorporation expressly resolves the question in dispute.

The *Marriott* court did recognize, however, that if the certificate of designation does not address the matter at issue fully, a fiduciary duty may be owed to the preferred shareholders. As Chancellor William Allen stated: "the question whether duties of loyalties are implicated by corporate action affecting preferred stock is a question that demands reference to the particularities of context to fashion a sound reply."[84]

For example, a duty of full disclosure is owed by a board of directors to both preferred shareholders and common shareholders when the preferred shareholders possess voting rights.[85] The extent of this fiduciary duty owed to the preferred stockholders is comparable to the duty owed to the corporation's common stockholders. Moreover, the board of directors cannot benefit and further the interests of the common stockholders to the detriment of the preferred shareholders unless permitted to do so under the contract.[86]

Particularly difficult questions arise in the context of a corporate transaction where the board is required to assess or apportion consideration between preferred and common stock. For example, preferred stockholders have prosecuted claims alleging breach of the fiduciary duty of loyalty in a merger context challenging the directors' decisions regarding the allocation of the merger consideration between the common and preferred stock.[87] Delaware courts have recognized such claims under the duty of loyalty and have stated that directors are "obligated to treat the preferred fairly."[88]

Although the preferred stockholders are owed fiduciary duties where their contract is silent, the actual breadth of this protection is questionable. The scope of the fiduciary duty imposed on a board of directors vis-à-vis preferred stock can be limited. By specifying in the certificate of incorporation or the certificate of designation the rights to be accorded to preferred shareholders in as many circumstances as can be contemplated, the fiduciary duty running to preferred stock could (theoretically, at least) be eliminated.[89]

As a practical matter, therefore, in all transactions affecting the rights of preferred stock, the board will want to consider carefully the contract rights of the preferred holders.

The Business Judgment Rule

Much has been written about the so-called "business judgment rule." There is at least one entire treatise devoted to the subject,[90] and the articles in print on the topic run into the hundreds, if not thousands. Here, we address the topic in only brief form, trusting that the interested reader will pursue the subject at greater length in the wealth of available resources.

The Nature of the Rule

At its simplest, the business judgment rule is a series of presumptions relating to decisions made by directors. It should be noted that the presumptions constituting the rule attach only to a director's *judgment*, although a conscious decision not to act is entitled to exactly the same treatment as a decision to take action.[91] To be entitled to rely on the protections of the rule, however, the director must have made a decision.[92]

A board's decision will be protected unless it is shown that a majority of the directors on the board were not disinterested with respect to that decision; the decision was made without prior consideration of all reasonably available material information; or a majority of the board is shown to have failed to act in the honest belief that the decision was in the best interests of the corporation. In a leading case, the Delaware Chancellor has described the rule from the perspective of a reviewing court:

> The business judgment form of judicial review encompasses three elements: a threshold review of the objective financial interests of the board whose decision is under attack (i.e., independence), a review of the board's subjective motivation (*i.e.*,

good faith), and an objective review of the process by which it reached the decision under review (*i.e.,* due care).[93]

The rule, when invoked to shield a decision made outside the control context provides a powerful presumption that, in making a decision, the directors acted "on an informed basis, in good faith and in the honest belief that the action taken was in the best interests of the company."[94] If a plaintiff is unable to rebut the presumptions inherent in the rule at trial (and it is plaintiff's burden to do so), the directors are protected from liability arising out of that decision, even if it later proves to be unwise.[95]

The rationale that supports such a sweeping limitation on judicial review of directors' decisions often is stated in different ways. First, the rule is said to encourage competent individuals to serve as directors by limiting liability and recognizing "human fallibility." Second, the rule recognizes that business decisions involve a certain degree of risk and that a system of law that subjects the risk takers to constant second-guessing by courts and shareholders alike would be highly inefficient. Third, the rule reflects the institutional shortcomings of the courts, which are not well suited to review often complex and technical business decisions.[96]

The Prerequisites for Invoking the Rule

When and under what circumstances may this powerful series of presumptions be invoked to shield a board's decisions? In the ordinary course of business, the presumptions of the rule protect director decision making provided the four elements of the rule are present. In each case, the reviewing court will seek to determine: whether the board made a decision to act or refrain from acting; whether a majority of the board was disinterested with respect to the decision in the sense that it had no financial interest in the outcome; whether the board carefully considered the issue and all reasonably available material information before acting; and whether the decision was taken in the good-faith belief that it was appropriate and in the best interests of the corporation. Here, we examine briefly each of these elements in light of the relevant law.

Did the board make a decision?
The law does not protect directors' inaction. The law does, however, distinguish between inaction and a conscious decision to re-

frain from acting. As noted previously, the latter decision is entitled to the presumptions of the rule, just as any other business decision of the board.

Was a majority of the board financially interested in the decision?

The decision of a director who has a financial interest in the underlying transaction is not entitled to the benefit of the business judgment rule. The rule proceeds from the commonsense observation that an "interested" director is likely to be affected by that personal interest. The courts also have held that the presence of fewer than a majority of "interested" directors will not strip the board's decision of the protection of the business judgment rule, without special circumstances.[97] The special circumstances under which the interest of less than a majority of the board could deprive the board's decision of the protections of the business judgment rule were described in *Cinerama, Inc. v. Technicolor, Inc.* In that case, the court concluded that the financial interest of one or more (but less than a majority of) directors stripped board action of the presumptions of the business judgment rule where the interested director "*controls* or *dominates* the board as a whole" or where the interested director fails to disclose his or her interest to the board and a reasonable director would have regarded the existence of the interest "as a significant fact in the evaluation of the proposed transaction."[98] Under either circumstance, the burden then shifts to the full board to show that the transaction is entirely fair to the corporation. This is so even where a single director fails to disclose his or her interest to the board. In such a situation, the good faith or "innocence" of the other board members, while relevant in the court's creation of a remedy, does not impact the necessity of showing the entire or inherent fairness of the transaction.[99]

What constitutes "interest"? Directors are ordinarily thought to be "interested" in a decision if they have a direct financial interest in the outcome, or stand on both sides of the transaction.[100] Put differently, a director is "independent" when "he or she is in a position to base his or her decision on the merits of the issue rather than being governed by extraneous considerations or influences."[101] The mere receipt of customary fees for service as a director does not render a director "interested."[102] Nonetheless, the payment of elaborate perquisites to board members may call into question their "interestedness," at least in the context of a suit challenging the award of such perquisites.[103] Moreover, to deprive the director or the board of the presumptions of the business judgment rule, the interest must be "material."[104]

Several corporations have attempted to define independent or disinterested directors in their bylaws. Section 2.12 of the GM bylaws requires that a majority of the board be made up of independent directors, which it defines as directors who have not been employed by the corporation within five years, are not "significant" advisers or consultants, are not affiliated with significant customers or suppliers, do not have significant personal services contracts with the company, are not affiliated with a tax-exempt entity that receives significant contributions from the company, and are not closely related to insiders at the company. Chrysler Corporation has adopted a similar bylaw that provides an objective measure of the "significant" affiliations identified in the GM bylaws by using the Securities and Exchange Commission (SEC) regulations as a trigger to disqualification as an "independent" director. Under Article II, Section 7 of Chrysler's bylaws, a director is not classified as "independent" if his or her affiliations are required to be disclosed under particular federal disclosure regulations.

More difficult issues arise in connection with what could fairly be termed directors' "indirect" interest in particular decisions. For example, in the *Revlon* case, the Delaware Supreme Court suggested that the board might not be entitled to the presumptions of the business judgment rule because several of the directors "were associated at some point with entities that had various business relationships with Revlon."[105] In a different case, the independence of a board composed of various professionals who rendered accounting, legal, and consulting services to the corporation or its dominant director was called into question where the case challenged the issuance of supervoting stock designed to assure the success of the incumbent board in a proxy fight.[106]

Before leaving the subject of director interest, however, it should be noted that the special scrutiny afforded to cases arising against the backdrop of a proxy or written consent fight and alleging manipulation of the election by the incumbent board also may be reflected in findings regarding the "interestedness" of directors who act to frustrate a proxy or consent fight. In one "franchise" case, for example, the court concluded that all directors were "interested" in the decision to postpone an annual meeting where the decision was made after the company's proxy solicitor informed the board that it would be likely to lose a proxy fight for control of the company if the scheduled meeting went forward.[107]

Did the board act with due care?

Directors owe a duty to consider all reasonably available material information on a topic prior to making a decision. At least under Delaware law, without a provision in the certificate of incorporation of the company exculpating directors from monetary liability for breach of the duty of care, a director may be held to respond in damages for a breach of his or her duty of care. Moreover, a decision taken in the absence of due care is not one to which the business judgment rule will attach.

Nonetheless, the courts have recognized that assembling information has certain costs and, in some circumstances, risks as well.[108] Take, for example, the case where a bidder offers to buy the company for a substantial premium to market at what appears to be a very attractive price, but makes clear that if the offer is not accepted unconditionally in some short period of time (for example, forty-eight hours) it will expire, not to be renewed. The board faced with such an offer is put to a difficult choice. While it appears relatively clear that a decision to reject such an offer on the grounds that the board has insufficient time in which to become fully informed would not be a basis for director liability,[109] a good faith decision that the company should be sold at the price offered could be subject to judicial second-guessing on the grounds that the board could not have had sufficient time to become fully informed prior to making a decision about such a critically important matter. In fact, this "hypothetical" tracks closely the facts of the *Van Gorkom* case, in which the directors were ultimately found personally liable for accepting an offer made at a not insubstantial premium to market by an acquiror who insisted on a response in a short period of time.

More recent decisions appear to provide some further elucidation. In *RJR Nabisco Shareholders Litigation*, for example, the Delaware court stated that "where an arm's length negotiating adversary imposes time limits, a board is forced to contend with that circumstance. If it exercises informed judgment in the circumstances, considers the risks posed by the deadline imposed, and concludes that it is prudent to act and acts with care, it has satisfied its duty."[110]

Did the board act in the honest belief that its decision would benefit the corporation?

The requirement of "good faith" has been expressed in various ways. Put most simply, directors must act "in the honest belief that their actions are in the corporation's best interests" and not for any personal gain.[111] Also subsumed within the notion of "good faith" is that the action taken has a "rational business purpose." Where the court concludes that a board's decision is not rational, it likewise may conclude that the decision was in good faith.[112]

The Delaware Modification of the Rule and Other Approaches to Business Judgment in the Takeover Context

As we noted previously, directors confronted with a takeover proposal must show that before acting they reasonably perceived a "danger to corporate policy and effectiveness" and that the action was "reasonable in relation to the threat posed."[113] If a majority of the board is able to make these showings, the board will be entitled to the presumptions of the business judgment rule, provided that all of the prerequisites for invocation of the rule are present. The imposition of the threshold requirements in the takeover area is a judicially crafted attempt to acknowledge the "omnipresent specter" of self-interest implicated whenever a board is required to make decisions that directly implicate its own tenure.

Not all jurisdictions track the Delaware approach to judicial review of director decision making in the takeover context. Indiana has enacted legislation rejecting the Delaware approach.[114] Pennsylvania also appears to have rejected the *Unocal* approach by statute.[115] New York, California, and New Jersey all appear to approach the subject somewhat differently from the Delaware model. While less than clear, it appears that neither New York nor California law places any *Unocal*-type threshold burden on directors, regardless of whether the directors act in the face of a takeover threat or not. Under this approach, however, once a plaintiff is able to make a prima facie showing that the board used its corporate powers to retain control, the burden falls on the directors to prove the intrinsic fairness of the transaction.[116] Courts interpreting New Jersey law have been less clear, one applying the Delaware approach, one following more closely the New York approach.[117]

The American Bar Association (ABA) Committee on Corporate Laws, which is the drafter of the Model Business Corporation Act, set out to codify the business judgment rule in connection with its overhaul of the Model Act during the 1980s. The project eventually was abandoned, apparently in light of concerns that no codification of the rule can accommodate all of the circumstances that a board might possibly address.[118] The American Law Institute (ALI) was not similarly dissuaded from its attempts to codify the rule, however. Section 4.01(c) of the *Principles of Corporate Governance: Analysis and Recommendations,* approved by the members of the ALI in May, 1985, provides:

> A director or officer who makes a business judgment in good faith fulfills his duty [of care] if:
>
> (1) he is not interested [a defined term] in the subject of his business judgment;
> (2) he is informed with respect to the subject of his business judgment to the extent he reasonably believes to be appropriate under the circumstances; and
> (3) he rationally believes that his business judgment is in the best interests of the corporation.[119]

This formulation has been the subject of extensive critique and debate.[120]

Statutory Liabilities of Directors

Directors of most large corporations are faced with an imposing array of statutory duties and liabilities that are imposed outside of the basic state law duties of loyalty, care, good faith, and full disclosure. The ABA Criminal Laws Committee has observed that the trend toward legislating directorial duties has increasingly led to the "criminalization" of business conduct.[121] While directors are at risk for criminal liability, both state and federal statutory law may impose civil liability as well.

State Statutory Liability

State statutes imposing liability on directors track many of the federal statutes. For example, states have enacted legislation requiring the registration of securities. Like their federal counterparts, these statutes impose liability on directors for wrongs committed in connection with the offer, purchase, or sale of securities. Likewise, states have enacted legislation that tracks and/or supplements federal regulation of the environment, trade, and taxes, among others. For example, most states regulate the disposal of hazardous wastes.[122]

In addition to liability for acts also prohibited by federal law, state statutory liability may be imposed on directors for illegal distributions to stockholders in the form of dividends, stock redemptions, liquidations, or transactions with individual directors. As discussed in Chapter 4, directors are jointly and severally liable for the declaration and payment of illegal dividends, e.g., where the corporation has insufficient legally available funds to pay dividends; where the board pays dividends without observing statutory formalities; or where the dividend is not proportionate among shareholders of the same class of stock.[123] Additionally, directors are liable for improper stock redemptions, for example, where a corporation's capital is impaired upon the redemption.[124] Under Delaware law, the potential for civil liability of directors for improper distributions by way of dividends or stock redemptions may be premised on conduct found to be merely negligent. In light of the lower standard and given that the statute of limitations for such liabilities is six years,[125] directors need to be particularly aware of such potential liabilities. In addition to civil liability, some states' statutory schemes provide for the imposition of criminal liabilities on directors for improper distributions.[126]

Federal Statutory Liability

Various federal statutes also impose personal liability on directors for statutorily prohibited actions. Examples of federal statutory schemes under which directors may be found criminally or civilly liable include: antitrust and trade regulation statutes; statutes relating to employee benefits; tax statutes; environmental and occupational health and safety statutes; intellectual property statutes; the Racketeer Influenced and Corrupt Organization Act (RICO);[127] and securities statutes. Although each statute differs, certain statutes may be enforced not only by governmental agencies, but also by private individuals. A few of the federal statutes more frequently litigated against directors are as follows.

Liability under the Federal Securities Laws

One of the most common and significant forms of potential statutory liability arises under the federal securities laws. Practically every corporate "statement" or communication, whether communicated in writing or orally, is heavily scrutinized by the investing public and the plaintiffs' bar. Indeed, the statutory scheme imposes potential liability from the first offering of securities by a public corporation onward.

In addition to liability for the registration statement and prospectus disseminated to the stockholders in connection with the initial public offering, directors of a reporting company have continuing obligations to inform the investing public. One of the most often litigated sections of the federal securities laws is Rule 10b-5, which implements Section 10(b) of the Securities Exchange Act of 1934. This rule governs any business transaction involving the purchase or sale of securities. While negligent representations or omissions are not actionable, fraudulent or reckless statements may be the basis for imposing liability on directors.[128] Actions employing Rule 10b-5 are frequent given that the rule applies to all public "statements" made by a company, including reports on Forms 8-K, 10-Q, and 10-K, as well as other periodic reports and press releases.

The federal securities laws also impose liability for misrepresentations or omissions made in proxy statements or solicitations, and/or any document filed with the SEC. Other sections of the federal securities laws impose liability on directors for short-swing profits relating to purchases and sales of company securities.

In sum, federal securities laws contain an imposing array of potential liabilities for directors. Directors should assure themselves that experienced counsel has advised the company prior to making any disclosure decisions.

Liability under the Employee Retirement Income Securities Act (ERISA)

The Employee Retirement Income Securities Act (ERISA) of 1974, as amended,[129] governs the conduct of fiduciaries of most employee benefit plans, including directors who exercise discretionary authority or control of such plans. Directors who are fiduciaries of benefit plans are charged with certain reporting and disclosure requirements, as well as acting solely in the interest of the plan beneficiaries and abstaining from any transactions that involve a conflict of interest. Transactions typically challenged include change-of-control transactions, such as tender offers and insider buy-out proposals, where the directors must consider the potentially competing interests of shareholders and plan participants.[130] Because this situation arises not infrequently, certain practitioners have suggested that directors avoid becoming fiduciaries under a plan governed by ERISA or resigning at the first hint of a conflict of interest.[131] Under ERISA, liability may be enormous, given that directors face personal liability for improper personal profits and possibly punitive damages.

Liability under the Racketeer Influenced
Corrupt Organizations Act (RICO)

RICO also has been applied against corporate directors. A RICO claim is predicated upon a pattern of racketeering activity in connection with interstate commerce and the operation of an "enterprise" through racketeering activity. Creative lawyers have attempted to expand RICO's reach to directors of public corporations because an "enterprise" for purposes of RICO includes a corporation. RICO claims have been litigated against directors based on allegations of common-law business fraud, securities fraud in mergers, and in connection with improper loans approved by a board of directors. Potentially staggering liability is faced by directors for violation of RICO, given its treble-damage provision.

Liability under the Environmental Laws

Protection of the environment has received an increasing amount of attention in the past few years and promises to continue to be the focus of legislatures and the courts. Both state and federal governments have enacted statutes regulating air quality, water quality, and the transportation and disposal of hazardous waste. Perhaps the most important and far-reaching of such statutes is the Comprehensive Environmental Response, Compensation, and Liability Act (CERCLA) and the Resource Conservation and Recovery Act (RCRA).[132] These statutory schemes impose significant liability risk on directors who direct or have knowledge of any act in violation of the statutes.[133] Liability is imposed on a director under the theory of agency. For example, if a corporate employee violates an environmental law, the person who directed that employee to perform the violative act likewise will be subject to liability. While on its face this liability would be unlikely to reach directors of a large company, courts have expanded liability to those who had the "capacity to control" or were "in a position to control" the employees' illegal activity.[134] This extension of the statutes is potentially very significant. Directors also could potentially face criminal charges under the federal environmental laws, although criminal enforcement actions under the environmental laws appear to be less frequent than civil actions.

Given the increased public awareness of environmental risks, the severity of injury caused by environmental violations, and the high costs of remedial efforts, directors are well advised to be sensitive to operations that have the potential to adversely impact the environment.

Notes

1. Solash v. Telex Corp., C.A. Nos. 9518, 9525, 9528, slip op. at 17–18 (Del. Ch. Jan. 19, 1988); *and see* Guth v. Loft, Inc., 5 A.2d 503, 510 (Del. 1939) (footnote omitted).

2. All but five states have statutes providing that an interested transaction is not automatically void or voidable. *Model Act* § 8.61 commentary, at 1142.42-2.

3. *See* 8 DEL. CODE ANN. § 144; and *see* 1 R. FRANKLIN BALOTTI & JESSE A. FINKELSTEIN, THE DELAWARE LAW OF CORPORATIONS AND BUSINESS ORGANIZATIONS, § 4.8, at 4–196 (2d ed. Supp. 1995) [hereinafter "BALOTTI & FINKELSTEIN § ___"].

4. Nixon v. Blackwell, 626 A.2d 1366 (Del. 1993); Marciano v. Nakash, 535 A.2d 400 (Del. 1987).

5. Weinberger v. UOP, Inc., 457 A.2d 701 (Del. 1983).

6. *Weinberger,* 457 A.2d at 711. The Delaware Supreme Court has stated that the *Weinberger* "fair dealing" test is designed to guarantee to shareholders certain "procedural protections" in conflicted transactions. Rabkin v. Phillip A. Hunt Chem. Corp., 498 A.2d 1099, 1105 (Del. 1985).

7. *Weinberger,* 457 A.2d at 711; *cf.* Cinerama, Inc. v. Technicolor, Inc., C.A. No. 8358 (Del. Ch. Oct. 6, 1994), *aff'd,* 663 A.2d 1156 (Del. 1995) (applying *Weinberger* analysis).

8. Rabkin v. Phillip A. Hunt Chem. Corp., 480 A.2d 655 (Del. Ch. 1984), *rev'd,* 498 A.2d 1099 (Del. 1985); Rabkin v. Phillip A. Hunt Chem. Corp., 547 A.2d 963 (Del. Ch. 1986); Rabkin v. Phillip A. Hunt Chem. Corp., C.A. No. 7547 (Del. Ch. Dec. 17, 1987); Rabkin v. Olin Corp., C.A. No. 7547 (Del. Ch. Apr. 17, 1990), *aff'd,* No. 164, 1990 (Del. Dec. 20, 1990), *disposition reported at* 586 A.2d 1202.

9. *Rabkin,* 498 A.2d at 1106–07.

10. Rabkin v. Olin Corp., C.A. No. 7547 (Del. Ch. Apr. 17, 1990), *aff'd,* No. 164, 1990 (Del. Dec. 20, 1990), *disposition reported at* 586 A.2d 1202.

11. Marciano v. Nakash, 535 A.2d 400, 405 (Del. 1987); and *see* Rosenberg v. Oolie, C.A. No. 11134 (Del. Ch. Oct. 16, 1989) (loans likely to be found entirely fair at trial where evidence showed opportunity to make loans offered to all directors, corporation unable to secure financing elsewhere, and funds desperately needed to avoid collapse of enterprise).

12. Rosenblatt v. Getty Oil Co., 493 A.2d 929, 938 n.7 (Del. 1985). The court pointed out, however, that the existence of a functioning independent committee is not "conclusive" of fairness. *Id. See also* Weinberger v. UOP, Inc., 457 A.2d 701, 709 n.7 (Del. 1983); Rabkin v. Phillip A. Hunt Chem. Corp., 498 A.2d 1099, 1106 n.7 (Del. 1985).

13. *See, e.g.,* Kahn v. Lynch Communication Sys., Inc., 638 A.2d 1110 (Del. 1994); *In re* Trans World Airlines, Inc. Shareholders Litig., C.A. No. 9844 (Del. Ch. Oct. 21, 1988); and *cf.* Mills Acquisition Co. v. Macmillan, Inc., 559 A.2d 1261 (Del. 1989).

14. Rabkin v. Olin Corp., C.A. No. 7547, slip op. at 14–15 (Del. Ch. Apr. 17, 1990), *aff'd,* No. 164, 1990 (Del. Dec. 20, 1990), *disposition reported at* 586 A.2d 1202.

15. Kahn v. Lynch Communications Systems, Inc., 638 A.2d 1110, 1119 (Del. 1994) (quoting *In re* First Boston, Inc. Shareholders Litig., C.A. No. 10338 (Del. Ch. June 7, 1990) (alteration in original)).

16. *See, e.g.,* William T. Allen, *Independent Directors in MBO Transactions: Are They Fact or Fantasy?,* 45 Bus. Law. 2055 (1990) [hereinafter *"Independent Directors at ___"*]; Scott V. Simpson, *The Emerging Role of the Special Committee — Ensuring Business Judgment Rule Protection in the Context of Management Leveraged Buyouts and Other Corporate Transactions Involving Conflicts of Interest,* 43 Bus. Law. 665 (1988).

17. *See* Mills Acquisition Co. v. Macmillan, Inc., 559 A.2d 1261 (Del. 1989) (court criticized the selection process of committee members where members "hand-picked" by CEO).

18. *Id.* at 1268 n.9 (court notes relationship of certain committee members to CEO's family); Lewis v. Fuqua, 502 A.2d 962 (Del. Ch. 1985), *appeal denied,* 504 A.2d 571 (Del. 1986) (one-person Litigation Committee found conflicted because of committee member's relationship to university to which corporation had made significant contributions).

19. Bayless Manning, *The Business Judgment Rule and the Director's Duty of Attention: Time for Reality,* 39 Bus. Law. 1477 (1984).

20. Aronson v. Lewis, 473 A.2d 805, 812 (Del. 1984).

21. *Id.;* Smith v. Van Gorkom, 488 A.2d 858 (Del. 1985) (reaffirming *Aronson* standard). Tomczak v. Morton Thiokol, Inc., C.A. No. 7861, slip op. at 31 (Del. Ch. Apr. 5, 1990).

22. *In re* RJR Nabisco, Inc. Shareholders Litig., C.A. No. 10389, slip op. at 51 (Del. Ch. Jan. 31, 1989), *appeal denied,* 556 A.2d 1070 (Del. 1989).

23. Rabkin v. Phillip A. Hunt Chem. Corp., 547 A.2d 963, 972 (Del. Ch. 1987).

24. Graham v. Allis-Chalmers Mfg. Co., 188 A.2d 125, 130 (Del. 1963).

25. Smith v. Van Gorkom, 488 A.2d 858 (Del. 1985).

26. Paramount Communications Inc. v. QVC Network Inc., 637 A.2d 34, 49 (Del. 1993).

27. The following is drawn, in part, from E. Norman Veasey's discussion of the topic appearing in Balotti & Finkelstein § 4.7. *See also* Simpson, *The Emerging Role of the Special Committee—Ensuring Business Judgment Rule Protection in the Context of Management Leveraged Buyouts and Other Corporate Transactions Involving Conflicts of Interest, supra* note 16, at 665, 678.

28. *See* Citron v. Fairchild Camera & Instrument Corp., 569 A.2d 53, 67 (Del. 1989). Professors Jonathan R. Macey and Geoffrey P. Miller have sug-

gested that the holding in the *Trans Union* case "eliminates the possibility that the board of a Delaware corporation will be held liable to shareholders if it delays making a decision and the bidder thereupon drops its offer." Jonathan R. Macey & Geoffrey P. Miller, *Trans Union Reconsidered,* 98 YALE L.J. 127, 136 (Nov. 1988).

29. In practice, outside experts often are consulted by boards of large companies. Recent jurisprudence suggests, however, that directors should not overlook the insights available from inside staff. For example, where the board was considering the adoption of an employee stock ownership plan (ESOP), a reviewing court found that the board had neglected to seek the views of the company's own in-house benefits staff before acting, an oversight of which the court was critical. *See* NCR Corp. v. American Tel. & Tel. Co., 761 F. Supp. 475 (S.D. Ohio 1991).

30. 85 A. 446 (Pa. 1912).

31. 493 A.2d 929 (Del. 1985).

32. There are notable exceptions. Indiana, for example, has enacted legislation explicitly rejecting the Delaware approach. New York, California, and New Jersey also appear to have developed a different approach, which may afford directors less protection than the Delaware rule. *See, e.g.,* Hanson Trust PLC v. ML SCM Acquisition Inc., 781 F.2d 264 (2d Cir. 1986) (New York law); Klaus v. Hi-Shear Corp., 528 F.2d 225 (9th Cir. 1975) (California law); Minstar Acquiring Corp. v. AMF Inc., 621 F. Supp. 1252 (S.D.N.Y. 1985) (New Jersey law).

33. Unocal Corp. v. Mesa Petroleum Co., 493 A.2d 946, 955 (Del. 1985); *cf.* Cheff v. Mathes, 199 A.2d 548, 555 (Del. 1964).

34. Ivanhoe Partners v. Newmont Mining Co., 535 A.2d 1334, 1341 (Del. 1987).

35. *Id.* at 1341–42; *cf.* Mills Acquisition Corp v. Macmillan, Inc., 559 A.2d 1261, 1282 n.29 (Del. 1988).

36. Of course, as noted in Chapter 1, where the sale of the corporation has become "inevitable," a director may not act to protect "constituencies" other than shareholders, unless doing so helps maximize shareholder return. *See* Revlon, Inc. v. MacAndrews & Forbes Holdings, Inc., 506 A.2d 173, 182 (Del. 1986).

37. *Mills Acquisition,* 559 A.2d at 282 n.29.

38. Commentators have suggested other factors. *See* Bayless Manning, *Reflections and Practical Tips on Life in the Boardroom After Van Gorkom,* 41 BUS. LAW. 1 (1985); *see also* ABA Committee on Corporate Laws, *Guidelines for Directors: Planning for and Responding to Unsolicited Tender Offers,* 41 BUS. LAW. 209 (1985); Martin Lipton, *Takeover Bids in the Target's Boardroom,* 35 BUS. LAW. 101 (1979).

39. *See* City Capital Assocs. v. Interco, Inc., 551 A.2d 787, 796–98 (Del. Ch.), *appeal denied,* 556 A.2d 1070 (Del. 1988) (citing Ronald J. Gilson & Reinier Kraakman, *Delaware's Intermediate Standard for Defensive Tactics: Is There Substance to Proportionality Review?* 44 BUS. LAW. 247 (1989)); Grand Metro. PLC v. Pillsbury Co., 558 A.2d 1049 (Del. Ch. 1988).

40. Paramount Communications, Inc. v. Time Inc., 571 A.2d 1140, 1153 (Del. 1990).

41. *See Paramount* at 1154 ("Time's board was under no obligation to negotiate with Paramount"); *cf.* TW Servs., Inc. v. SWT Acquisition Corp., C.A. No. 10427 (Del. Ch. Mar. 2, 1989).

42. *Ivanhoe*, 535 A.2d at 1337; *Unocal*, 493 A.2d at 954.

43. *Ivanhoe*, 535 A.2d at 1345.

44. *Unocal*, 493 A.2d at 954 (explicitly rejecting passivity arguments put forward in Frank H. Easterbrook & Daniel R. Fischel, *Takeover Bids, Defensive Tactics, and Shareholders' Welfare*, 36 BUS. LAW. 1733 (1981) and Frank H. Easterbrook & Daniel R. Fischel, *The Proper Role of a Target's Management in Responding to a Tender Offer*, 94 HARV. L. REV. 1161 (1981)).

45. *Unocal*, 493 A.2d at 955.

46. *See, e.g.*, Moran v. Household Int'l, Inc., 500 A.2d 1346 (Del. 1985) (adoption of poison pill); Polk v. Good, 507 A.2d 531 (Del. 1986) (upholding settlement of litigation challenging defensive stock repurchase from raider); *Unocal* (upholding discriminatory self-tender); Ivanhoe Partners v. Newmont Mining (upholding extraordinary dividend designed to allow related party to conduct "street sweep," i.e., large-scale open-market purchase of stock, coupled with standstill agreement with third party in order to defeat hostile bid); Shamrock Holdings, Inc. v. Polaroid Corp., 559 A.2d 278 (Del. Ch. 1989) (upholding stock placement to self-described "white knight"); Shamrock Holdings, Inc. v. Polaroid Corp., 559 A.2d 257 (Del. Ch. 1989) (upholding sale of 14 percent of outstanding common stock to ESOP in the face of hostile bid); Paramount Communications, Inc. v. Time Inc., 571 A.2d 1140 (Del. 1990) (upholding decision to change merger (that required shareholder vote) to tender offer (that did not require a vote)).

47. *See, e.g.*, City Capital Assocs. v. Interco, Inc., 551 A.2d 787 (Del. Ch. 1988) (ordering target board to redeem poison pill in the face of all cash, all shares offer); *but cf.* Paramount Communications, Inc. v. Time Inc. (expressly disapproving *Interco* and progeny); AC Acquisitions Corp. v. Anderson, Clayton & Co., 519 A.2d 103 (Del. Ch. 1986) (enjoining corporate restructuring as coercive where stockholders were unable to choose between restructuring and competing outside bid); Robert M. Bass Group, Inc. v. Evans, 552 A.2d 1227 (Del. Ch. 1988), *appeal denied*, 548 A.2d 498 (Del. 1988) (enjoining restructuring that left management with 40 percent stake in one of two surviving businesses); Phillips v. Insituform of N. Am., Inc., C.A. No. 9173 (Del. Ch. Aug. 27, 1987) (enjoining stock issuance); Frantz Mfg. Co. v. EAC Indus., Inc., 501 A.2d 401 (Del. 1985) (upholding injunction against issuance of shares to ESOP in attempt to dilute acquiror's stake); *but cf.* Unitrin, Inc. v. General Corp., 651 A.2d 1361 (Del. 1995) (reversing injunction against stock repurchase adopted in response to a hostile bid on grounds that repurchase not preclusive).

48. Unitrin, Inc. v. American General Corp., 651 A.2d 1361, 1367 (Del. 1995).

49. 506 A.2d 173 (Del. 1986).

50. *Revlon*, 506 A.2d at 182.

51. Mills Acquisition Co. v. Macmillan, Inc., 559 A.2d 1261, 1285 (Del. 1988).

52. *Macmillan*, 559 A.2d at 1284, n.32, 1285.

53. Paramount Communications Inc. v. QVC Network Inc., 637 A.2d 34, 44 (Del. 1994).

54. *Id.* at 44 (citing Barkan v. Amsted Indus., Inc., 567 A.2d 1279, 1287 (Del. 1989)).

55. *Id.* at 48.

56. Barkan v. Amsted Indus., Inc., 567 A.2d 1279, 1286 (Del. 1989). *See also* Mills Acquisition, Inc. v. Macmillan, Inc., 559 A.2d 1261, 1284–85 (Del. 1989); Paramount Communications Inc. v. QVC Network Inc., 637 A.2d 34, 44 (Del. 1994).

57. *See* TCG Secs., Inc. v. Southern Union Co., C.A. No. 11282 (Del. Ch. Jan. 31, 1990).

58. Mills Acquisition Co. v. Macmillan, Inc., 559 A.2d at 1288.

59. It is something of a misnomer to refer to a "standard" or "ordinary" form of no-shop clause, and it is unclear from the cases exactly what prohibitions were imposed by the provisions under consideration. Certainly, one could argue that a clause that prohibited further solicitation *and receipt* of further bids should be scrutinized far more carefully than a form of provision that prohibited dissemination of information unless the target's board was advised that the board needed to provide such information to fulfill its fiduciary duties. Such "fiduciary-out" provisions are frequently inserted in no-shop agreements. *In re* Vitalink Communications Corp. Shareholders Litig., Cons. C.A. No. 12085, slip op. at 23 (Del. Ch. Nov. 8, 1991) (where no-shop clause was "subject to a fiduciary out clause" court concludes it was only a "minimal impediment to a . . . market test"); and *see generally* Gregory V. Varallo & Daniel A. Dreisbach, *Amsted Industries: Structuring the Sale of Corporate Control Outside the Auction Context*, 4 INSIGHTS, May 1990, at 31.

60. *Macmillan*, 559 A.2d at 1284; *Revlon*, 506 A.2d at 183–85; *see also* Hanson Trust PLC v. ML SCM Acquisition, Inc., 781 F.2d 264, 274 (2d Cir. 1986).

61. *Macmillan*, 559 A.2d at 1286.

62. *Paramount*, 637 A.2d at 51.

63. *Id.* at 49 n.20 (citing *Barkan*, 567 A.2d at 1288).

64. *Id.* at 48.

65. *In re* Amsted Indus., Inc. Litig., C.A. No. 8224, slip op. at 19–20 (Del. Ch. Aug. 24, 1988), *aff'd sub nom.* Barkan v. Amsted Indus., Inc., 567 A.2d 1279 (Del. 1989).

66. *See, e.g.*, Evelyn Sroufe, *A Bird in the Hand or Pie in the Sky: The Market Check in the '90s*, 5 INSIGHTS, Oct. 1991, at 12; Varallo & Dreisbach, *Amsted Industries: Structuring the Sale of Corporate Control Outside the Auction Context, supra* note 256; Gregory V. Varallo, *The "Market Check" in the Market Place for Corporate Control*, 3 INSIGHTS, May 1989, at 30.

67. Typically, the parties will agree to hold their deal in place for somewhat longer than the twenty-day period required by the tender offer regula-

tions. *See* Varallo, *The "Market Check" in the Market Place for Corporate Control*, 3 INSIGHTS, May 1989, at 30.

68. The Delaware courts have consistently acknowledged that "break-up" or "topping" fee provisions requiring payment to the original bidder of a reasonable fee in the event his or her deal is "topped" by a third party are permissible. Although no hard-and-fast rule has emerged against which to measure "reasonableness" of such a fee, the cases that have examined the subject have approved fees in the range of 2 percent to 3 percent of the value of the original deal. *See In re* Vitalink Communications Corp. Shareholders Litig., Cons. C.A. No. 12085, slip op. at 14 (Del. Ch. Nov. 8, 1991) (finding 1.9 percent fee did not prevent effective market check and citing cases); Sroufe, *A Bird in the Hand or Pie in the Sky: The Market Check in the '90s, supra* note 66. Of course, evidence of negotiation of the breakup fee provision will be likely to enhance the chances of the provision surviving judicial scrutiny and because a lower fee is less likely to impede the emergence of other bidders, the directors of the selling company should focus upon the size of such a fee in negotiations.

69. *Amsted*, 567 A.2d at 1288.

70. Sutton Holding Corp. v. DeSoto, Inc., C.A. No. 11221 (Del. Ch. Feb. 5, 1990).

71. *See* Phillips v. Insituform of N. Am., Inc., C.A. No. 9173 (Del. Ch. Aug. 27, 1987); *cf.* Blasius Indus., Inc. v. Atlas Corp., 564 A.2d 651 (Del. Ch. 1988).

72. *Blasius Indus., Inc.,* 564 A.2d at 661.

73. *Id.* at 663.

74. 559 A.2d 278 (Del. Ch. 1989).

75. C.A. No. 11510 (Del. Ch. Aug. 9, 1990).

76. *Stahl,* slip op. at 17.

77. 606 A.2d 75 (Del. 1992).

78. Stroud v. Grace, 606 A.2d at 92 n.3 (citing Gilbert v. El Paso Co., 575 A.2d 1131, 1144 (Del. 1990)).

79. *Id.; see also* Unitrin Inc. v. American General Corp., 651 A.2d 1361 (Del. 1995) (reversing injunction against stock repurchase adopted in response to a hostile bid).

80. Jedwab v. MGM Grand Hotels, 509 A.2d 584 (Del. Ch. 1986).

81. Giammalvo v. Sunshine Mining Co., C.A. No. 12842, slip op. at 17 (Del. Ch. Jan. 31, 1994), *aff'd,* No. 121, 1994 (Del. Oct. 28, 1994) (ORDER) (*citing* Cede & Co. v. Technicolor, Inc., 634 A.2d 345, 361 (1994), *modified in part,* 636 A.2d 956 (Del. 1994)). *Accord* Robert B. Robbins and Barton Clark, *Directors' Liability: The Board's Fiduciary Duty to Preferred Stockholders,* 7 INSIGHTS, Nov. 1993, at 18 [hereinafter *"Directors' Liability* at ___"].

82. C.A. No. 12922 (Del. Ch. June 9, 1993).

83. "In most instances, given the nature of the acts alleged and the terms of the certificate, this contractual level of analysis will exhaust the judicial review of corporate action challenged as a wrong to preferred stock." *HB Korenvaes,* slip op. at 10; *accord* Judah v. Delaware Trust Co., 378 A.2d 624 (Del. 1977).

84. *HB Korenvaes,* slip op. at 11.

85. *See* Eisenberg v. Chicago Milwaukee Corp., 537 A.2d 1051, 1062 (Del. Ch. 1987) (remarking that the board of directors has a fiduciary duty to safeguard the interests of the preferred shareholders).

86. Porges v. Vadsco Sales Corp., 32 A.2d 148 (Del. Ch. 1943); MacFarlane v. North Am. Cement Corp., 157 A. 396 (Del. Ch. 1928). *See also In re* FLS Holdings, Inc. Shareholders Litig., C.A. No. 12623, slip op. at 8 (Del. Ch. Apr. 2, 1993, *revised* Apr. 21, 1993) (commenting that "[i]n allocating the consideration of this merger, the directors, although they were elected by the common stock, owed fiduciary duties to both the preferred and common stockholders, and were obligated to treat the preferred fairly").

87. *In re* FLS Holdings, Inc. Shareholders Litig., C.A. No. 12623 (Del. Ch. Apr. 2, 1993, *revised* Apr. 21, 1993); Eisenberg v. Chicago Milwaukee Corp., 537 A.2d at 1062; Jedwab v. MGM Grand Hotels, 509 A.2d at 593–94.

88. *In re* FLS, slip op. at 8; *see* Rothschild, 474 A.2d at 136. Because relatively few cases have asserted such claims, the courts have yet to determine conclusively which party bears the burden of establishing the fairness of the allocation. *Compare In re* Trans World Airlines, Inc. Shareholders Litig., C.A. No. 9844, slip op. at 18–19 (Del. Ch. Oct. 21, 1988) (burden on plaintiff) *with In re* FLS, slip op. at 2 (burden on defendants).

89. *See Directors' Liability* at 22.

90. DENNIS J. BLOCK, ET AL., THE BUSINESS JUDGMENT RULE (3d ed. 1989) [hereinafter "THE BUSINESS JUDGMENT RULE at ____"]; and *see* E. Norman Veasey, *in* BALOTTI & FINKELSTEIN, *supra* note 3, Ch. 4.

91. Aronson v. Lewis, 473 A.2d 805, 813 (Del. 1984) (the rule "operates only in the context of director action . . . it has no role where directors have either abdicated their functions, or absent a conscious decision, failed to act") (footnote omitted); Rabkin v. Philip A. Hunt Chem. Corp., 547 A.2d 963, 972 (Del. Ch. 1986) (the rule "may apply to a deliberate decision not to act, but it has no bearing on a claim that directors' inaction was the result of ignorance").

92. *See* BALOTTI & FINKELSTEIN § 4.6, *supra* note 3, at 4-41; THE BUSINESS JUDGMENT RULE at 12.

93. *In re* RJR Nabisco, Inc. Shareholders Litig., C.A. No. 10389, slip op. at 34–35 (Del. Ch. Jan. 31, 1989), *appeal denied*, 556 A.2d 1070 (Del. 1989).

94. *Aronson*, 473 A.2d at 812; and *see* Smith v. Van Gorkom, 488 A.2d 858, 872 (Del. 1985). The authors of *The Business Judgment Rule, supra* note 90, note that courts in at least sixteen states other than Delaware have described the rule in terms of these presumptions. *Id.* at 8-9.

95. *See* Grobow v. Perot, 526 A.2d 914, 928 (Del. Ch. 1987) (rule protects decision "[h]owever controversial, unpopular, or even wrong such a decision might turn out to be . . ."), *aff'd*, 539 A.2d 180 (Del. 1988).

96. *See* THE BUSINESS JUDGMENT RULE, *supra* note 90, at 6; *In re J.P. Stevens & Co., Inc. Shareholders Litig.*, 542 A.2d 770, 780 (Del. Ch.), *appeal denied*, 540 A.2d 1088 (Del. 1988); Solash v. Telex Corp., C.A. Nos. 9518, 9525, 9528, slip op. at 19 (Del. Ch. Jan. 19, 1988) ("Because businessmen and women are correctly perceived as possessing skills, information and judgment not possessed by re-

viewing courts and because there is great social utility in encouraging the allocation of assets and the evaluation and assumption of economic risk by those with such skill and information, courts have long been reluctant to second-guess such decisions when they appear to have been made in good faith.").

97. Aronson v. Lewis, 473 A.2d 805, 812 (Del. 1984); Cinerama, Inc. v. Technicolor, Inc., C.A. No. 8358 (Del. Ch. Oct. 6, 1994), aff'd, 663 A.2d 1156 (Del. 1995).

98. Cinerama, Inc., slip op. at 51.

99. Cinerama, Inc., slip op. at 52.

100. Note that in this regard, Delaware, as most states, has statutorily mandated that the interest of some members of the board in a particular decision is not necessarily fatal to the decision. Where the interested directors disclose their interest to their fellow board members and the board acts by an independent majority, or by an independent committee of the board, or the directors' interest is disclosed and the shareholders vote to approve the transaction, or the transaction itself is objectively fair to the corporation, it is not "void or voidable" solely because of the participation of "interested" directors. 8 DEL. CODE ANN. § 144.

101. Kaplan v. Wyatt, 499 A.2d 1184, 1189 (Del. 1985).

102. Grobow v. Perot, 539 A.2d 180, 188 (Del. 1988).

103. Heineman v. Datapoint Corp., C.A. No. 7956 (Del. Ch. Oct. 9, 1990) (finding that pleading that recited receipt of annuities by all directors and severance contracts by two members of the board created a reasonable doubt regarding the directors' disinterest); and see Tate & Lyle PLC v. Staley Continental, Inc., C.A. No. 9813 (Del. Ch. May 9, 1988) (enjoining funding of $65 million irrevocable "rabbi trust" designed to preserve director benefits adopted in the face of a hostile takeover proposal).

104. Cede & Co. v. Technicolor, Inc., 634 A.2d 345, 363 (Del. 1993).

105. Revlon, Inc. v. MacAndrews & Forbes Holdings, Inc., 506 A.2d 173, 176 note 3 (Del. 1986).

106. Packer v. Yampol, C.A. No. 8432 (Del. Ch. Apr. 18, 1986).

107. Aprahamian v. HBO & Co., 531 A.2d 1204 (Del. Ch. 1987); and cf. Packer v. Yampol. In a similar case, Good v. Texaco, C.A. No. 7501 (Del. Ch. May 14, 1984), the court concluded preliminarily that the allegations of a complaint sufficiently plead director "interest" where the board, in connection with a corporate repurchase of approximately 5 percent of Texaco's common stock, structured the acquisition to provide that the stock would be voted as the board directed for some period of time. The court's preliminary findings as to the interest of the board in this setting was buttressed by the fact that the company's stock was widely held and the 5 percent voting block dramatically exceeded the small individual stockholdings of the directors, thus greatly magnifying their ability to cause their own reelection, entirely at corporate expense. See also Abajian v. Kennedy, C.A. No. 11425 (Del. Ch. Jan. 17, 1992).

108. See In re RJR Nabisco Shareholders Litig., C.A. No. 10389 (Del. Ch. Jan. 31, 1989), appeal denied, 556 A.2d 1070 (Del. 1989).

109. *See* Lewis v. Honeywell, C.A. No. 8651 (Del. Ch. July 28, 1987).

110. RJR Nabisco Shareholders Litig., C.A. No. 10289, slip op. at 52 (Del. Ch. Jan. 31, 1989), *appeal denied*, 556 A.2d 1070 (Del. 1989). In Citron v. Fairchild Camera & Instrument Corp., 569 A.2d 53 (Del. 1989), the Delaware Supreme Court revisited the case where a board was faced with a tight deadline to accept or reject a premium offer for the company. Although it cautioned that in the past, boards who allowed themselves to be rushed in decision making were more likely to be subject to criticism for failing to exercise due care, the court nonetheless affirmed the lower court's decision, finding that in the circumstances the board could have concluded that it had sufficient information to sell the company, notwithstanding the very short time frame involved.

111. *See* Aronson v. Lewis, 473 A.2d at 812.

112. *See* Sutton Holding Corp. v. DeSoto Inc., C.A. No. 11221, slip op. at 20 (Del. Ch. Feb. 5, 1990). *See also In re* RJR Nabisco Shareholders Litig., slip op. at 36–37 note 13 (noting that the court, in the appropriate circumstance, could infer bad faith from "an 'egregious' or 'irrational' decision").

113. *See* Unocal Corp. v. Mesa Petroleum Co., 493 A.2d 946, 955 (Del. 1985).

114. 35 IND. CODE ANN. § 23-1-35-1(f) (Burns 1988).

115. 15 PA. STAT. ANN. § 1715(d) (Purdon's 1988).

116. *See* Hanson Trust PLC v. ML SCM Acquisition, Inc., 781 F.2d 264, 273 (2d Cir. 1986) (New York law); *cf.* Klaus v. Hi-Shear Corp., 528 F.2d 225 (9th Cir. 1975) (California law); E. Norman Veasey, *in* BALOTTI & FINKELSTEIN Ch. 4, *supra* note 3, at 4-54, 4-55.

117. *Compare* Asarco Inc. v. M.R.H. Holmes A Court, 611 F. Supp. 468 (D. N.J. 1985); Minstar Acquiring Corp. v. AMF Inc., 621 F. Supp. 1252 (D. N.J. 1985).

118. *See* E. Norman Veasey & Julie M.S. Seitz, *The Business Judgment Rule in the Revised Model Act, the Trans Union Case, and the ALI Project — A Strange Porridge*, 63 TEX. L. REV. 1483, 1496 (1985); and *see* THE BUSINESS JUDGMENT RULE, *supra* note 90, at 24–25.

119. *Principles of Corporate Governance: Analysis and Recommendations* § 4.01(c) (Tentative Draft No. 4 Apr. 12, 1985); and *see* THE BUSINESS JUDGMENT RULE, *supra* note 90, at 25–26.

120. *See, e.g.*, Michael P. Dooley & E. Norman Veasey, *The Role of the Board in Derivative Litigation: Delaware Law and the Current ALI Proposals Compared*, 44 BUS. LAW. 503 (Feb. 1989); Roswell B. Perkins, *The ALI Corporate Governance Project in Midstream*, 41 BUS. LAW. 1195 (Aug. 1986); E. Norman Veasey & Julie M.S. Seitz, *The Business Judgment Rule in the Revised Model Act, the Trans Union Case, and the ALI Project — A Strange Porridge, supra* note 118.

121. ABA Criminal Laws Committee, *The Increasing Criminalization of Business Conduct: An Overview*, 11 BUS. LAW. UPDATE (Jan./Feb. 1991).

122. 3 JOHN F. OLSON & JOSIAH O. HATCH, III, DIRECTOR & OFFICER LIABILITY: INDEMNIFICATION AND INSURANCE § 3.05[2] (1994).

123. *See* 8 DEL. CODE ANN. § 174.

124. *Id.* at § 160.

125. *Id.* at § 174.

126. *See N.Y. Penal Law* § 190.35(1)(a) (authorization of illegal dividends may result in finding of class B misdemeanor).

127. 18 U.S.C. §§ 1961 *et seq.*

128. McLean v. Alexander, 599 F.2d 1190, 1197 (3d Cir. 1979).

129. 29 U.S.C. §§ 1001 *et seq.*

130. *Director and Officer Liability, supra* note 122, at § 3.03[1].

131. Jesse A. Finkelstein, *et al., Protecting Corporate Directors and Officers from Liability,* 27 Bus. Law Monographs § 2.03[5] (May 1992).

132. *See* 42 U.S.C. § 7401 *et seq.*; 42 U.S.C. § 6901–6991; 16 U.S.C. §§ 1601, 1801; 49 U.S.C. §§ 1801–1812; 42 U.S.C. §§ 9601–9615.

133. *See, e.g.,* United States v. Mottolo, 605 F. Supp. 898 (D.N.H. 1985); *United States v. Ward,* 618 F. Supp. 884 (E.D.N.C. 1985).

134. *Director and Officer Liability, supra* note 122, at § 3.05[3].

CHAPTER 4

Dividends

Directors of most public corporations are regularly called upon to declare dividends. Although dividends often are declared as a routine matter in many boardrooms, the exercise should be anything but routine, for payment of an illegal dividend can subject directors to personal liability for the full amount of the dividend paid—a potentially staggering amount. In this chapter we review the basic legal principles applicable to the declaration and payment of dividends while also addressing director "due diligence" in that regard and legally permissible payment of dividends in circumstances where "surplus" for payment of dividends is not available.

Statutory Authority for Payment of Dividends

Every state corporation code provides statutory authority for the declaration and payment of dividends. Delaware's statute provides that directors may declare and pay dividends out of surplus or, where no surplus exists, out of net profits for the current or immediately preceding fiscal year.[1]

Dividends Paid from Surplus

To determine whether a dividend lawfully may be paid, directors first must determine whether there are sufficient funds legally available to pay the dividend. Assuming that the dividend is to be paid from "surplus" (rather than profits), the board first must determine the amount of surplus of the corporation.

Under Delaware law, the amount of the corporation's surplus is defined in relation to its "capital." Capital, in turn, is defined as that portion of the consideration received by the corporation for the issued shares of its capital stock that the directors determine to be capital, but in no event less than the aggregate par value of the issued shares.[2] In other words, if a corporation receives $10 for each share of its $1 par-value stock, at least $1 must be deemed capital. Any or all of the remaining $9 may be deemed surplus.

If the board fails to determine the amount of capital in connection with an issuance of stock, a default provision in the Delaware statute provides that the amount of consideration to be deemed capital will be equal to the par value of the stock multiplied by the number of shares issued.[3] In the case of no par stock, without action by the board, the capital account of the corporation is credited with the total consideration received for stock.

Once the amount of capital has been determined, the board can determine the available surplus. Surplus, also a defined term under many corporate statutes, is the amount equal to the present fair value of the total assets of the corporation, minus the present fair value of the total liabilities of the corporation, minus the capital of the corporation.[4] If surplus exists, dividends may be declared and paid from this amount without regard to the current profitability of the corporation.[5]

Dividends Paid from Profits or "Nimble" Dividends

In addition to a declaration and payment of dividends out of surplus, under Delaware law, dividends may be declared and paid out of net profits for the fiscal year in which the dividend is declared and/or the preceding fiscal year, absent a limitation in the certificate of incorporation. Dividends paid out of profits, also known as "nimble" dividends, may be so paid when the surplus of the corporation is insufficient, but only when and to the extent that the capital representing shares of preferred stock is not impaired.[6] In other words, dividends may be paid to stockholders out of profits notwithstanding the lack of available surplus, so long as the capital account representing shares of preference stock outstanding contains an amount that equals or exceeds the amount determined to be capital.

Dividends of "Wasting Assets" Companies

Delaware's statute also permits companies that are engaged in the exploitation of wasting assets (including natural resources or patents or otherwise engaged primarily in the liquidation of specific assets) to declare and pay dividends. Directors of such corporations are permitted to determine net profits derived from exploitation of such wasting assets without regard to the depletion of assets of the corporation "resulting from lapse of time, consumption, liquidation or exploitation of such assets."[7] This provision is extremely important to the ability of oil and gas, timber, and similar companies to declare and pay dividends.

Applicability of the Business Judgment Rule to Decisions Respecting Dividends

The Board Customarily Has Discretion to Set Dividend Policy

Decisions concerning whether to declare and pay dividends rest within the discretion of the board of directors. Courts repeatedly have upheld the right of directors to determine whether to pay dividends, in what amount and in what form. A leading case discussing the decision to declare and pay dividends is *Gabelli & Co., Inc., Profit Sharing Plan v. Liggett Group Inc.,* There, the Delaware Supreme Court strongly reaffirmed the presumption of validity afforded directors' decisions respecting the payment of dividends, holding that the decision whether and when to declare a dividend was a decision protected by the business judgment rule.[8]

While disgruntled shareholders sometimes have challenged board decisions not to declare dividends, the burden on the shareholder bringing such a challenge is heavy. To strip the business judgment rule's presumption of validity from a decision to pay or not pay dividends, a shareholder must demonstrate that the directors acted fraudulently, in bad faith, to oppress the rights of shareholders, or in abuse of their discretion. The Delaware court has described the circumstances under which it would interfere with the decision of a board of directors regarding the payment of dividends as follows:

> That courts have the power in proper cases to compel the directors to declare a dividend, is sustained by respectable authorities. But that they should do so on a mere showing that an asset exists from which a dividend may be declared, has

never . . . been asserted anywhere. In such a case the court acts only after a demonstration that the corporation's affairs are in a condition justifying the declaration of the dividend as a matter of prudent business management and that the withholding of it is explicable only on the theory of an oppressive or fraudulent abuse of discretion.[9]

If a shareholder successfully establishes bad faith, oppression, fraud, or abuse of discretion, the board of directors then must establish the "entire fairness" of its decision not to declare dividends.[10] Clearly, however, it is only in the rarest of cases that the stockholder will meet his or her initial burden.

While the business judgment rule normally will protect directors' decisions regarding dividends, a board should exercise great care prior to determining whether to pay dividends. Here, we review the process by which the assets and liabilities should be valued, a necessary exercise where dividends are paid out of surplus. As a practical matter, however, the decision to pay a dividend is complex and must extend beyond a mere investigation into the availability of funds from which a dividend may be declared. Of course, a board must determine the amount and form of payment if a dividend is declared. The board also will want to consider several other factors. While many of these factors are obvious, we note several to emphasize the far-reaching consequences of a board's decision with respect to dividends.

One of the concerns that should be addressed by the board in determining whether to pay dividends is the overall financial condition of the company. This issue is separate and apart from the arcane legal rules governing whether directors may legally declare dividends. Instead, this inquiry is designed to address the practical question: Is the corporation best served by paying out funds now or reinvesting those same funds for future growth? In considering this issue, the board might want to consider the corporation's short-term and long-range goals. Despite the legal availability of funds from which to declare and pay a dividend, for example, a board may determine to preserve cash or other assets of the corporation in favor of an ongoing or planned program to reinvest in the corporation's business. Alternatively, the board may determine to utilize any excess funds to reduce a company's debt or eliminate other liabilities. As might be imagined, a host of considerations are involved in these determinations and the input of the corporation's chief financial officer, outside financial advisers, and other members of management is likely to be important.

Another factor that the board will want to consider when making this business decision is the public and investor reaction to the board's decision. Indeed, public corporations traded on major stock exchanges sometimes are viewed primarily (or importantly) in terms of their dividend streams. Any change in dividend policy, whether to increase or decrease dividends, often triggers immediate reaction in the market and is reflected in the price of the corporation's securities. A board, therefore, will want to consider carefully any change in dividend policy and reflect on any consequences that change may have on the market's perception of the company and on the business of the company itself, including the ability to obtain credit on favorable terms.

Of course, these factors are but a few of those the board will want to consider when discussing dividends. While the specific factors vary from corporation to corporation, we emphasize only that the dividend decision is complex and should not be treated merely as a technical matter depending only on the availability of legally sufficient funds.

Dividends May Be Made Mandatory

Under certain circumstances, directors also may validly contract away their discretion regarding dividend policy. In other words, dividend payments may be made mandatory subject, of course, to the existence of a legal source of funds. Contracts for the mandatory payment of dividends usually involve preferred stock. As a general matter, however, courts are reluctant to limit directors' discretion over whether and when to declare dividends. A certificate of incorporation provision requiring the payment of dividends must be exceedingly clear and precise before a court will require that it be observed.[11]

Protections Afforded Reliance on Reports and Books of Corporation in Declaring Dividends

While the business judgment rule protects decisions of directors with respect to dividends, directors are personally liable for their willful or negligent conduct in connection with the payment of an "unlawful dividend." An unlawful dividend is a dividend made in violation of the governing statute or certificate of incorporation.[12] In particular, under Delaware law, directors are liable to the corporation, and in the event of dissolution or insolvency, to its creditors, at any time within six years from the date the unlawful dividend was paid, for the full amount of the payment of any unlawful dividend.[13] Directors may be found liable for either a willful or negligent declaration and payment of an unlawful dividend.[14]

Notwithstanding the heightened standard for director conduct in this area (recall that directors ordinarily are liable only for "gross negligence"), directors are not left wholly without defense. Many corporate statutes provide protection to directors who rely in good faith on the books of the corporation or on reports of an independent appraiser selected with reasonable care in determining whether there are sufficient funds legally available for the payment of a dividend.

The Delaware statute specifically addressing reliance on experts in connection with the decision to declare and pay a dividend provides, in substance, that directors are protected from liability for wrongful declaration and payment of a dividend where they rely in good faith upon the books and records of the corporation, or rely in good faith upon the report of an officer or employee of the company or any outside expert selected with reasonable care, in determining whether there are sufficient funds legally available for the payment of a dividend.[15] As with reliance on any expert, directors must assure that the expert is chosen with care and that the expert's report is otherwise worthy of reliance. The courts have held that the statute protects "reasonable" not "blind" reliance.

While retention of independent advisers certainly is persuasive evidence that the directors exercised due care in their decision to declare dividends, the advice of outside experts is not required to demonstrate compliance with directors' fiduciary duties. As the courts have recognized, "often insiders familiar with the business of a going concern are in a better position than are outsiders to gather relevant information; and under appropriate circumstances . . . directors may be fully protected in relying in good faith upon valuation reports of [corporate] management."[16] This is particularly true in the area of dividends, where a corporation's chief financial officer may be able to provide the board with a reliable and informed report regarding the value of corporate assets and liabilities. Reliance on experts, however, is not a substitute for thoughtful judgment by each director. Reliance on a report to the board that is patently incorrect, and that any alert director should have known was incorrect, may not afford the board any protection whatsoever.

Valuation of Assets

As noted previously, surplus is determined in light of a corporation's assets and liabilities that should be valued if dividends are to be paid out of surplus. Questions of how particular assets should be valued in a dividend declaration context often are difficult. Courts have held that directors have "a duty to evaluate the assets on the basis of acceptable data and by standards that they are entitled to believe reasonably reflect present 'values.'"[17] No specific guidelines on what factors or methods a board of directors should consider in performing such valuations have been approved by the courts.

Nonetheless, the question of the proper method for valuing assets was directly considered by the court in *Morris v. Standard Gas & Electric Co.* There, the defendant corporation was a public utility holding company whose assets consisted of ownership of various stock interests in public utility companies. The plaintiff in *Morris* challenged the result of the valuation process employed by the defendant corporation. Among other things, the plaintiff challenged the defendant corporation's valuation on the ground that an actual appraisal of the assets in the underlying companies whose stock was owned by the defendant was required to comply with the directors' statutory duty to value the assets of the corporation prior to paying a dividend.

Although the analysis in *Morris* focused primarily on the valuation of the stock held by the holding company, the broad principles enunciated by the court are similarly applicable in the context of valuing assets other than stock. The valuation process used by the board of the defendant corporation in determining to pay the dividend in question in the *Morris* case demonstrates an almost faultless decision-making process. There, the board had three meetings to consider the dividend, during which directors were provided with extensive information, including: (1) the financial records of the corporation; (2) the report of an independent outside appraiser regarding the value of the corporation's assets; (3) the report of the treasurer of the corporation as to his valuation of the corporation's assets; (4) opinions of legal counsel stating that payment of the dividend was permissible under Delaware law; and (5) approval of the SEC of the payment of the dividend. Based on this record, the court found that the board of the defendant corporation "took great care to obtain data on the point in issue, and exercised an informed judgment on the matter."[18] Recognizing that "directors must be given reasonable latitude in ascertaining value," the court also held that under the circumstances presented, it could not substitute "either plaintiff's or its own opinion of value for that reached by the directors where there is no charge of fraud or bad faith."[19]

By way of contrast, in *Farland v. Wills*, the court criticized the board involved in that case for not having made a reasonable effort to value the assets of the corporation in connection with certain stock purchase arrangements. In invalidating the challenged stock purchases, the court cited a statute that forbids a corporation from purchasing its own capital stock "when the capital of the corporation is impaired or when such [purchase] would cause any impairment of the capital of the corporation." Following the decision in *Morris*, the court held that even though the directors were not required to make a formal appraisal, they did have a duty to evaluate the assets and liabilities of the corporation on the basis of acceptable data by standards that they reasonably believed reflected present "values."[20] The court found that the directors of the defendant company had made no effort in that regard.

The purpose of the limitation on the sources of permissible dividends is to protect creditors (and in some cases stockholders as well) from fraud. Because it is usually only fair market value that represents a potential fund from which creditors' claims may be satisfied, the authors believe that the reference to "value" in the cases should be read as a reference to fair market value of assets and liabilities. It follows that a board of directors is permitted to value the shares of capital stock of other companies on a "going-concern" basis without engaging in a formal evaluation of each of such companies' assets.

Nonstock assets, however, require different valuation methodologies. To the extent that assets consist of plants, equipment, or divisions, and such assets could be sold together as a whole, an appropriate methodology would likely be to value these assets as if they were sold on a going-concern basis (i.e., as if a particular plant or unconsolidated division were sold as a whole to a third party). Implicit in such an analysis is the recognition that corporate assets such as a division or particular plant may be sold at a price in excess of the breakup value of the assets of such division or plant. On the other hand, to the extent that assets of a corporation are not susceptible to being sold on a going-concern basis, or to the extent that the company has any significant assets that are unique in the sense of having particular value attributes, such assets should be valued on an individual basis to determine the amount that could be realized by the corporation were it required to sell such assets to satisfy creditors.[21]

Valuation of Liabilities

In addition to the asset side of the balance sheet, the directors also must review the liabilities of the company. While fixed liabilities are easily valued, the hard question faced by directors is how and at what amount contingent liabilities should be valued.

There are no specific guidelines in statutory or case law as to how a board of directors should treat contingent liabilities for determining the existence and amount of surplus. In our view, a board should consider the probability that such contingent liabilities and commitments may become payable and assign a value to such liabilities. While there is no Delaware case law directly on this point, there is some case law outside of Delaware that addresses the issue, as well as some discussion by commentators.[22]

The Committee on Corporate Laws in its report accompanying the recent amendments to the Model Business Corporation Act also takes the position that contingent liabilities should be considered by directors before declaring a dividend:

> To the extent that the corporation may be subject to asserted or unasserted contingent liabilities, the directors are required and entitled to make judgments as to the likelihood, amount and time of any recovery against the corporation, after giving consideration to the extent to which the corporation is insured or otherwise protected by others against loss.[23]

While there is general agreement that contingent and other liabilities not recognized by generally accepted accounting principles (GAAP) should be considered by the directors before declaring a dividend, the case law and commentators provide little guidance about valuing such liabilities properly. If called upon to review a board's determination on this issue, a court first may consider whether the board's treatment was in accordance with GAAP. The mere fact that a contingent or other liability need not be carried on the books of the corporation at face value for accounting purposes would not seem dispositive in the dividend context; rather, it seems incumbent upon the board to make such investigation and receive such advice as is appropriate in each particular instance to assess the proportionate risk of the contingent liability and to make a business judgment with respect to such liability. If a contingent liability is treated at less than its face value for the purpose of determining surplus, it likely would be incumbent upon the board to substantiate why.[24] The need to value such liabilities may occur more frequently than one might expect. Contingent environmental liabilities, for example, likely of assertion, might need to be valued prior to declaration of a dividend. For corporations in industries dealing in hazardous substances, such contingent liabilities could be quite large and may make the dividend decision very difficult.

Payment of Dividends If Sufficient Surplus or Profits Exist

Once a board determines that funds sufficient to declare and pay dividends exist and the amount of dividends to be paid, the form of payment must be set. Dividends to stockholders of Delaware corporations may be paid in cash, in property, or in shares of the corporation's capital stock. Payment in cash or property requires only a simple adjustment to the corporation's balance sheet to reflect the reduction in assets. If payment is made in stock, however, the board of directors is required to cause the transfer of the amount representing capital in respect of the stock to the capital account to satisfy the minimum capital requirements discussed previously.[25] Once the type of dividend is determined, the board must pass a resolution to declare and pay that dividend to holders of stock as of a record date, also to be determined by the board. The payment itself then is customarily accomplished through agents of the corporation and is a simple procedure assuming no prior dividends have been declared but not paid.

Where dividends are in arrears, there is some question regarding which of the old or new dividend declaration is to be paid first. The authors believe that without contrary language in the corporation's certificate of incorporation, dividends declared are payable first with respect to the current dividends and then with respect to accumulated, unpaid dividends. A leading commentator affirmatively states the rule as follows: "[C]urrent dividends should be paid before paying arrearages."[26] Likewise, in *Kennedy v. Carolina Public Service Co.*, a Georgia federal court, interpreting Delaware law, held that where a company's certificate of incorporation did not address the issue, the more equitable rule under the facts of that case would be to pay the dividend on a current basis before paying off accumulated arrearages.[27]

Payment of Dividends without Current Surplus or Profits

Often, corporations wishing to maintain a dividend stream may be legally unable to declare dividends for lack of surplus and profits. In certain cases the problem may be solved by increasing surplus either through reduction of capital or revaluation of assets and liabilities.

Reduction of Capital

A board of directors is permitted to reduce the capital of the corporation (to create surplus) in a number of ways, but first must determine that the corporate assets remaining after the reduction in capital are sufficient to pay debts of the corporation for which payment has not been "otherwise provided."[28] A corporation desiring to transfer capital to surplus, therefore, must have assets after the transfer equal to or greater than the amount that is necessary to pay its debts as they become due. In making the determination of whether the assets of the corporation sufficiently cover its debts, the board should evaluate all of the assets and liabilities of the corporation on the basis of acceptable data and pursuant to standards it believes reasonably reflect present values. In particular, the board is not restricted to—and should not limit itself to—an inquiry regarding book values only.[29]

When determining whether to reduce capital, the board again may rely on the records of the corporation or the reports of the corporation's employees or agents, or on the opinions of outside experts if such reliance is reasonable and in good faith.[30] Assuming a board of directors determines that the corporation satisfies the net assets test discussed previously, the board has flexibility to transfer to surplus some or all of the former capital of the company.[31] Excess surplus also may be created by reducing the stated par value of the capital stock.[32]

Revaluing Assets and Liabilities

Other than reducing the capital of the corporation, the board may create a surplus out of which dividends may be declared and paid by revaluing the assets and liabilities of the corporation. Courts and legislatures long have permitted the directors of a corporation to "revalue" all of the corporation's assets and liabilities on the basis of current data and by standards that the directors are entitled to believe reasonably reflect the present fair value of the assets and liabilities for the purpose of determining the amount of surplus available for payments of dividends. As already discussed, no particular method of valuation has been specified by the courts or legislature. As with other decisions, directors must base their new valuation of the assets and liabilities of the corporation on data that reasonably reflect present value. Dividends then may be declared and paid out of the newly created surplus that results from the revaluation of assets and liabilities, subject to the various cautions detailed previously.

Discrimination among Stockholders Regarding Dividend Payments and Kinds of Payments

The general rule is that the distribution of dividends among shareholders of the same class "must be without discrimination and pro rata unless it is otherwise agreed by all."[33] A corporation may, however, with the consent of the nonreceiving shareholders, declare a dividend to some, but not all, shareholders of the same class of stock. The test regarding the validity of the dividend would appear to be one of overall fairness to all stockholders.[34]

There is substantial authority that any arrangement to pay a liquidating distribution in one form to some stockholders and in a different form to other stockholders is illegal, and these cases provide a useful analogy to the dividend situation.[35]

Dividends, however, may differ between separate classes of stock. Indeed, courts that have invalidated discriminatory dividend payments among stockholders of the same class have indicated that the same action might have been permissible had separate classes of stock been established.[36] Of course, it is not improper for a corporation to discriminate among stockholders with respect to dividends provided that the "nonrecipient" stockholders consent.[37]

Where the class of stock to which a dividend is to be paid is held by a majority stockholder, however, the declaration and payment of a dividend only on shares of that class may be deemed a self-dealing transaction subject to review under a standard of entire fairness.[38] As discussed before, Delaware courts have recognized the declaration and payment of dividends as an area particularly within the broad discretionary powers of directors.[39] Under the business judgment rule, a court will not second-guess the decision of a board of directors unless the party challenging the decision establishes facts indicating a lack of due care or good faith or that indicate an abuse of discretion by the directors.

Rights of Stockholders upon Declaration of a Dividend

The declaration of cash dividends creates a debtor-creditor relationship between the corporation and the stockholders and, if such dividend is not paid when due, it may be recovered in an action by the stockholders.[40] Once declared, a cash dividend may not be rescinded, and the corporation is obligated to pay such dividend on the designated payment date. The right of the stockholders to a cash dividend becomes "vested" upon declaration and "it necessarily follows that neither the same board of directors nor their successors can afterward reconsider their action and revoke the declaration of a legally declared dividend without the stockholders' consent."[41]

In contrast, it generally is held that the declaration of dividends payable in stock of the paying corporation creates no such debtor-creditor relationship, and that stock dividends, therefore, are revocable by the board of directors after declaration but prior to actual issuance of the stock.[42] The rationale for the different treatment of cash and stock dividends appears to lie in the different nature of a stock dividend. Unlike a cash dividend, the declaration of a stock dividend results merely in a proportionate alteration of the corporation's capital structure, leaving the stockholder in exactly the same economic position.

Consistent with these rationales, courts from certain jurisdictions have suggested that a *property* dividend, such as a dividend payable by a corporation in the stock of another corporation, "has all of the characteristics" or "is regarded" as a cash dividend.[43] This matter, however, is not definitively settled.

Although not common, it sometimes happens that a corporation has legally available funds to pay a dividend on the dividend declaration date but that because of financial reversals lacks such funds on the payment date. Because the statutory prohibition (and concomitant liability to directors) arises upon *payment*, a board aware of the absence of legally available funds on the date of dividend payment is well advised to halt such payment, even at the risk of defending lawsuits brought by disgruntled stockholders.

Notes

1. 8 DEL. CODE ANN. § 170(a).
2. *Id.* at § 154.
3. *Id.*
4. *Id.;* Morris v. Standard Gas & Elec. Co., 63 A.2d 577; Farland v. Wills, C.A. No. 4888 (Del. Ch. Nov. 12, 1975).

5. Note, however, that payment of dividends by an insolvent corporation may subject the directors and/or the corporation to liability under fraudulent conveyance statutes. Throughout this discussion, we assume that the corporation is solvent and that the payment of dividends will not render the corporation insolvent.

6. *Id.* at § 170(a).

7. *Id.* at § 170(b). The statute is also self-limiting, for it may be restricted by any provision contained in the corporation's certificate of incorporation.

8. Gabelli & Co., Inc. Profit Sharing Plan v. Liggett Group, Inc., 479 A.2d 276, 280 (Del. 1984).

9. Eshleman v. Keenan, 194 A. 40, 43 (Del. Ch. 1937), *aff'd,* 2 A.2d 904 (Del. 1938).

10. *See generally* Gabelli & Co., Inc. Profit Sharing Plan v. Liggett Group, Inc., 444 A.2d 261, 264 (Del. Ch. 1982); Litle v. Waters, C.A. No. 12155, slip op. at 8–11 (Del. Ch. Feb. 10, 1992); 1 R. FRANKLIN BALOTTI & JESSE A. FINKELSTEIN, THE DELAWARE LAW OF CORPORATIONS AND BUSINESS ORGANIZATIONS § 5.21 (2d ed. Supp. 1995) [hereinafter "BALOTTI & FINKELSTEIN § ___"].

11. 11 WILLIAM M. FLETCHER, FLETCHER CYCLOPEDIA OF THE LAW OF PRIVATE CORPORATIONS § 5325 (perm. ed. rev. vol. 1986) [hereinafter "11 CYCLOPEDIA CORPORATIONS § ___"]. *Accord* DeJonge v. Zentgraf, 169 N.Y.S. 377 (N.Y. App. Div. 1918) (clause divesting discretion enforced only if no other possible meaning).

12. *See* 8 DEL. CODE ANN. § 173 ("No corporation shall pay dividends except in accordance with this chapter.").

13. *Id.* at § 174.

14. *Id.* at § 174(a).

15. *Id.* at § 172.

16. Smith v. Van Gorkom, 488 A.2d 858, 876 (Del. 1985).

17. Morris v. Standard Gas & Electric Co., 63 A.2d at 582.

18. *Id.* at 585.

19. *Id. See also In re* Amsted Indus., Inc. Litig., Cons. C.A. No. 8224 (Del. Ch. Aug. 24, 1988), *aff'd sub nom.* Barkan v. Amsted Indus., Inc., 567 A.2d 1279 (Del. 1989).

20. Farland v. Wills, C.A. No. 4888, slip op. at 12 (Del. Ch. Nov. 12, 1975).

21. Similarly, the board is entitled to consider assets that are not reflected on the balance sheet of the corporation, such as unconsolidated joint ventures and other assets that the board reasonably believes are valuable to the corporation.

22. *See* L.L. Constantin & Co. v. R.P. Holding Corp., 153 A.2d 378 (N.J. Super. Ct. Ch. Div. 1959).

23. (*Quoted in Current Issues on the Legality of Dividends from a Law and Accounting Perspective: A Task Force Report,* 39 BUS. LAW. 289, 305 (Nov. 1983)). *See also* Committee on Corporate Laws, *Changes in the Model Business Corporation Act—Amendments Pertaining to Distributions,* 42 BUS. LAW. 259, 263 (Nov. 1986).

24. *Cf.* Boesky v. CX Partners, L.P., C.A. No. 9739 (Del. Ch. Apr. 28, 1988) (questioning the appropriateness of reserving only a discounted amount for a contingent claim under the dissolution provisions of the Delaware Revised Uniform Limited Partnership Act and the General Corporation Law).

25. 8 DEL. CODE ANN. § 173.

26. 12 WILLIAM M. FLETCHER, FLETCHER CYCLOPEDIA OF THE LAW OF PRIVATE CORPORATIONS § 5446, at 174 (perm. ed. 1985) (footnote omitted).

27. Kennedy v. Carolina Public Service Co., 262 F. 803, 807 (N.D. Ga. 1920).

28. 8 DEL. CODE ANN. § 244(b).

29. *Cf.* Morris v. Standard Gas & Elec. Co., 63 A.2d 577 (Del. Ch. 1949); Farland v. Wills, C.A. No. 4888 (Del. Ch. Nov. 12, 1975).

30. *See* 8 DEL. CODE ANN. § 141(e). As will be discussed later, the board of directors also may determine that the books and records of the corporation do not accurately reflect the value of the corporation's assets and liabilities and may revalue them.

31. 8 DEL. CODE ANN. § 244(4).

32. *Id.* at §§ 151(g) and 242.

33. HENRY W. BALLANTINE, BALLANTINE ON CORPORATIONS § 239, at 563 (rev. ed. 1946). *Cf.* Unocal Corp. v. Mesa Petroleum Co., 493 A.2d 946 (Del. 1985); Hannigan v. Italo-Petroleum Corp. of Am., 47 A.2d 169 (Del. 1945).

34. *See* Shrage v. Bridgeport Oil Co., 71 A.2d 882 (Del. Ch. 1950).

35. Zimmerman v. Tidewater Associated Oil Co., 143 P.2d 409, 412 (Cal. Ct. App. 1943); *In re* San Joaquin Light & Power Corp., 127 P.2d 29 (Cal. Ct. App. 1942); Shrage v. Bridgeport Oil Co., 71 A.2d 882 (Del. Ch. 1950).

36. Scott v. P. Lorillard Co., 154 A. 515 (N.J. Ch.), *aff'd,* 157 A. 388 (N.J. 1931).

37. *See* 11 *Cyclopedia Corporations, supra* note 11, § 5352, at 848 ("While, ordinarily, dividends must be apportioned among the stockholders pro rata to their several holdings, 'it cannot be doubted that the stockholders may, by unanimous consent, adopt and become bound by a different mode of division.' And stockholders who assent to a discriminatory arrangement may thereby be estopped to object") (footnotes omitted).

38. *See* Sinclair Oil Corp. v. Levien, 280 A.2d 717, 720–21 (Del. 1971).

39. *See* Giammalvo v. Sunshine Mining Co., C.A. No. 12842, slip op. at 9 (Del. Ch. Jan. 31, 1994), *aff'd,* No. 121, 1994 (Oct. 28, 1994) (ORDER); Eshleman v. Keenan, 194 A. 40 (Del. Ch. 1937), *aff'd,* 2 A.2d 904 (Del. 1938); Gabelli & Co., Inc. Profit Sharing Plan v. Liggett Group, Inc., 444 A.2d 261 (Del. Ch. 1982); Baron v. Allied Artists Pictures Corp., 337 A.2d 653; BARBARA BLACK, CORPO-RATE DIVIDENDS AND STOCK REPURCHASES § 4.03[1], at 4–26 (1990) ("Determination of a corporation's dividend policy is the quintessential business decision protected by the business judgment rule") (footnote omitted).

40. Wilmington Trust Co. v. Wilmington Trust Co., 15 A.2d 665 (Del. Ch. 1940); Selly v. Fleming Coal Co., 180 A. 326 (Del. Super. 1935); 11 CYCLOPEDIA CORPORATIONS, *supra* note 11, § 5323.

41. 11 Cyclopedia Corporations, *supra* note 11, §5323, at 736 (footnote omitted).

42. 11 Cyclopedia Corporations, *supra* note 11, §5323.1, at 741; *Corporate Dividends* §59, at 185–86; *see* Staats v. Biograph Co., 236 F. 454, 458–60 (2d Cir. 1916); *cf.* Rutherford Nat'l Bank v. Black, 32 A.2d 86, 98 (N.J. Ch. 1943).

43. Union & New Haven Trust Co. v. Taintor, 83 A. 697, 699 (Conn. 1912); Commissioner v. Scatena, 85 F.2d 729, 731 (9th Cir. 1936); *see also* Staats v. Biograph Co., 236 F. at 461 (quoting 1 Arthur Machen, Jr., Modern Law of Corporations §601, at 498 (1908) ("therefore a dividend payable in shares which had been purchased by the company should be in this respect assimilated to a cash dividend, and is irrevocable") (footnote omitted)).

CHAPTER 5

Derivative Litigation: Managing a Unique Corporate Asset

Although management of corporate assets is ordinarily the exclusive province of the board, the law empowers stockholders with a procedural mechanism to remedy perceived wrongdoing that harms the corporation. This mechanism, known as a derivative action, has the effect of removing from the board management of a potentially important asset in certain circumstances. Examples of derivative actions include those challenging alleged breaches of fiduciary duty, mismanagement, self-dealing, or waste of corporate assets.

The derivative suit is a corporate asset because any recovery from litigation is a recovery for the corporation. The derivative suit is unique because, in many cases, management of the asset (i.e., prosecution of the litigation) rests solely with one or more disgruntled stockholders. The law recognizes the power of the board to take control of this asset in appropriate circumstances, however, even over the opposition of the plaintiff-stockholder. Following, we examine briefly the nature of derivative litigation and the use by corporations of various techniques to assert control over this asset, including the use of committees of the board and the advantages and disadvantages of the committee process.

The Nature of Derivative Litigation

A derivative action is a suit brought to enforce a corporate right that the corporation has refused to assert. Derivative plaintiffs, if successful, win a recovery only for the corporation itself, and any recovery in such an action belongs to the corporation and stockholders benefit only indirectly from the recovery in proportion to their ownership interests.

Prior to prosecuting derivative litigation, a stockholder must comply with a series of rules that have been created to balance the potentially disruptive effects of derivative litigation on a corporation's ability to manage its day-to-day business. The most frequently discussed (and perhaps most easily misunderstood) rule relating to derivative actions is the demand rule.

The Demand Rule

Prior to instituting a derivative suit, a stockholder is required to demand, formally and in writing, that the board of directors take action to remedy the wrong the stockholder believes has been done to the corporation. Alternatively, if a demand is not made prior to a stockholder bringing suit, the stockholder must allege with "particularity" in his or her complaint the reasons for not making a demand.[1]

The purpose of the demand requirement is "to give a corporation the opportunity to rectify an alleged wrong without litigation, and to control any litigation that does arise."[2] Demand is required because the "shareholder derivative action is an exception to the normal rule that the proper party to bring a suit on behalf of a corporation is the corporation itself, acting through its directors or a majority of its shareholders."[3] Put more simply, before the law will allow a stockholder to take control of the management of the company's lawsuit from the board, the stockholder must establish either that he or she has requested the board to take action and the board has wrongfully failed to do so, or that the board is not in a position to manage the litigation.

Stockholder demands, while simple in concept, must meet certain minimal requirements: The demand must "identify the alleged wrongdoers, describe the factual basis of the wrongful acts and the harm caused to the corporation, and request remedial relief."[4] If a demand is adequate, the board of directors to assert control over the process must investigate (where appropriate) and respond to the demanding stockholder within a reasonable period of time. While it has been held that there is no "magical period of time within which a board must respond to a demand," the courts are likely to consider the timeliness of the board's response in the context of the facts surrounding the alleged wrong.[5] The appropriate response time will vary, of course, depending upon the complexity of the issues raised. If the board allows this period to expire without response by the corporation, the demanding stockholder can "assume control" of the litigation. Accordingly, if a corporation receives a proper demand, a careful, thorough investigation should be undertaken, albeit with one eye on the calendar to assure the response to the demand is communicated within a reasonable period under the circumstances.[6]

Where the board of directors considers the demand and determines to bring an action to enforce the corporation's rights, the issue of a stockholder suit becomes moot, for there is no need for the stockholder to become enmeshed in the board's management of the company's litigation. Where the board considers the demand and determines *not* to bring suit, the matter likewise is concluded unless the stockholder is able to demonstrate that the board's refusal to litigate was "wrongful."

Alternatively, where the stockholder is able to demonstrate that the making of a demand would have been "futile" (i.e., that the board, because of inherent conflicts, should not be permitted to take charge of the matter) or, if after making a demand no timely response is forthcoming from the corporation, he or she may proceed with litigation. At least under Delaware law, however, the corporation may later determine to assume control of the litigation or, after investigation, seek to dismiss the litigation.

Is Demand "Futile" and Thus Excused?

As mentioned previously, a stockholder need not make a demand if he or she can show that the board is disqualified from managing the litigation.[7] In other words, a stockholder may commence litigation if demand on the board would be "futile." As the Delaware Supreme Court has held: "[t]he application of the demand futility test . . . presupposes that the corporation has taken a hostile position regarding the derivative litigation" and the corporation "cannot effectively stand neutral."[8]

The Delaware courts have formulated a two-part test for determining whether demand is futile and, therefore, not necessary. Under that test, the court looks to see whether the complaint pleads facts that raise a reasonable doubt that a majority of the board are disinterested and independent or that the transaction was otherwise the product of a valid exercise of business judgment.[9]

Interestedness and Lack of Independence

Demand will be excused if the complaining stockholder can plead specific facts evidencing that a majority of the current board of directors is interested in the transaction or lacks independence. A director must be a direct and substantial beneficiary of the challenged transaction for a court to conclude that the director is interested or lacks independence. The type of self-interest in a transaction that would taint a director's independence has been described as follows:

> Directorial interest exists whenever divided loyalties are present, or a director either has received, or is entitled to receive, a personal financial benefit from the challenged transaction which is not equally shared by the stockholders. The question of independence flows from an analysis of the factual allegations pertaining to the influences upon the directors' performance of their duties generally, and more specifically in respect to the challenged transaction.[10]

The Delaware Supreme Court in *Cede & Co. v. Technicolor, Inc.*, rejected the contention that any self-interest, standing alone and without evidence of disloyalty, is enough to disqualify the board from acting. Rather, the court determined that a director's self-interest must be material.[11] Without such director interest, courts will not excuse demand under the first prong of the test.

The determination of whether a stockholder has adequately pled demand futility has been the subject of much litigation. The procedural nature of these motions has been criticized as wasteful, time-consuming, and not in the best interests of stockholders. While a detailed review of those opinions would not be productive here given the wealth of authority discussing this issue, we do pause to note that at least under Delaware law, a stockholder does not establish that a board should be disqualified from considering a demand (i.e., that a demand would have been "futile") merely by naming all the directors as defendants,[12] by the bare assertion that directors did not take action before suit was filed,[13] or because the directors approved the challenged transaction.[14] Similarly, the mere allegation that a board has rejected a prior demand is insufficient to excuse demand,[15] nor will the refusal to rescind a transaction demonstrate futility.[16]

With respect to independence, the relevant question "whether a director is controlled by a third party . . . [which question] is 'an intensely factual one,'" and the courts have "require[d] that a plaintiff 'assert the facts from which it is believed an inference of control could be drawn.'"[17] For example, it has been held that a complaint sufficiently called into question the independence of a majority of the board where an action is taken by a board comprised of six members, five of whom also were officers of other entities controlled by the majority stockholder, and three of whom had a family relationship with that stockholder.[18] Mere financial ties by a majority of directors to the corporation, however, will not necessarily excuse demand.[19]

Valid Business Judgment

Without a showing that the directors are interested, the courts look to see if a complaining stockholder has established a reasonable doubt that "the challenged transaction was otherwise the product of a valid exercise of business judgment."[20] To make such a showing, the plaintiff must demonstrate that "the directors were not *capable* of exercising their business judgment with respect to any of the transactions."[21] A court will excuse demand, for example, if a stockholder alleges particularized facts evidencing that the challenged transaction was wasteful, i.e., that the consideration received by the corporation was so inadequate that no person would reasonably conclude that it was adequate in light of the consideration given.[22] Other theories of relief that have been found to excuse demand include: issuance of stock for inadequate consideration to entrench directors in office and arbitrarily rejected offers to acquire stock of the corporation.[23]

Determining Whether Demand Is Excused Where No Business Decision Has Been Made

In *Rales v. Blasband*, the Delaware Supreme Court clarified that in circumstances where no decision has been made by a board or where a challenged business decision had been made by directors *other* than those who were asked to consider a stockholder demand, a reviewing court will examine the "interest" and "independence" of the board called upon to consider the demand, not the board that made the challenged decision.[24] This is a sensible rule that gives appropriate deference to the decision makers who make up the board at the time of the demand.

Where Demand Is Made and Refused, the Stockholder Must Show "Wrongfulness" of the Rejection to Proceed

If demand is made and refused, the board's decision not to litigate will be protected unless it was "wrongful," i.e., unless it was not the product of a valid exercise of business judgment. It is not enough for a stockholder merely to state that the refusal was "wrongful." Rather, under Delaware law, the stockholder must allege with particularity facts sufficient to rebut the presumption that the board's rejection is protected by the business-judgment rule.[25] When a board refuses a demand, the only issues that will be examined by a reviewing court are the good faith and reasonableness of the board's investigation.[26] Where the business judgment rule protects a board's refusal to sue, the stockholder "lacks the legal managerial power to continue the derivative action, for that power is terminated by the refusal."[27]

Asserting Control of the Process: The Role of the Presuit Investigation Committee

If a proper demand is made on a board of directors, a committee of independent directors often is appointed and charged with the task of investigating the allegations of the demand and recommending to the board the appropriate action to be taken, if any, in response to the demand. Although the law does not require that this work be performed by a committee, rather than the full board, practical considerations often make the appointment of a committee useful for this task. If, for example, a majority of the board were implicated in the alleged wrongdoing identified in the demand, investigation by a committee of untainted directors could help alleviate the perception of a conflict of interest. Likewise, where the board itself is large, it often is more efficient simply to delegate the task of investigating a demand to a smaller working group of the board. The board's reliance upon the recommendation of such a committee customarily is entitled to the full protection of the business judgment rule if the committee is comprised of disinterested and independent directors, and has conducted a good faith, reasonable investigation into the allegations of the demand.

Use of the committee process is not without costs to the corporation, given that it has become customary (but by no means required) for the committee to retain its own legal and financial advisers. Further, where the committee's investigation is protracted, the disruption of the business and management of the corporation and the impact of the investigation on employees is difficult, if not impossible, to measure. Nonetheless, the alternative (i.e., litigation by a stockholder) also carries with it certain costs, and the adversarial setting is likely to lead to a higher level of disruption and distraction than would the work of a committee.

The Charge and Composition of the Committee

The resolutions that create the committee are likely to be of importance from the legal perspective. The first issue that must be confronted in this regard is whether the committee is to be charged with making a recommendation for consideration and decision by the full board of directors, or whether the committee itself is to be empowered to take action. Because the latter approach may implicate certain doctrines of law that will be dealt with later, we assume for purposes of this discussion that the committee is formed to investigate and make recommendations to the full board.

The resolution forming the committee should state specifically the purpose of the committee (e.g., "to investigate the allegations set forth in the demand and to recommend to the full board of directors appropriate action to be taken with respect thereto"); the composition of the committee (including the board's conclusion that the members of the committee are independent and disinterested with respect to the challenged transaction); and, where appropriate, the fact that the committee is authorized to retain counsel and other advisers or experts to assist it in its investigation.

Only those independent directors with no direct financial interests in the challenged action should be appointed as members of the committee. Accordingly, directors who directly participated in the challenged action should not be appointed to serve as committee members, although mere approval of the action does not disqualify a director from serving on a committee.[28] If a board of directors does not have any current members who are independent and disinterested with respect to the challenged actions, the board may consider either filling any existing vacancies on the board or expanding the board, if possible, with independent directors who then may be appointed to investigate the subject matter of the demand.

The Work of the Committee

The first outward step a corporation takes in response to a demand is to acknowledge its receipt. This acknowledgment should refer to the existence of the committee, if formed prior to the response, and should assure the author of the demand that he or she will be advised of the corporation's decision with respect to the demand immediately after it is made. If a timetable for the investigation has been set and is likely to be met, the drafter also may want to consider informing the demanding stockholder of the expected response date to prevent any preemptive filing of litigation. Often, however, a schedule for the investigation is not accurately predictable at this early stage of the investigation. If not, the initial response should not speculate regarding the timing of the investigation.

The committee often will turn first to the task of retaining counsel. Although no rule of law requires a committee to retain outside counsel, it has become the generally accepted practice, a practice that the authors believe is advisable to follow. Factors that the committee will want to consider in retaining counsel are the same as those considered in other circumstances: expertise and experience in advising committees; the ability of the firm adequately to staff the matter; the absence of a disabling conflict of interest; and whether the members of the committee feel comfortable with the lawyers. The last factor is extremely important in this context, for interaction between counsel and the committee members typically is quite frequent and sometimes spans lengthy time periods. Moreover, as will be described, the use of independent committees in certain circumstances has received a fair degree of healthy skepticism from the judiciary. This skepticism is tempered by the recognition that the committee's advisers play a crucial role in assuring the integrity of the committee process. One of the most important tasks of retained counsel is to provide each of the members of the committee with an understanding of his or her legal obligations and duties as a committee member.[29] This understanding should be reinforced throughout the process. The committee also should consider whether it desires to retain any nonlegal expert advisers, such as financial analysts, investment bankers, or technical experts, depending, of course, on the nature of the transaction being investigated. The issue of whether such additional expertise is necessary is one that the committee should revisit as the investigation proceeds.

As the committee begins its substantive investigation into the matters contained in the demand, it typically will request copies of documents relevant to its investigation. After a thorough review of the documents, which the committee at some point must conclude is sufficient for its accurate understanding of the events called into question, the committee's investigation likely will turn to interviewing various persons knowledgeable about the matters to be investigated. Indeed, even prior to requesting, reviewing, and assimilating documents produced by the company, the committee may wish to interview certain people to give the committee a basic understanding of the matters at issue. Particularly where the matters complained of in the demand already have been or currently are the subject of litigation, the committee might best be able to obtain an overview of the matter from in-house or outside lawyers involved in the litigation.[30] Such preliminary interviews are likely to help the committee determine which other persons to interview. The committee should not feel constrained, however, to interview each and every person possibly with relevant knowledge. To the contrary, as with its review of relevant documents, the committee should interview as many persons as the committee feels reasonably necessary to enable it to make an informed recommendation to the full board of directors.

Eventually, the committee will enter the decision-making stage. While the committee should take as much time as is necessary to investigate the matter carefully and thoroughly,[31] excessive delay without justification may allow a stockholder to establish a right to prosecute the litigation based on the delay.[32] There is no formula to determine when enough documents have been collected and reviewed or when sufficient interviews have been conducted, nevertheless, most committees seem intuitively to know when they have reached that point in their investigation. The factors that the committee may wish to consider in reaching its conclusions include: the magnitude of any injury to the corporation; the legal responsibility of corporate directors, officers, employees, or agents for that injury; the likelihood of recovering damages in litigation and the costs that would have to be incurred to recover such damages; the effect of litigation on the morale of employees; the value to the corporation of continuing the employment of any employees responsible for the injury; the effect of litigation on the corporation's relationships with customers, suppliers, etc.; and remedial steps already taken by the corporation to prevent a recurrence of the challenged actions.[33]

After discussing the results of its investigation, the committee may wish to reach tentative, as opposed to final, conclusions. With such tentative conclusions in hand, counsel for the committee customarily drafts a report of the committee. While no two committee reports are identical, these reports typically include: (1) a discussion of the chronology of the committee investigation (i.e., the formation of the committee, retention of counsel, gathering of documents, conducting of interviews and meetings, etc.); (2) a discussion of the facts relevant to the committee's investigation; (3) a discussion of any limitations on the investigation, whether self-imposed or because of factors beyond the committee's control; and (4) a discussion of the committee's conclusions and recommendations. The committee should review the draft report and, if appropriate, suggest revisions to the draft report. Once the committee is satisfied with the report, the committee may wish to further deliberate to arrive at its final conclusions and, if appropriate, approve the report.

The Role of the Full Board

At this point in the process, the report typically is forwarded by the committee or its counsel to the corporate secretary for presentation to the full board of directors. At the board meeting, committee members and/or counsel typically make a presentation to the full board, reviewing the charge of the committee and explaining the process employed by the committee, the limitations on the investigation, if any, and the conclusion reached. Assuming that the charge of the committee was limited to reporting to the board, the full board then will determine whether to accept the report and the recommendations of the committee.

Once the full board of directors has determined how to respond to the demand, the corporate secretary or general counsel usually is instructed to communicate that decision. Again, there is no legally required format for the board's formal response. Given the current state of law providing for minimal, if any, discovery into the committee process, where the board determines to reject the demand, careful practitioners usually respond by indicating only that the demand was refused by the board of directors after a thorough and deliberate review of all relevant facts.

The Role of the Postfiling or Zapata Committee

The Context and the Legal Analysis

Even where demand is deemed excused and derivative litigation may be maintained validly by the stockholder, the board nonetheless may appoint a committee of independent directors to determine whether the continuation of the litigation is in the corporation's best interests and, where appropriate, to seek a dismissal or take over prosecution of the litigation.[34] Typically, in this context it is the committee—and not the full board—that is given the task of determining whether litigation should continue. This is so because if the litigation has proceeded, there likely has been a prior determination, either in court or in the boardroom, that a majority of the board was "interested" in the action. Thus, in staffing a postfiling committee, considerations of the independence of committee members are paramount.

A number of states have determined that a special litigation committee of disinterested directors has the ability, in its business judgment, to determine whether the action should be continued. This ability derives from the duty of the board of directors to govern the affairs and manage the assets of the corporation. Among the states that have allowed a special litigation committee to terminate derivative litigation (by state or federal decision) or by statute are Alabama, California, Colorado, Connecticut, Delaware, Georgia, Iowa, Maryland, Massachusetts, Michigan, Minnesota, New York, North Carolina, Ohio, and Virginia.[35]

Courts have taken at least two different approaches in reviewing a committee's decision to terminate a derivative action when demand is initially excused. For example, the New York court has determined that, under New York law, a board of directors has the power to seek the dismissal of a derivative action, subject only to judicial review on the question of whether an appropriate and sufficient investigation has been made by disinterested members of the board of directors making the decision.[36]

The Delaware Supreme Court also has held that the board has the power to appoint a special litigation committee and that the committee has the power to petition the court to dismiss the action if, after investigation, it determines that dismissal would be in the best interests of the corporation. Under this approach, however, the court is required to apply a two-step analysis in determining whether to dismiss the action, which analysis requires: (1) a judicial determination of whether the committee acted independently and in good faith and demonstrated a reasonable basis for its determination that the action should be dismissed; and (2) an application by the court of its "own independent business judgment" to determine whether the action should be dismissed.

The Work of the Committee

Much like a presuit committee, a so-called "special litigation" or postfiling committee may wish to retain separate counsel before beginning its investigation. In pursuing its work, a special litigation committee may wish to consider, inter alia, the following factors in determining whether a derivative action should be dismissed:

1. *Merits of the Claim.* Does the derivative plaintiff's complaint state a claim under state corporation law, federal securities, or other law?[37] If so, is the cause of action supported by substantial evidence?

2. *Injury to the Corporation.* Were the underlying acts or transactions fair or did they subject the corporation to substantial injuries?[38] If the corporation has been injured, will the defendant directors be able or required to respond in damages?[39]

3. *Costs of Prosecution.* Is there a likelihood that the corporation will incur substantial legal expenses?[40] Will prosecution of the derivative action result in substantial indemnification expenses for the corporation?[41]

4. *Effect on Operations.* Will prosecution of the derivative action have an adverse effect on the management's ability to manage the corporation,[42] or on the morale of the corporation's employees and executives?[43] Will there be an adverse customer, supplier, banker, or stock market reaction to the prosecution of the derivative action?[44]

5. *Cost-Benefit Analysis.* Does the likelihood of success on the merits justify the additional cost of pursuing the additional claims?[45]

6. *Knowledge and Motivation.* Did the defendant directors knowingly authorize the alleged misconduct? Did the defendant directors authorize the transactions in question to serve their personal interests or to serve the corporation's best interest?

7. *Effect of Remedial Action.* If sanctions were imposed, were they effective on the individuals involved in the allegedly improper transactions?[46] Has the corporation taken corrective measures or adopted new policies designed to prevent the recurrence of similar misconduct?[47]

If the special litigation committee concludes, after considering the foregoing and all other relevant factors, that further prosecution of the derivative action is not in the corporation's best interests, the committee should file a motion to dismiss the action.[48]

Consequences and Pitfalls of Using the Committee Process

The decision to employ a committee to investigate the allegations contained in a stockholder's demand or to determine whether to move to dismiss a derivative action using a committee is not without consequences. As described below, not only has the use of special committees itself been criticized, but that process contains many pitfalls for the inexperienced.

"Structural Bias"—Skeptical Views of the Committee Process

Several leading jurists and commentators have expressed skepticism regarding the validity of the hypothesis supporting the use of special committees in the first place: that they will act as truly independent extensions of the board, without overt or concealed bias for or against any position.[49] Judicial skepticism over the use of special committees stems from the perception that the process may be "subverted and rendered less than useful."[50] This perspective appears to allow for the possibility of so-called "structural bias" working subtly (or not so subtly) to subvert the committee process in favor of directors who may well be social friends or business colleagues of committee members. Moreover, the argument has been made that, in practice, committee members often are chief executive officers of their own corporations who may "view the roles of directors in the same way that they probably wish outside directors on the board of their own companies view their role—as a source of expert advice and judgment, on call to the CEO but not to be officiously interjected."[51]

In light of this criticism, perhaps the best way to ensure that a special litigation committee receives proper deference by a reviewing court is to ensure that the committee follows an intellectually rigorous process in its analysis and avoid the appointment of committee members with ties to those under scrutiny—even if it means bringing in new board members especially to staff the committee.

As commentators have suggested, after an appointment as a member of a special committee, only one factor stands between interested management and the interests of the nonaffiliated stockholders. That factor, a "sense of duty," must be impressed upon the committee members by their advisers so that the members understand that "as a result of accepting the special assignment, they have a new duty and stand in a new and different relationship to the firm's management or its controlling shareholder."[52] The committee's lawyers play the crucial role in establishing and assuring the integrity of the committee process and are charged with explaining to the committee members the "radical change" in their relationship with the board of directors as a whole and the corporate enterprise.[53] Thus, "if the special committee process is to have integrity, it falls in the first instance to the lawyers to unwrap the bindings that have joined the directors into a single board; to instill in the committee a clear understanding of the radically altered state in which it finds itself and to lead the committee to a full understanding of its new duty."[54]

Accordingly, the judicial skepticism regarding the committee process must be considered in the decision whether to employ that process. While a truly independent committee can make an informed and good faith decision that, if properly presented, will be given due deference by a reviewing court, care should be exercised not only in selecting the members of that committee, but also in selecting experienced counsel to guide the committee and, perhaps most important, help the committee understand its special role.

Authority of the Special Committee

Courts also have recognized that the appointment of a special committee, delegated complete authority to act on a demand, may be a concession by the board that the full board is unable to act on the demand, and that demand, therefore, is "excused."[55] The current view is that where a corporation files a motion to dismiss for failure to make demand before it appoints a special litigation committee, the challenged board has not conceded its disqualification and demand, therefore, is not excused.[56]

In light of the current state of the law, if a corporation's board appoints a special litigation committee after filing a motion to dismiss, or if the board does not completely delegate its decision-making powers to the special litigation committee, the business judgment rule should be the standard used to evaluate the board's decision to terminate the litigation. Careful use of the committee process and delegation of board authority can alleviate many of these pitfalls.

Waiver of the Attorney-Client Privilege

Another pitfall of the use of a special committee is the potential waiver of the attorney-client privilege otherwise applicable to corporate communications or documents. While in theory this risk can be dealt with adequately by retaining separate counsel for the corporation and its agents, the realities of the investigation process nevertheless may lead to harmful results. As described previously, during the investigation, committee members who also are directors customarily request information from corporate employees.

While any request for an interview or for documents will, if properly presented, reflect that the committee and its counsel do not represent the corporation or any of its employees, those employees, particularly those unsophisticated in legal proceedings, will feel tremendous pressure to produce and discuss any and all events, regardless of their relevance and whether the corporation has a valid privilege against disclosure of such information.

Even for those experienced in litigation or those adequately counseled, care must be taken not to draw too aggressive a line concerning privilege issues. Given that the validity of the committee process rests in large part on the amount and the nature of information the committee has reviewed, circumstances exist that may justify the waiver of the attorney-client or other privilege. Accordingly, the use of the committee may, in some circumstances, lead to a waiver of the corporation's privilege. While circumstances may justify waiver of the applicable privilege, care should be taken to assure the protection of privileged information in future proceedings, if possible.

Uncovering Wrongdoing during the Investigation

As previously described, after a committee is formed to investigate the allegations contained in the demand or the claims made in a derivative suit, the committee must pursue a course of action designed to arm it with sufficient information to make an informed decision in good faith. Once sufficient information has been obtained, the committee must determine whether to institute suit or, in the case of demand-excused derivative litigation, whether to terminate that litigation.

In addition to often difficult questions regarding the institution or maintenance of derivative litigation, a special committee may face other difficult issues during its investigation. One of the most difficult of these issues may arise if, during the investigation, the committee uncovers evidence of wrongdoing that was committed by a director, officer, or agent of the corporation. This wrongdoing, of course, may relate to the subject of the investigation itself or may relate to matters wholly outside the allegations contained in the stockholder's demand.

For example, the committee may uncover criminal or civil wrongdoing committed by one or more corporate actors. If so, committee members, indeed the whole board, will be faced not only with an ethical dilemma, but with a very serious business decision. The United States Sentencing Commission has promulgated, effective November 1, 1991, guidelines to be followed in sentencing convicted defendants that are organizations.[57] These guidelines establish base fines for convictions "which are determined by the nature of the offense alleged and its economic effect."[58] A formula then is applied to yield a culpability score, which ultimately determines the multiplier to be applied to the loss incurred by the victims. The culpability score is itself determined by the organization's demonstrated involvement in or tolerance of criminal activity, prior history of any criminal misconduct, the violation of a judicial order or injunction, or the obstruction of justice. Importantly, however, the culpability score can be reduced if the organization has an effective program to prevent and deter violations of law and if the corporation reported the violation and thereafter cooperated and accepted responsibility for the criminal conduct. Under the sentencing guidelines, the culpability score will be reduced most greatly if:

> The organization (A) prior to an immediate threat of disclosure or government investigation; and (B) within a reasonably prompt time after becoming aware of the offense, reported the offense to appropriate governmental authorities, fully cooperated in the investigation, and clearly demonstrated recognition and affirmative acceptance of responsibility for its criminal conduct. . . .[59]

Accordingly, if the committee discovers criminal or potentially criminal conduct, the interest of the corporate body as a whole may be best served by reporting the conduct to the appropriate authority, thus entitling the corporation to the greatest possible reduction in the culpability score and, as a result, reducing the potential fine to the corporation.[60] Of course, depending on the seriousness of the violation and the ultimate fine, the potential risk to the corporate enterprise as a viable entity may be impacted by the disclosure of this information. In short, use of the committee process may lead to unexpected and vexing issues.

Discovery of the Committee's Work

Members of committees often wonder whether the mass of papers produced by the committee in the course of its investigation, including its report, will ever be made available to the stockholder who asserted the demand it was charged with investigating. At least in Delaware, the answer to that question is that without a showing by a plaintiff that the committee failed to conduct a good faith, reasonable investigation of the demand, the plaintiff is not entitled to discovery from the committee.[61] A careful practitioner, however, will assume that any document he or she creates in the course of representing the committee may well be produced at some point in the process.

Courts have noted that "[t]he corporation should have the burden of proving independence, good faith and a reasonable investigation, rather than presuming independence, good faith and reasonableness."[62] To develop a record to assist the court's inquiry into the committee's good faith and independence, and the bases supporting the committee's conclusion, limited discovery may be ordered by the court. The scope of discovery is limited to "what the Committee did or did not do, and the actual existence of the documents and persons purportedly examined by it. . . ."[63] A plaintiff, however, is "not entitled to discover all the information relating to the Committee's report" but only "sufficient means to discover and examine the independence and good faith of the Committee's investigation."[64]

Notes

1. These requirements are set forth in Rule 23.1 of the Federal Rules of Civil Procedure and in comparable state rules.

2. Aronson v. Lewis, 473 A.2d 805, 809 (Del. 1984).

3. Daily Income Fund, Inc. v. Fox, 464 U.S. 523, 542 (1984). *See also* DENNIS J. BLOCK, ET AL., THE BUSINESS JUDGMENT RULE 447 (3d ed. 1989) [hereinafter "THE BUSINESS JUDGMENT RULE at ___"].

4. Allison v. General Motors Corp., 604 F. Supp. 1106, 1117 (D. Del.), *aff'd mem.*, 782 F.2d 1026 (3d Cir. 1985). Moreover, the alleged wrong must have occurred prior to the demand, Cottle v. Standard Brands Paint Co., C.A. No. 9342, slip op. at 17 (Del. Ch. Mar. 22, 1990), and the identity of the stockholder must be set forth in the demand. Smachlo v. Birkelo, 576 F. Supp. 1439, 1444 (D. Del. 1983).

5. BTZ, Inc. v. National Intergroup, Inc., C.A. No. 11388, slip op. at 8 (Del. Ch. Apr. 7, 1993) (quoting Rubin v. Posner, 701 F. Supp. 1041, 1045 (D. Del. 1988)).

6. *Allison,* 604 F. Supp. at 1117. Before examining the traditional standards to see if demand is excused, a court must determine what position has been taken by the corporation on whose behalf the derivative action was brought. The Delaware Supreme Court has determined that a corporation "cannot effectively stand neutral . . . [and the] failure to object to a suit brought on its behalf must be viewed as an approval for the shareholders' capacity to sue derivatively." Thus, taking a position of neutrality will lead to excusal of a plaintiff's requirement to make a demand. Kaplan v. Peat, Marwick, Mitchell & Co., 540 A.2d 726, 731 (Del. 1988).

7. Indeed, "[b]y making a demand, a stockholder tacitly acknowledges the absence of facts to support a finding of futility." Spiegel v. Buntrock, 571 A.2d 767, 774–75 (Del. 1990).

8. Kaplan v. Peat, Marwick, Mitchell & Co., 540 A.2d 726, 731–32 (Del. 1988).

9. Aronson v. Lewis, 473 A.2d at 814. *See also* Grobow v. Perot, 526 A.2d 914, 920 (Del. Ch. 1987), *aff'd,* 539 A.2d 180 (Del. 1988); Levine v. Smith, 591 A.2d 194, 206 (Del. 1991).

10. Pogostin v. Rice, 480 A.2d 619, 624 (Del. 1984) (citations omitted).

11. Cede & Co. v. Technicolor, Inc., 634 A.2d 345, 363–64 (Del. 1993), *modified on other grounds and remanded,* 636 A.2d 956 (Del. 1994).

12 *See* Brook v. Acme Steel Co., C.A. No. 10276, slip op. at 5-6 (Del. Ch. May 11, 1989).

13. Richardson v. Graves, C.A. No. 6617, slip op. at 8 (Del. Ch. Mar. 7, 1983); Stotland v. GAF Corp., C.A. No. 6876, slip op. at 16 (Del. Ch. Sept. 1, 1983); Cramer v. General Tel. & Elec. Corp., 582 F.2d at 276–77; Allison v. General Motors Corp., 604 F. Supp. at 1113.

14. Aronson v. Lewis, 473 A.2d at 817.

15. Kaufman v. Safeguard Scientifics, Inc., 587 F. Supp. 486 (E.D. Pa. 1984).

16. Grobow v. Perot, 526 A.2d at 926. *See, e.g.,* Lewis v. Graves, 701 F.2d 245, 248 (2d Cir. 1983).

17. Weiss v. Temporary Inv. Fund, Inc., 516 F. Supp. 665, 671 (D. Del.), *reargument denied,* 520 F. Supp. 1098 (D. Del. 1981), *aff'd,* 692 F.2d 928 (3d Cir. 1982), *vacated and remanded on other grounds,* 465 U.S. 1001 (1984) (quoting Vernars v. Young, 539 F.2d 966, 968 (3d Cir. 1976)).

18. *In re* NVF Co. Litig., Cons. C.A. No. 9050, slip op. at 12 (Del. Ch. Nov. 21, 1989).

19. Haber v. Bell, 465 A.2d 353, 360 (Del. Ch. 1983). The mere receipt by directors of fees for their services as directors is insufficient to render them interested. *See, e.g., In re* Rexene Corp. Shareholders Litig., C.A. No. 11300, slip op. at 7 (Del. Ch. May 8, 1991), *aff'd sub nom.* Eichorn v. Rexene Corp., 604 A.2d 416 (Del. 1991) (citing Sinclair Oil Corp. v. Levien, 280 A.2d 717, 721–22 (Del. 1971); Hannigan v. Italo Petroleum Corp. of Am., 77 A.2d 209, 212 (Del. 1949)); Grobow v. Perot, 539 A.2d at 188; Day v. Quotron Sys., Inc., C.A. No. 8502, slip op. at 16 (Del. Ch. Nov. 20, 1989); *In re* E.F. Hutton Banking Practices Litig., 634 F. Supp. 265, 271 (S.D.N.Y. 1986). Otherwise, "every director who receives a director's fee would be biased." 634 F. Supp. at 271.

20. Aronson v. Lewis, 473 A.2d at 814. *See also* Levine v. Smith, 591 A.2d at 207.

21. Scopas Technology Co. v. Lord, C.A. No. 7559, slip op. at 9 (Del. Ch. Nov. 20, 1984).

22. Saxe v. Brady, 184 A.2d 602, 610 (Del. Ch. 1962).

23. Avacus Partners, L.P. v. Brian, C.A. No. 11001, slip op. at 13 (Del. Ch. Oct. 24, 1990); Cottle v. Standard Brands Paint Co., C.A. Nos. 9342, 9405 & 9151, slip op. at 6 (Del. Ch. Mar. 22, 1990); Lewis v. Spencer, No. 494, 1989, order at 3–4 (Del. May 11, 1990) (ORDER), *disposition reported at* 577 A.2d 753.

24. Rales v. Blasband, 634 A.2d 927, 934 (Del. 1993).

25. *See In re* General Motors Class E Stock Buyout Secs. Litig., 694 F. Supp. 1119, 1132 (D. Del. 1988); Mount Moriah Cemetery v. Moritz, C.A. No. 11431, slip op. at 5 (Del. Ch. Apr. 4, 1991), *aff'd,* 599 A.2d 413 (Del. 1991). In determining the wrongfulness of the demand refusal, a plaintiff is not entitled to discovery. Levine v. Smith, C.A. No. 8833, slip op. at 13 (Del. Ch. Dec. 22, 1987); Allison v. General Motors Corp., 604 F. Supp. at 1117; Lewis v. Hilton, 648 F. Supp. 725, 727 n.1 (N.D. Ill. 1986).

26. Spiegel v. Buntrock, 571 A.2d 767, 777 (Del. 1990).

27. Aronson v. Lewis, 473 A.2d at 813; Zapata Corp. v. Maldonado, 430 A.2d at 784. *See also In re* General Motors Class E Stock Buyout Sec. Litig., 694 F. Supp. at 1133.

28. As noted before, mere approval of a transaction by a director should not disqualify that director from serving as a member of a committee appointed to investigate a demand challenging that transaction. *See* Aronson v. Lewis, 473 A.2d 805 (Del. 1984).

29. *See* William T. Allen, *Independent Directors in MBO Transactions: Are They Fact or Fantasy?,* 45 BUS. LAW. 2061 (1990) [hereinafter "*Independent Directors* at ___"].

30. While the committee always should be concerned about the protection of its own attorney/client relationship, as well as any privilege attaching to the corporation's dealing with its lawyers, ongoing litigation necessarily heightens this concern.

31. *See* Allison v. General Motors Corp., 604 F. Supp. at 1117–19 ("There can be no precise rule as to how much time a Board must be given to respond to a demand."); Rubin v. Posner, 701 F. Supp. 1041, 1045 (D. Del. 1988) ("no magical period at time exists by which to measure whether suit was filed prematurely").

32. *Allison,* 604 F. Supp. at 1117.

33. Gregory P. Williams, *Advising Committees of Boards of Directors Formed to Investigate Stockholder Demands,* 5 INSIGHTS, Jan. 1991, at 30.

34. Zapata Corp. v. Maldonado, 430 A.2d at 785–89. Federal courts may be reluctant to allow a special litigation committee to terminate a derivative action if it would frustrate any relevant federal policies. *See* Burks v. Lasker, 441 U.S. 471, 486 (1979).

35. *See generally* THE BUSINESS JUDGMENT RULE, *supra* note 3, at 501–02 and Appendix D (4th ed. 1993).

36. Auerbach v. Bennett, 393 N.E.2d 994 (N.Y. 1979). Accord Roberts v. Alabama Power Co., 404 So.2d 629 (Ala. 1981); Genzer v. Cunningham, 498 F. Supp. 682 (E.D. Mich. 1980) (construing Michigan law); Lewis v. Anderson, 615 F.2d 778 (9th Cir. 1979), *cert. denied,* 449 U.S. 869 (1980) (construing California Law).

Although the Supreme Court of North Carolina originally adopted the *Auerbach* approach, *see* Alford v. Shaw, 349 S.E.2d 41 (N.C. 1986), the court withdrew that decision and issued a new opinion in which the *Zapata* test was adopted. *See* Alford v. Shaw, 358 S.E.2d 323 (N.C. 1987).

The Iowa Supreme Court has addressed the special litigation committee issue by holding that the directors whose conduct is in question are prohibited from being involved in choosing the members of the committee. Miller v. Register & Tribune Syndicate, Inc., 336 N.W.2d 709 (Iowa 1983).

37. *See* Mills v. Esmark, Inc., 544 F. Supp. 1275, 1282 n.2 (N.D. Ill. 1982) (committee's recommendation to seek dismissal based on, *inter alia*, its conclusion that the "conduct of the individual defendants violated neither state nor federal law"); Mills v. Esmark, Inc., 573 F. Supp. 169, 172 n.2 (N.D. Ill. 1983) (committee's recommendation to seek dismissal based on, *inter alia*, "merits of the claims"); Stein v. Bailey, 531 F. Supp. at 690 (committee's recommendation to seek dismissal based on, *inter alia*, its reliance on special counsel's opinion that the claims "are without legal merit"); Robert K. Payson, et al., *After Maldonado—The Role of the Special Litigation Committee in the Investigation and Dismissal of Derivative Suits*, 37 BUS. LAW. 1199, 1206 (1982) [hereinafter *"After Maldonado* at ___"].

38. *See* Kaplan v. Wyatt, 499 A.2d 1184, 1188 (Del. 1985) (committee concluded that the underlying transactions were "reasonably fair" to the corporation); Mills v. Esmark, Inc., 573 F. Supp. at 172 n.2 (committee considered, *inter alia*, the "fairness of the results of the challenged actions" and the "damages resulting from the challenged actions"); *After Maldonado* at 1206.

39. *See, e.g.,* 8 DEL. CODE ANN. § 102(b)(7).

40. *After Maldonado* at 1206. *See also* Abella v. Universal Leaf Tobacco Co., 546 F. Supp. 795, 801 n.13 (E.D. Va. 1982) (committee concluded that the benefit to be derived from a successful decision on the merits was outweighed by, *inter alia*, the "[l]arge attorneys' fees and expenses"); Mills v. Esmark, Inc., 573 F. Supp. at 172 n.2 (committee's recommendation to seek dismissal based on, *inter alia*, the "cost of pursuing the claims"); Lewis v. Fuqua, 502 A.2d 962, 971 (Del. Ch. 1985), *appeal refused,* 504 A.2d 571 (Del. 1986) (expense was one of the "decisive factors" in committee's recommendation that the company move for dismissal of the derivative action).

41. *See* Lewis v. Fuqua, 502 A.2d 962, 971 (Del. Ch. 1985), *appeal refused,* 504 A.2d 571 (Del. 1986) (possible obligation to indemnify the defendant directors among the "decisive factors" in committee's recommendation that the corporation move for dismissal of the derivative litigation); *see also After Maldonado* at 1206.

42. Abella v. Universal Leaf Tobacco Co., 546 F. Supp. at 801 n.13. *See also* Stein v. Bailey, 531 F. Supp. at 690 (court considered, *inter alia*, the cost of litigation in terms of its "disruption of management"); Lewis v. Fuqua, 502 A.2d at 971 (disruptive effect on corporate management was one of the "decisive factors" in committee's recommendation that the corporation move for dismissal of the derivative action); *After Maldonado* at 1207 (committee should consider whether the prosecution of a derivative suit will affect the "[a]bility of senior management to manage the corporation").

43. *See* Mills v. Esmark, Inc., 544 F. Supp. at 1282 n.2 (committee considered, *inter alia*, the effect on the morale of the company's executives); Mills v. Esmark, Inc., 573 F. Supp. at 172 n.2 (committee based its report and recom-

mendation on, *inter alia*, the "effects on morale if the challenged awards were to be invalidated"); Abella v. Universal Leaf Tobacco Co., 546 F. Supp. at 801 n.13 (committee concluded that there would be an "overall reduction in morale" if the derivative litigation were continued); Lewis v. Fuqua, 502 A.2d at 971 (committee considered, *inter alia*, disruptive effect of derivative litigation on corporate morale); *After Maldonado* at 1207.

44. *See* Abella v. Universal Leaf Tobacco Co., 546 F. Supp. at 801 n.13 (committee concluded that, *inter alia*, any benefit to be derived from a successful decision on the merits was outweighed by the cost to the corporation of "[a]dverse customer, banker and stock market reaction"); Stein v. Bailey, 531 F. Supp. at 690 (committee's recommendation not to pursue derivative claims based on, *inter alia*, the expected "loss of business and renewal of negative publicity"); *After Maldonado* at 1207 (committee may consider the effect of derivative litigation on the corporation's relations with its customers, suppliers, and the public.)

45. *See* Lewis v. Fuqua, 502 A.2d at 971 (the low probability of recovery and the possibility of a meager recovery were among the "decisive factors" in committee's recommendation that the corporation move for a dismissal of the derivative action); Mills v. Esmark, Inc., 544 F. Supp. at 1282 n.2 (committee's determination that continuation of the litigation would not advance the best interests of the corporation was based on, *inter alia*, the committee's conclusion that the corporation's "chance of succeeding on the merits . . . would be too small to justify the expenditure of substantial legal fees").

46. Stein v. Bailey, 531 F. Supp. at 690 (committee based its recommendation not to pursue the derivative claims on, *inter alia*, the "sufficiency of the sanctions previously imposed by the Board against the executives most directly involved with the improper payments").

47. *Stein,* 531 F. Supp. at 60 (committee based its recommendation not to pursue the derivative claims on, *inter alia*, the fact that changes in management, which were specifically designed to prevent the recurrence of misconduct, were implemented following the committee's investigation and the changes appeared to have succeeded); Abramowitz v. Posner, 672 F.2d at 1028 (committee's conclusion that pursuing the derivative action was not in the company's best interest was based on, *inter alia*, its conclusion that "corrective measures already being taken by the companies, and the policies, procedures and controls adopted by the [committees], should prevent recurrence of these matters"); *After Maldonado* at 1206 (committee should consider whether the "corporation established internal controls to prevent recurrence").

48. Zapata Corp. v. Maldonado, 430 A.2d at 788. If, however, a second shareholder claim is raised based on the same transaction, a special committee must look independently at the second claim before determining whether to refuse demand. Avacus Partners, L.P. v. Brian, C.A. No. 11001, slip op. at 17 (Del. Ch. Oct. 24, 1990).

49. *Independent Directors, supra* note 29, at 2059. While the chancellor's comments were delivered in connection with an analysis of the work of independent committees in buyout transactions, many of the same shortcomings

identified there appear to apply with equal force when committee members are asked to determine whether to sue (rather than sell to) a fellow board member. *See also* Victor Brudney, *The Independent Director—Heavenly City or Potemkin Village?* 95 HARV. L. REV. 597 (1982).

50. *Independent Directors, supra* note 29, at 2056.

51. *Id.* at 2057.

52. *Id.* at 2061; *see also* Amitai Etzioni, *The Moral Dimension: Toward a New Economics* (1988).

53. *Independent Directors, supra* note 29, at 2061.

54. *Id.* at 2061–62.

55. Spiegel v. Buntrock, 571 A.2d at 777; *but cf.* Abbey v. Computer & Communications Technology Corp., 457 A.2d 368 (Del. Ch. 1983).

56. Spiegel v. Buntrock, 571 A.2d at 777; *see also* Richardson v. Graves, slip op. at 10–11; *but cf.* Peller v. Southern Co., 911 F.2d 1532, 1536–37 (11th Cir. 1990).

57. UNITED STATES SENTENCING COMMISSION, FEDERAL SENTENCING GUIDE-LINES MANUAL ch. 8, Introductory Commentary at 347 (1992 ed.) [hereinafter "SENTENCING GUIDELINES at ___"].

58. Thomas E. Holliday, *et al., Tilting the Balance: The Effect of the Sentencing Guidelines on Organizational Defendants,* 5 INSIGHTS, Aug. 1991, at 2.

59. *Sentencing Guidelines, supra* note 57, at § 8(c)2.5(g)(1).

60. *See* Anton R. Valukas & Robert R. Stauffer, *Corporate Liability: Internal Investigations of Corporate Misconduct,* 6 INSIGHTS, Feb. 1992, at 17 ("Voluntary disclosure of wrongdoing, combined with internal disciplinary measures, can be a determinative factor in convincing the government not to prosecute."). In a related area, the U.S. Environmental Protection Agency (EPA) recently asserted publicly that voluntary environmental audits coupled with disclosure of adverse findings to the EPA have "never" led to federal criminal prosecutions. The EPA also is reported to be considering proposals to provide privilege and/or use immunity to companies who voluntarily report results of audits. *Voluntary Audits Haven't Triggered Prosecutions, EPA Official Maintains,* CORP. COUNS. WKLY. (BNA) (May 6, 1992).

61. Levine v. Smith, C.A. No. 8833, slip op. at 12–13 (Del. Ch. Dec. 22, 1987). *See also* Allison v. General Motors Corp., 604 F. Supp. at 1120–21; Lewis v. Hilton, 648 F. Supp. 725, 727 note 7 (N.D. Ill. 1986). It should be noted, however, that one court has expressed its "concern" over a committee's refusal to provide plaintiff copies of memoranda prepared by counsel summarizing interviews. Peller v. Southern Co., 707 F. Supp. 525 (N.D. Ga. 1988), *aff'd,* 911 F.2d 1532 (11th Cir. 1990).

62. Zapata Corp. v. Maldonado, 430 A.2d at 788. *Accord* Kaplan v. Wyatt, 499 A.2d at 1188; Lewis v. Fuqua, 502 A.2d at 967.

63. Kaplan v. Wyatt, 484 A.2d at 519.

64. Kaplan v. Wyatt, 499 A.2d at 1192.

CHAPTER 6

Corporate Governance of the "Troubled" Company

Perhaps no area of corporate governance has received less attention than the law pertaining to governance of the "troubled" company. Comparatively few judicial precedents exist in this area. Those that do share few unifying characteristics. In this chapter we address the law pertaining to directors of companies operating in the "vicinity" of insolvency; directors of clearly insolvent companies; and directors of bankrupt companies operating as debtors in possession. Finally, we address the subject of fights for control of bankrupt companies and the governance restructurings opportunities available to companies emerging from bankruptcy.

Duties of Directors of the "Nearly Insolvent" Company

Until recently, nearly all of the discussion devoted to governance of "troubled" companies focused on the implications of insolvency for governance. In late 1991, however, the Delaware Court of Chancery had occasion to address briefly the duties of directors of a company operating "in the vicinity of insolvency" (admittedly a less than precise term). The case featured a direct conflict between MGM's majority stockholder (who owned 98.5 percent of the company) and the company's creditors. As a condition to bankruptcy financing, MGM's creditors negotiated for and received certain concessions in the governance of MGM. An "executive committee" of the board was put in place to operate the postbankrupt company, and all board powers that could be delegated to the committee under Delaware law were expressly so delegated, with minor exception.

Importantly, however, the executive committee retained the right to approve (or decline to approve) the expected MGM asset sales that would be used to pay down the company's debt.

The conflict arose when the creditor-appointed executive committee declined to approve the majority stockholder's proposed asset sales on the grounds that the proposed sale prices were too low and would impair the ability of the company to function.

Finding that the challenged decisions were made when the corporation was operating in the "vicinity of insolvency," the court held that there was no breach of any duty owed in the circumstances.[1] The court began its analysis by noting that "[a]t least where a corporation is operating in the vicinity of insolvency, a board of directors is not merely the agent of the residu[al] risk bearers [i.e., the stockholders], *but owes its duty to the corporate enterprise.*"[2] The court stated that the MGM board "had an obligation to the community of interest that sustained the corporation, to exercise judgment in an informed, good faith effort to maximize the corporation's long-term wealth creating capacity."[3] It followed, reasoned the court, that there was no per se breach of duty by the board when it failed to "immediately facilitat[e] whatever asset sales were in the financial best interest of the controlling shareholders."[4]

In a footnote to the opinion, which quickly received widespread attention among both practitioners and academics, the court set out a hypothetical business problem that dramatically illustrates the potential divergence of economic interests between shareholders and other constituencies in the "vicinity" of insolvency. Specifically, the hypothetical problem assumes a solvent corporation with $12 million in debt and one asset, a $51 million judgment against a solvent debtor. Assuming a 25 percent chance of affirmance on appeal, a 70 percent chance of substantial modification, and a 5 percent chance of reversal, the issue presented is should the board settle, and, if so, at what price. Analyzing the probabilities, the court concludes that the board should settle the judgment for the best available offer greater than $15.5 million, the mathematically derived "expected value" of the judgment on appeal.[5]

In a $15.5 million settlement, however, the residual value of the equity would be $3.5 million ($15.5 million – $12 million debt = $3.5 million). In this hypothetical situation, equity holders likely would prefer the company to prosecute the appeal, which, although risky, if successful would yield a residual value to equity of $9.75 million ($51 million judgment − $12 million debt = $39 million × 25 percent = $9.75 million). Thus, the decision whether to litigate or settle depends importantly upon the directors' view of to whom they owe fiduciary duties in this circumstance. About this question, the court wrote:

> [I]f we consider the community of interests that the corporation represents it seems apparent that one should in this hypothetical accept the best settlement offer available providing it is greater than $15.55 million. . . . But that result will not be reached by a director who thinks he owes duties directly to shareholders only. It will be reached by directors who are capable of conceiving of the corporation as a legal and economic entity. Such directors will recognize that in managing the business affairs of a solvent corporation in the vicinity of insolvency, circumstances may arise when the right (both the efficient and the fair) course to follow for the corporation may diverge from the choice that the stockholders (or the creditors, or the employees, or any single group interested in the corporation) would make if given the opportunity to act.[6]

Credit Lyonnais, therefore, appears to hold that a board operating in the "vicinity of insolvency" may owe its duty not only to stockholders but to *the corporation*, at least where there exists a potential conflict between shareholders' interests and the interests of other corporate constituencies. As explained in the opinion, the duty is "to maximize the corporation's long-term wealth creating capacity."[7]

The *Credit Lyonnais* court did not, however, discuss the availability of the business judgment rule to protect decisions made in the "vicinity" of insolvency. There appears to be no reason why the rule would not apply in the case of decisions made by a solvent corporation. Recognizing a shift in the duties of the board (or perhaps the supervening duty to the corporation) should not render the rule inapplicable.[8] Indeed, one could argue persuasively that the policy supporting application of the rule is even more critical where the board is forced to make the difficult decisions that arise when the corporation is in poor financial health. In short, it appears that the board of the nearly insolvent firm must pay special attention to the long-term interests of the corporation, even if in so doing it pursues a course contrary to the wishes of its shareholders. In addressing the needs and interests of the corporation, these directors should pay special attention to all of the constituencies that make up that entity, including creditors. The expanded nature of the director's duties in this area, however, should not preclude risk taking or entrepreneurship, provided the decision to pursue such activities is made in the informed, good faith belief that it is reasonably likely to enhance the long-term wealth-generating abilities of the firm.

How does a board discharge its duty to take account of the needs of constituencies other than shareholders, for example, creditors? There is little, if any, guidance on the process the board should follow in considering nonshareholder interests, and the board may easily find itself in uncharted waters when it attempts to apply the rules of law developed in this area.

The director who starts the process of decision making by attempting to assure that he or she has all available material information on the subject upon which he or she is called to pass will undoubtedly have taken the most important first step toward discharging his or her fiduciary duties. As with any corporate decision, the director is entitled to statutory protection if he or she relies on the report of experts chosen with reasonable care. While reliance on expert reports alone may not discharge the director's duty of due care, it is an important part of the discharge of that duty, especially in light of the statutory protection for such reliance afforded by Delaware law.

Who might the board choose as an expert when faced with the financial, and often timing, exigencies of a corporation in the vicinity of insolvency? While outside experts should not be overlooked, they may not be preferable if time, or money, is short. The board should not ignore the fact that it often can look inside the corporation for expert reports and information. The board, for example, reasonably could conclude that the company's chief financial officer, who probably will find himself or herself in close contact with the company's creditors during this period in the corporation's history, is the best possible expert available to the board in the circumstances. Provided the board has confidence in the competence and integrity of the CFO, it could be that this officer's intimate knowledge of the company's financial situation makes him or her the best possible source of expert reports and/or information.

On what should the expert report? Certainly, the board will want full information on the company's financial situation and the company's projections for the foreseeable future. The directors also will want to know certain particulars about the creditors of the company. Are they secured or unsecured and who are the individual large creditors? What impact, if any, would the action being considered by the company have on the security of secured creditors and on the probability of unsecured creditors being paid? Likewise, to the extent that it is not immediately obvious, the directors will want input on the reasons for the company's financial distress: Why is the company doing poorly, and what needs to be done to return it to profitability? The answers to these questions may, in turn, lead to consideration of whether the company may best be able to achieve its goals in a bankruptcy reorganization. Alternatively, depending upon the reasons for the company's financial distress, it may be wise to consider the possibility of an organized liquidation of the company. At the least, the board, under certain circumstances, may want to investigate the liquidation value of the company and attempt to compare that value to the likely future of the company, to the extent that can be projected with reasonable accuracy.

While much of the information suggested here will be important to almost any troubled corporation, the decision whether to review liquidation scenarios or reorganization alternatives will be driven by the particular circumstances facing the firm. While there is no set formula by which the board must build its record of consideration of nonstockholder constituencies when acting in the vicinity of insolvency, careful consideration of at least some of the foregoing factors may be desirable.

Duties of Directors of the "Clearly Insolvent" Corporation

When the financial health of the corporation deteriorates from "nearly" to "clearly" insolvent, that insolvency brings with it profound changes in the ordinary scheme of corporate governance. The "majority view," which appears to be the law in several jurisdictions including New York,[9] is that upon insolvency (and perhaps even immediately prior to insolvency),[10] corporate assets become impressed with a constructive trust for the benefit of corporate creditors.

The "Trust Fund" Doctrine

The so-called "trust fund doctrine," where strictly applied, dictates that upon insolvency directors no longer owe duties to stockholders, who no longer have any viable economic interest in the entity. Instead, directors are said to owe their duty to corporate creditors. Importantly, the nature of the directors' duty also shifts from long-term value maximization to preservation of existing asset value for eventual distribution to creditors.[11]

For those jurisdictions applying the trust fund doctrine in the form articulated before, the implications for the board are staggering. Unnatural as it may seem, the board is expected to undergo a radical metamorphosis in its approach to management of the enterprise upon the occurrence of insolvency. Entrepreneurship and risk taking, the hallmarks of corporate activity prior to insolvency, suddenly expose directors to new potential liabilities. Asset preservation, the ordinary province of the trustee, will likely seem to be unduly conservative to the ordinary board. Obviously, recognizing when insolvency has become "clear" is critical, and a failure to recognize "clear" insolvency and to act accordingly may lead to personal liability for board members. Unfortunately, there is little guidance in the case law on how insolvency should be determined, i.e., whether directors should consider the entity insolvent when it is unable to meet debts as they come due or insolvent when the fair value of liabilities exceeds the fair value of corporate assets. As to the latter test, it has been noted that because the corporate balance sheet shows only historical information, directors may not be able to rely on the balance sheet to determine solvency.[12] Moreover, as some commentators have pointed out, the approach to valuing corporate assets and liabilities is unclear. Should the enterprise be valued on a "going-concern" or "liquidation" basis? If on a "going-concern" basis, does there come a time when a "liquidation" methodology becomes appropriate? One Delaware court has pronounced that "an entity is insolvent when it has liabilities in excess of a reasonable *market value* of assets held."[13] This standard seems to be particularly troublesome, as directors rarely may be aware of the "market value" of the assets of an industrial enterprise.

The existence of business judgment–type protection for directors in this area is of special importance, in light of the many questions left unanswered in the legal pronouncements governing the area. While the New York decisions can be read to reject business judgment–rule protection for directors of a clearly insolvent firm on the basis that directors of such an enterprise should be considered to be strict trustees,[14] the Delaware law does not appear quite so inflexible. For example, in *In re* RegO Co.[15] the Delaware Chancellor made several significant observations about the so-called trust fund doctrine and its application in Delaware.

In discussing the doctrine and its historical evolution, Chancellor William T. Allen identified the "core concepts" of the doctrine as follows:

> [the] core concepts are that *on dissolution* corporate directors have obligations to creditors and that creditors, at least creditors to whom the corporation had reason to know, have an equitable right to follow corporate assets and to impress a constructive trust upon them in the hands of shareholders.[16]

The court also expressly rejected the *New York Credit* case, at least to the extent it could be read to impose duties on directors of a dissolved corporation, signaling a rejection of the strict reading of the doctrine favored in some jurisdictions outside Delaware.[17]

Finally, the court extended the protections of the business judgment rule to directors of a dissolved corporation acting in the informed, good faith, and disinterested exercise of business judgment. Although the court's holding in this regard does not expressly address the predissolution stage, in light of the rejection of the *New York Credit* case, the holding strongly suggests that the protections of the business judgment rule also will extend to decisions made prior to dissolution, as well.

Moreover, in support of its holding regarding the business judgment rule, the court cited approvingly an Illinois bankruptcy court case where the bankruptcy judge, interpreting Delaware law, applied a form of business judgment rule protection where directors of an insolvent firm approved a sale of an important corporate division to an arms' length, third-party purchaser, while the company was insolvent.[18] Notwithstanding an attack on the transaction (which included a disclosed personal benefit to the company's chief executive) by the company's creditors in bankruptcy, the court held in favor of the board, having found that the directors acted in a good faith manner, after appropriate deliberations and with the best interests of the corporation in mind.

The policy rationale for application of some type of business judgment-rule protection in this realm is strong. When directors act in the informed exercise of good faith business judgment in an attempt to work out a business plan that they reasonably believe could lead to the salvation of the corporate enterprise, assessing liability for failure of that plan is likely to chill all attempts at work-outs outside of the bankruptcy arena.

Practical Problems Arising from the Imposition of Fiduciary Duties to Creditors

The imposition of fiduciary duties to creditors upon insolvency or before creates numerous practical problems for the board and its legal advisers.

First: When do the duties arise? If, as the case law suggests, the duties arise upon or just prior to insolvency, how is a director (or a lawyer for the director) to know at the point in time a decision is presented whether or not the duty has arisen? As "insolvency" is defined differently in various contexts and often is not clear until *after* the fact, the imposition of fiduciary duties upon or prior to insolvency could result in a rule of virtually strict liability in certain circumstances.

The only apparent practical solution to the issue of "when" the duty arises is for directors of a troubled company to take advice from the company's financial officers regarding the solvency of the company before taking action as a board. Of course, this would be a marked departure from ordinary practice and the solvency determination might be quite burdensome to make on an interim basis.

Second: Precisely to whom are the duties owed and how are conflicting duties to be resolved? While the case law makes it clear that a duty to creditors arises, it is unclear whether or not the springing duty to creditors entirely displaces other groups to whom directors may owe duties. For example, does the board still owe fiduciary duties to stockholders or the corporation as a whole when the duty to creditors arises? If so, which duty takes precedence in the case of an irreconcilable conflict between the interests of the different constituencies? If the insolvency is likely to be short-lived, does the forecast of a near-term recovery affect the calculus?

While the Delaware court's formulation of the duty in the *Credit Lyonnais* case provides a workable construct in which to answer these and other issues, when the duty is posited as one to creditors qua creditors (outside of the dissolution context), rather than creditors as part of the universe of constituencies that make up the corporation, that alternative construct is rife with problems. While judicial recognition of the business judgment rule in this area would likely make informed and judicious board action somewhat less problematic, few courts have directly addressed the availability of the protections of the rule in this area, although the Delaware court appears to point the way.

Third: Does insolvency deprive directors of statutory protection? Under Delaware law, stockholders may choose to adopt a charter provision limiting or eliminating monetary liability of directors for breach of certain fiduciary duties. The statute allows the charter to limit a director's liability "to the corporation or its stockholders." Creditors are not mentioned. It appears, therefore, that unless the statute is further amended, in certain circumstances, creditors could impose monetary liability on directors where stockholders could not.

Risk Taking and Insolvency

While bankruptcy in some instances may be preferable as a forum for the resolution of financial difficulties, strict application of the trust fund doctrine creates substantial incentives for directors to consider alternative courses of action. The goal of law relating to fiduciary liability should be to promote rational decision making with flexibility to confront varying circumstances. Once prerequisites to application of the business judgment rule (e.g., independence, due care, etc.) have been satisfied, there are strong policy reasons to protect directors' decisions. Where that latitude for good faith proactive governance is lost to a strict liability doctrine, corporate directors will have no incentive to consider alternatives to bankruptcy, where all of their important decisions will be made with judicial protection.

Moreover, we suggest that the traditional policies invoked to support the business judgment rule outside the insolvency context are equally applicable in that context. We perceive no basis to conclude that courts are likely to be any better equipped to make business decisions for an insolvent corporation than they are for a solvent one. Nonetheless, it would be a mistake to conclude that the courts will or should treat directors' decisions made in the insolvency context with a "business as usual" approach.

Perhaps a two-step analysis not unlike that used in evaluating directors' actions taken in the face of a threat to corporate control will evolve,[19] requiring directors to demonstrate their consideration of creditor interests and the reasonableness of their business plan in connection with those interests, prior to invocation of the ordinary protections of the business judgment rule. Such an approach would ensure that creditors' interests were considered, but would afford latitude to the board in dealing with the enormous practical difficulties of executing a business plan designed to work the corporation out of insolvency.

Practically speaking, however, until the law is further clarified, risk-adverse directors of an insolvent corporation may be protected best under the federal bankruptcy laws. Although the authors believe that a Delaware court likely would afford some level of deference to a rational and informed decision *not* to seek bankruptcy protection[20] and, therefore, would not be likely to impose liability for an honest (but failed) attempt to work a company out of financial difficulties, provided the directors were able to demonstrate that they acted in a fully informed manner and after consideration of the interests of all relevant constituencies had concluded that their workout plan was in the best interests of the corporation,[21] no Delaware case squarely so holds. Until the law is further developed, directors of an insolvent or nearly insolvent corporation should proceed with the greatest caution and only upon informed, thorough, and well-documented deliberation. Without the umbrella of bankruptcy court approval of major initiatives, the "downside risk" of failed initiatives is likely to be daunting.

Governance in Bankruptcy

The decision to file bankruptcy is one that should be made only after careful investigation of available alternatives and consultation with qualified experts in the field.[22] The operating management of a corporation that determines to attempt to reorganize under Chapter 11 of the Bankruptcy Code is likely to encounter significant changes in the day-to-day life of the bankrupt company. The relief provided from litigation by virtue of the automatic stay, coupled with the so-called period of exclusivity during which only the management of the debtor corporation is permitted to propose a plan of reorganization, are both designed to allow those that know the company best the opportunity to propose a solution that, if accepted by the court, will be the groundwork for a successful reorganization. Both management and the board also may welcome the fact that, during the pendency of the bankruptcy process, virtually all major operational decisions are examined and approved by the court.[23]

The filing of a Chapter 11 proceeding transforms the role of the board of directors of the company. By statute, directors of a Chapter 11 debtor become trustees of the estate created by the bankruptcy and are obligated to perform the same duties that would be performed by a trustee for the estate. It has been said that the filing changes the nature of the director's duties "from helmsman to guardian."[24] Under the Bankruptcy Code, the principal duties of the directors of the Chapter 11 debtor are to: (1) Safeguard and recover assets, including examining claims made against the estate and objecting to improper claims; (2) operate the business of the debtor; and (3) formulate promptly and file a plan of reorganization.[25]

In discharging these duties, the directors are said to be fiduciaries for all parties to the reorganization, including both creditors and shareholders. The nature and extent of that duty seem less than clear, however, and there appears to be disagreement among the courts that have addressed the issue regarding whether directors of a Chapter 11 debtor are liable for simple negligence as trustees, or whether decisions made by the board of the debtor are entitled to the protection of the business judgment rule. Practically speaking, the board of the debtor in possession often may avoid the issue by seeking court approval of any significant decision.

Formulating the Plan of Reorganization

Perhaps the single most important power given to the management of the debtor in possession under Chapter 11 is the *exclusive* right to formulate a plan of reorganization. Under the Bankruptcy Code, unless a trustee is appointed or the court otherwise orders, management retains this exclusive right for a period of 120 days from the filing of the bankruptcy petition. If the debtor does propose a plan within the first 120 days of filing, the Bankruptcy Code grants the debtor an additional sixty days to obtain acceptances before any competing plan may be proposed, and none may be proposed if the debtor is able to obtain the requisite acceptances in that period. Moreover, unless a strong showing can be made by creditors regarding why the exclusive period should not be extended, bankruptcy judges often appear willing to extend the exclusivity period for additional periods at times for up to a year or more.

In formulating the plan, management will want to take a hard look at the company and its current operations, with special focus on the probable amount of cash flow from the reorganized businesses and appropriate levels of postreorganization debt. Consideration should be given to the advisability of continuing each line of business in which the company operates and the feasibility of divestiture or liquidation of subsidiaries or divisions that are not likely to enhance the performance of the reorganized company. It is from such an economic analysis of the reorganized company that several important pillars of the plan of reorganization will emerge. How much debt will the reorganized company realistically be in a position to service? Would other alternatives such as the sale or merger of part—or all—of the business be likely to enhance the value of the estate?

Perhaps the most difficult issue confronting every Chapter 11 debtor in formulating a plan is how the available assets of the estate will be divided and/or distributed among the various different groups making claims. As commentators have suggested, how a board perceives its duties and to whom it believes those duties are owed may dramatically impact the structure of the plan.[26] As fiduciaries to the *estate*, the members of the board must work to balance the claims of creditors and shareholders, mindful of the priority of each under the law and the fact that shareholders can, and often do, receive nothing as a result of the process.

In the event that the 120-day "exclusivity" period expires without the presentation by management of a plan of reorganization and the bankruptcy court does not extend the period of exclusivity, the bankruptcy proceeds into the so-called "nonexclusive period," during which any party in interest may (and many often do) file its own plan of reorganization. Once the exclusive period has run without a widely supported management plan having been filed, the board of the debtor is in danger of losing control of the process. In a large bankruptcy case, for example, there may be several competing plans filed and/or put to a vote of creditors. While there may be strategic reasons in any particular case to allow the bankruptcy to go into this phase, in general, just as it may be said that the exclusive right to propose a plan gives the board of the debtor control of the process, it also is true that the expiration of the period signals ascendancy of creditor groups or others.

Operating the Debtor in Possession

Another of management's important responsibilities in a Chapter 11 case is the operation of the company. Although the proposed plan of reorganization may call for the restructuring of the enterprise and the liquidation or sale of certain businesses or subsidiaries, until the court gives its approval to these structural changes, the business of the company continues. Employees must be paid, plants operated, and customers served.

As noted previously, the filing of the bankruptcy brings with it a stay of litigation against the company and an effective prohibition on further litigation during the pendency of the bankruptcy proceeding, unless the litigant is able to convince the bankruptcy court to allow the institution or continuation of specific litigation. This is often a welcome relief to the management of the company, who, prior to the bankruptcy filing, may have found itself enmeshed in the defense of litigation.

The filing also practically relieves the board of the necessity of making difficult business decisions in the face of uncertain liability. As pointed out before, the ordinary course for a company operating under bankruptcy law protection is to seek prior court approval for all significant business decisions. When forthcoming, this approval makes the directors' decisions much more difficult to second-guess or criticize.

Without court approval for new initiatives, the management of the debtor in possession is charged with operating the business of the company in the ordinary course. Doing so requires cash, however, and cash is likely to be a commodity the bankrupt estate finds in short supply. Fortunately, the Bankruptcy Code gives priority to certain types of debtor in possession (DIP) financing, and so-called DIP financing has become much more widely available to Chapter 11 debtors.

There are, however, several limitations upon the debtor's operation of the business of the company. While operating under Chapter 11, management of the debtor *must* seek court approval to:

1. pay any prepetition debts;
2. pay any lawyers, accountants, or other professionals;
3. use cash or borrow any money using security; and
4. sell or lease any property of the estate outside of the ordinary course of business.

Recovering the Assets of the Estate

In addition to ordinary operational responsibilities, the management of the debtor in possession also is charged with the responsibility to account for the property of the estate. Management, therefore, will review creditors' claims and proofs of claim and object to improper claims.

The Bankruptcy Code also provides that the debtor in possession shall have all the rights and powers of a trustee in bankruptcy.[27] Thus, under the Code, the debtor has the power to employ, with the prior approval of the court, one or more lawyers, accountants, appraisers, and other professionals, provided that such persons do not hold or represent interests adverse to the estate.[28]

The debtor also has the statutory power to reject, affirm, and assign executory contracts and unexpired leases of the company.[29] Similarly, the debtor has the power to avoid any transfer of property of the debtor or any obligation incurred by the debtor that is voidable by a creditor or bona fide purchaser of real property,[30] as well as any obligation incurred by the debtor that is voidable under applicable law by a creditor holding an unsecured claim in certain circumstances.[31]

Finally, the debtor in possession has the powers of a bankruptcy trustee to avoid certain liens and fraudulent conveyances, to recover preferential transfers, and to avoid certain transfers.

Fights for Control of the Bankrupt Company

Proxy Fights for Control of the Bankrupt Company

Under bankruptcy law, the filing of the Chapter 11 petition does not cut off management's responsibilities to shareholders. While the Bankruptcy Code appears to evidence a bias toward allowing management sufficient "breathing room" to attempt to formulate a workable plan of reorganization, management may not be wholly free from outside challenge, even during the period of exclusivity. Courts have held that the mere filing of the Chapter 11 petition does not relieve the incumbent management of its state law obligation to hold annual meetings to elect directors[32] and, in certain circumstances, the management of a debtor in possession may even find itself facing a hostile proxy battle.[33]

From the shareholders' perspective, the ability to influence management of the debtor prior to the confirmation of a plan of reorganization may be the only remaining leverage. As a plan can eliminate any economic interests of shareholders of the company, a proxy fight designed to install directors more sympathetic to a shareholder recovery, or the threat of such a challenge, may be the only bargaining chip left short of the threat to vote against ultimate confirmation of the plan. Of course, because the bankruptcy law allows a plan to be confirmed over the opposition of shareholders

where the plan is found to meet certain criteria, the threat of shareholder opposition to a plan is not likely to increase materially the
leverage of shareholders as a group.

In *In re Saxon Industries, Inc.*,[34] a committee of equity security
holders petitioned the bankruptcy court for an order authorizing
the committee to retain special counsel to represent it in an action
seeking to compel the holding of an annual meeting of shareholders under Delaware law. Creditors objected, arguing that the estate
was insolvent and the Saxon shareholders would have no interest
in the reorganized debtor. The court rejected this argument and
granted the equity committee's motion.

The case then was tried in Delaware state court, where the defendant company argued that it should not be required to hold an
annual meeting because of the pending bankruptcy. The Delaware
court rejected this argument and ordered that a meeting be held.
On appeal, the Delaware Supreme Court affirmed, noting the
strong policy of Delaware law requiring annual meetings and free
exercise of the stockholders' franchise.[35]

A similar result was reached in the Allegheny bankruptcy.
There, the district court for the Western District of Pennsylvania reversed the bankruptcy court's refusal to allow Allegheny shareholders to convene an annual meeting of the company. Reasoning
that there was no showing of "clear abuse" where shareholders
were attempting to elect directors who would block a company
from filing a plan shareholders disliked, the court allowed the
meeting to go forward.[36]

Where creditors are unable to show that the holding of an annual meeting is likely to impede the reorganization[37] or that the
shareholders seeking to compel the meeting are guilty of "clear
abuse,"[38] the courts have been unwilling to enjoin the shareholders
from exercising their franchise.

Takeover of the Bankrupt Company

While the board of directors of the bankrupt debtor in possession is
faced with difficult choices when confronted with a proxy contest
for control of the debtor, the issues that arise when a hostile acquiror attempts a takeover of the bankrupt debtor are daunting indeed. To begin with, the board's reaction to a takeover proposal
will not necessarily be judged by the same standards used to evaluate the conduct of a board in defending against a takeover outside
of the bankruptcy context. As fiduciaries for shareholders and creditors charged with maximizing the value of the estate, the conduct

of the board of a bankrupt debtor that defends against an unwelcome takeover proposal may not be entitled to the same level of deference afforded outside of the bankruptcy arena. Perhaps most problematic is the lack of any clear case law guidance in this area, which, except for a few widely noted cases, is virtually nonexistent. This relative lack of authority masks the fact that takeovers of debtors in bankruptcy, which were apparently widespread during the 1930s,[39] appears again to be on the rise. Two prominent commentators note several recent and well-publicized transactions, including Allegheny International, Apex Oil Co., King Resources, Inc., and Baldwin United, Inc.[40] To this list can be added the more recent acquisitions of Schwinn Bicycles and Carter Hawley Hale Stores by the Zell/Chilmark Fund.[41]

Another widely noted problem is the dearth of federal regulation of the form of transaction likely to emerge into a takeover attempt in the bankruptcy arena. Although federal law governs tender offers outside the bankruptcy arena, a bankruptcy acquiror is likely to build a position by acquiring claims of various classes of debtors, a process that, unless accomplished via a tender offer, is virtually unregulated under existing law.[42]

The decision in the Allegheny bankruptcy and the technique employed to acquire Carter Hawley Hale both merit study. In Allegheny, the acquiror proceeded without prior bankruptcy court approval and during the period when votes on a plan of reorganization were being solicited. This resulted in an extremely negative decision by the bankruptcy judge, who, after determining that the offeror had proceeded in "bad faith," stripped the acquired claims of any right to vote on the plan and confirmed the plan over the acquiror's objection, even though the acquiror's claims would have given it a sufficient vote to block approval of the plan.[43]

By contrast, the friendly bankruptcy acquisition of Carter Hawley Hale by the Zell/Chilmark Fund avoided many of the pitfalls that became evident as a result of the Allegheny case. For example, the Fund made its offer before any plan of reorganization had been proposed. In addition, the Fund was careful to proceed only upon express court approval of its offer and full disclosure of all material information in the tender offer materials.[44]

Several interesting problems arose during the negotiations leading to the consummation of the tender. To begin with, the Carter Hawley Hale board was faced with deciding whether to take a position on the tender or to remain neutral. After weighing the difficulty of recommending the offer, which likely would have forced the board to come to some conclusion regarding the value of the claims for which the Fund was tendering, a determination some felt the board was simply unable to make,[45] the board eventually determined to remain neutral with respect to the offer.

Similarly, the form of no-shop agreement used by the company also created a significant degree of controversy, eventually leading to litigation. Apparently, the Fund originally had insisted on a classic no-shop limitation as a condition to its making an offer. The company, while agreeing not to initiate discussions with potential bidders, insisted on being able to make nonpublic information available to interested third parties. The Fund agreed, but only on the condition that the form of confidentiality agreement used by the company would contain restrictions on third parties that were no less restrictive than the restrictions already agreed to by the Fund. Thus, any third party receiving confidential information would have to agree not to make open market purchases of claims; to proceed only by tender offer open for at least thirty business days and subject to withdrawal rights; and to agree that upon completion of such an offer, no reorganization plan would be submitted without management approval for a full year. Creditors objected and brought the matter to the attention of the bankruptcy court. Upon consideration, the bankruptcy judge ordered that the form of confidentiality agreement be modified by removing the provisions that prohibited the potential acquiror from proposing any plan of reorganization for a one-year period. The court allowed the "standstill" provisions of the agreement to remain, ensuring that any other party to come forward would offer the same protections to tendering creditors as offered by the Fund.[46]

After modification of the confidentiality agreement, only two interested parties came forward. When neither one made an offer, the Fund's tender offer closed, assuring it control over both the outcome of the bankruptcy (having secured an order of the court assuring that it would be able to vote its claims) and the reorganized company.

Although Carter Hawley Hale appears to break new ground in the acquisition of a debtor in possession, the transaction dramatically illustrates how little guidance is available in this area. Although the target's board may have established a useful precedent by refusing to take a position with respect to the fairness of the offer, the issues that did appear to arise in this *friendly* acquisition may pale in comparison with the more thorny questions that could arise in the case of a hostile tender. Given the difficulty of valuing a bankrupt company before the confirmation of a plan of reorganization that sets the capital structure of the reorganized firm, it is unclear how the board of a bankrupt company ever will be in a position to inform itself before making critical decisions in the face of a hostile tender for debt—decisions such as whether to oppose or endorse such a tender. This difficulty inheres in the economic uncertainty surrounding the company, which, in turn, is exacerbated by the lack of clear legal guidelines in the bankruptcy context. Consider, for example, how poorly the precedents that have evolved outside the bankruptcy context are likely to translate into bankruptcy principles. As noted previously, under the *Revlon* case, directors faced with an inevitable sale of the company are charged with maximizing the value generated in that sale. How would directors of the bankrupt company, short of an affirmative mandate by the court, determine whether or not a sale of the enterprise is "inevitable"? If only one bidder emerged, how would the board determine whether or not to sell, in light of the enormous difficulties inherent in valuation? These and the myriad of other issues that have been settled outside the bankruptcy context eventually may be confronted in bankruptcy as so-called "value investors" find their attention attracted by bankrupt companies.

Restructuring Corporate Governance Pursuant to a Reorganization Plan

Without special statutory authority, the ability to effectuate a plan of reorganization could be impeded by certain creditors' refusal to permit the debtor's capital structure to be reorganized under state corporate law. As one would expect, the vote to change charter provisions to effectuate a plan could be difficult, if not impossible, to obtain, given the necessary approval of those adversely affected.[47] Accordingly, many states have enacted statutory provisions in their corporation codes to "accord plenary authority for the reorganization court to issue decrees and orders relative to the reorganization."[48] These provisions exist to coincide with the purpose of the Bankruptcy Code "to provide the opportunity to restructure obligations allowing the Debtor to continue as a viable and productive entity."[49] As such, in proposing a plan of reorganization in Chapter 11, a corporation has the ability to propose a wide range of governance changes in the reorganized company without the approval of the corporation's shareholders. The purpose behind these provisions is to prevent shareholders asserting their own parochial interests from obstructing the confirmation of the reorganization plan. In short, these provisions permit modification of corporate governance provisions without prior approval of the board of directors (where the board is not proposing the plan) or shareholders of the corporation.

For example, Section 303 of the Delaware General Corporation Law was enacted to facilitate the reorganization of Delaware corporations under the federal Bankruptcy Code. That section provides that a Delaware corporation may, pursuant to a plan of reorganization that "has been or shall be confirmed . . . take any proceeding and do any act . . . without further action by its directors or stockholders." Any action taken pursuant to this section will, according to the statute, have "like effect as if exercised and taken by unanimous action of the directors and stockholders of the corporation."

Pursuant to Section 303, a corporation may:

(i) alter, amend, or repeal its bylaws;

(ii) constitute or reconstitute and classify or reclassify its board of directors;

(iii) name, constitute, or appoint directors and officers in place of or in addition to all or some of the directors or officers currently in office;

(iv) amend its certificate of incorporation, including making any change in its capital or capital stock or otherwise amend, change, or alter any provision thereof provided it is consistent with the Delaware General Corporation Law;

(v) dissolve, transfer all or part of its assets, merge, or consolidate;

(vi) authorize and fix the terms, manner, and conditions of the issuance of bonds, debentures, or other obligations;

(vii) change its registered agent; and

(viii) lease its property and franchises, if otherwise permitted by law.[50]

Provisions such as Section 303 customarily are interpreted together with Sections 105(a) and 1107(a) of the Bankruptcy Code.[51]

Delaware's Section 303 applies to a corporation whose plan of reorganization "has been or shall be confirmed" but ceases to apply "upon the entry of a final decree in the reorganization proceedings closing the case and discharging the trustee or trustees, if any." Various litigants have argued that Section 303 should be construed narrowly, given the requirement that a plan of reorganization "has or shall be confirmed."[52] Courts addressing challenges to the use of Section 303 have uniformly rejected such arguments, holding instead that Section 303 is applicable whenever "there is a reasonably good prospect that a plan will be confirmed. . . ."[53]

Likewise, courts have rejected challenges to the use of Section 303 to strip the voting rights from an issue of preferred stock[54] and to a similar Idaho statute in a case where the statute was used to deny the right of a 50 percent stockholder from voting for removal or election of directors during the pendency of the plan of reorganization.[55]

In short, Section 303 and similar state statutes consistently have been upheld in the bankruptcy courts. These statutes provide wide leeway to reorganize the governance of the postbankruptcy company.

Notes

Portions of this chapter have appeared previously as Gregory V. Varallo & Jesse A. Finkelstein, *Fiduciary Obligations of Directors of the Financially Troubled Company*, 48 Bus. Law. 239 (1992). The authors wish to express their gratitude to their colleague Jesse Finkelstein for his assistance with this chapter.

1. Credit Lyonnais Bank Nederland, N.V. v. Pathe Communications Corp., C.A. No. 12150, slip op. at 84–85 (Del. Ch. Dec. 30, 1991).

2. *Id.* at 83 (emphasis supplied).

3. *Id.* at 85.

4. *Id.* at 84.

5. The "expected value" calculation was performed as follows:

$$
\begin{array}{ll}
25\% \text{ chance of affirmance (\$51mm)} = & \$12.75\text{mm} \\
70\% \text{ chance of modification (4mm)} = & \$\ 2.8\text{mm} \\
5\% \text{ chance of reversal (\$0)} \quad\quad = & \underline{\quad 0 \quad\quad} \\
& \$15.55\text{mm}
\end{array}
$$

Credit Lyonnais, slip op. at 84 n.55.

6. *Id.*

7. *Id.* at 85.

8. In an early analysis of the decision, one commentator has argued that the rule does apply to a decision made by directors who "rely on advice that a transaction will improve the corporation's long-term wealth creating capacity. . . ." John C. Coffee, Jr., *Court Has a New Idea on Directors' Duty*, Nat'l. L.J. 18 (Mar. 2, 1992).

9. Steven R. Gross, *et al.*, *Directors Face Risks in Workout*, Nat'l L.J. 19 (Apr. 15, 1991) (identifying New York rule as the "majority view"); and *see In re* STN Enters., 779 F.2d 901 (2d Cir. 1985).

10. *See* New York Credit Men's Adjustment Bureau, Inc. v. Weiss, 110 N.E.2d 397, 398 (N.Y. Ct. App. 1953) (directors are "trustees" even "[i]f the corporation was then technically solvent but insolvency was approaching and was then only a few days away . . .").

11. There are numerous variations on the theme. Some jurisdictions appear to recognize that once a company is insolvent, its directors continue to owe duties to shareholders, while duties to creditors also arise. *See, e.g.,* Hollins v. Brierfield Coal & Iron Co., 150 U.S. 371 (1893).

12. Lewis U. Davis, Jr., et al., *Corporate Reorganizations in the 1990s: Guiding Directors of Troubled Corporations Through Uncertain Territory,* 47 Bus. LAW. 1, 3–4 (1991) [hereinafter *"Reorganizations in the 1990s* at ____"].

13. Geyer v. Ingersoll Publications Co., 621 A.2d 784, 789 (Del. Ch. 1992) (emphasis supplied).

14. *See* New York Credit Men's Adjustment Bureau v. Weiss, 110 N.E.2d 397 (N.Y. Ct. App. 1953).

15. 623 A.2d 92 (Del. Ch. 1992).

16. *Id.* at 95 (emphasis supplied).

17. *Id.* at 109 n.35.

18. *In re* Xonics Inc., 99 B.R. 870, 872 (Bankr. N.D. Ill. E.D. 1989).

19. *See* Unocal Corp. v. Mesa Petroleum Co., 493 A.2d 946, 955 (Del. 1985).

20. *Compare In re* Xonics Corp., discussed previously, and *see Reorganizations in the 1990s, supra* note 12, at 10 (arguing that business judgment rule should protect decision regarding whether to restructure or seek bankruptcy protection regardless of solvency).

21. *Compare* Credit Lyonnais Bank Nederland, N.V. v. Pathe Communications Corp., C.A. No. 12150 (Del. Ch. Dec. 30, 1991); Geyer v. Ingersoll Publications Co., 621 A.2d 784 (Del. Ch. 1992).

22. An in-depth analysis of the factors that might be considered in deciding whether or not to seek bankruptcy protection, a topic beyond the scope of this chapter, is found in *Reorganizations in the 1990s, supra* note 12.

23. The Bankruptcy Code *requires* the board to seek approval prior to the corporation taking any action outside the "ordinary course" of its business. 11 U.S.C. §§ 1107, 1108.

24. *In re* Baldwin—United Corp., 43 B.R. 443, 459 note 22 (Bankr. S.D. Ohio 1984).

25. 11 U.S.C. 1106; and *see Reorganizations in the 1990s, supra* note 12, at 15–18.

26. *See Reorganizations in the 1990s, supra* note 12, at 24–25.

27. The sole exception is the trustee's right to compensation. *See* 11 U.S.C. § 1107(a).

28. *See* 5 *Collier on Bankruptcy* ¶ 1107.03; 11 U.S.C. § 327(a).

29. 11 U.S.C. § 365.

30. *See* 11 U.S.C. § 544(a); and *see* 5 *Collier on Bankruptcy* ¶ 1107.02.

31. *See* 5 *Collier on Bankruptcy* ¶ 1107.02; 11 U.S.C. §§ 544(b) and 502.

32. *In re* Saxon Indus., Inc., 39 B.R. 49 (Bankr. S.D.N.Y. 1984); *In re* Lifeguard Indus., Inc., 37 B.R. 3 (Bankr. S.D. Ohio 1983); *In re* Lionel Corp., 30 B.R. 327 (Bankr. S.D.N.Y. 1983).

33. There undoubtedly are limitations on the ability of shareholders to influence (or change) management during the course of a bankruptcy proceeding. Few, if any, of such limitations are statutory in nature and those that have been fashioned appear to reflect the reluctance of the bankruptcy courts to allow shareholders—who often have little or no economic interest left by the time bankruptcy is filed—to influence in any meaningful way the outcome of

the process. In addition, there is a recognition that a hostile proxy fight can be very expensive and may materially delay the bankruptcy process.

34. *In re* Saxon Indus., Inc., 39 B.R. 49 (Bankr. S.D.N.Y 1984).

35. *See* Saxon Indus., Inc. v. NKFW Partners, 488 A.2d 1298 (Del. 1984).

36. *In re* Allegheny Int'l, Inc., [1987–88 Transfer Binder] Bankr. L. Rep. (CCH) ¶ 72,328, at 93, 153–54 (W.D. Pa. May 31, 1988).

37. *See In re* Lionel Corp., 30 B.R. 327 (Bankr. S.D.N.Y. 1983); and *cf. In re* Heck's Inc., 112 B.R. 775, 798 (Bankr. S.D.W. Va. 1990), *aff'd in part and rev'd in part sub nom. In re* Heck's Properties, Inc., 151 B.R. 739 (S.D.W. Va. 1992).

38. *In re* Johns-Manville Corp., 801 F.2d 60, 64–69 (2d Cir. 1986).

39. C. Fortgang & T. Mayer, *Trading Claims and Taking Control of Corporations in Chapter 11*, 12 CARDOZO L. REV. 1, 62 (1990) [hereinafter "*Trading Claims* at ___"].

40. *Id.* at 76.

41. *See* James E. Millstein & Shari Siegel, *Strategies for Investing in Chapter 11 Debtors*, 6 INSIGHTS, Feb. 1992, at 3.

42. *Trading Claims, supra* note 39, at 47; *Reorganizations in the 1990s, supra* note 12, at 26 n.101.

43. *In re* Allegheny Int'l, Inc., 118 B.R. 282 (Bankr. W.D. Pa. 1990).

44. *See* Millstein & Siegel, *Strategies for Investing in Chapter 11 Debtors, supra* note 41, at 3.

45. *See* Corporate Control Alert, Vol. 8, No. 11 *In a Novel Takeover Tactic, Zell/Chilmark Buys Debt of Bankrupt Carter Hawley Hale* (Nov. 1991).

46. *Id.* at 6.

47. MODEL BUSINESS CORP. ACT ANN. § 65, ¶ 2 (3d ed. 1994).

48. *In re* United Press Int'l, Inc., 60 B.R. 265, 272 (Bankr. D.D.C. 1986).

49. *In re* Federated Dep't Stores, Inc., 133 B.R. 886, 891 (S.D. Ohio 1991) ("bankruptcy, by its very nature, provides the Debtor the opportunity to alter rights and obligations established pre-petition" [sic]).

50. 8 DEL. CODE ANN. § 303(b).

51. *See, e.g., In re* Gaslight Club, Inc., 782 F.2d 767, 771 (7th Cir. 1986). Section 105(a) of the Bankruptcy Code authorizes the court to "issue any order, process, or judgment that is necessary or appropriate to carry out the provisions" of the Code. 11 U.S.C. § 105(a). Section 1107(a) provides that the rights and powers of a debtor in possession are "subject to . . . such limitations or conditions as the court prescribes." 11 U.S.C. § 1107(a).

52. *See, e.g., In re* Federated Dep't Stores, Inc., 133 B.R. at 892.

53. *In re* Federated Dep't Stores, Inc., 1991 WL 116542, at *3 (Bankr. S.D. Ohio May 31, 1991). *See also In re* Federated Dep't Stores, Inc., 133 B.R. at 892 (S.D. Ohio) (approving amendment under Section 303 noting that "there is no indication from the Bankruptcy Court that there are any meritorious obstacles that may derail confirmation of the Plan").

54. *In re* Federated Dep't Stores, Inc., Consol. C.A. No. 1-90-00130, slip op. at 7 (Bankr. S.D. Ohio May 31, 1991), *aff'd*, Consol. C.A. No. 1-90-130 (S.D. Ohio Nov. 20, 1991).

55. *In re* Acequia, Inc., 787 F.2d 1352 (9th Cir. 1986) (applying Idaho Code § 30-1-65).

CHAPTER 7

Governance of
Nonprofit Corporations

Nonprofit corporations may be organized and maintained for various reasons. Most nonprofit corporations are organized and operated for some charitable, educational, or similar purpose, or to take advantage of a particular exemption from taxation. Clearly, however, nonprofit corporations are not limited solely to charitable organizations. The National Football League, the American Federation of Labor and Congress of Industrial Organizations (AFL-CIO), and the Girl Scouts of America are all nonprofit corporations.[1] Little has been written about the governance of such corporations, and the purpose of this chapter is not to cover the field in an exhaustive fashion.[2] Instead, we outline here several broad governance concepts. In doing so we assume that the nonprofit corporations addressed qualify for exemption from federal income tax under the Internal Revenue Code (IRC).

First, we explore the purpose of the nonprofit corporation and the duties of its directors, then turn to a judicial review of directors' actions and conflict transactions, and conclude with certain observations pertaining to the special issues implicated in the governance of cooperative organizations.

The Purpose of the Nonprofit Corporation
and the Duties of Its Directors

Importance of the Corporate Purpose

Unlike the ordinary for-profit corporation, nonprofit corporations usually are organized for some specific purpose other than profit generation. Under the relevant sections of the IRC, tax-exempt, nonprofit corporations may be organized for religious, scientific, charitable, and other specific purposes.[3] Most organizations that expect to qualify for tax-exempt status are organized with express restrictions on permissible corporate activity in their certificate of incorporation or bylaws.

The director of a nonprofit corporation should be intimately familiar with the purpose of the corporation. Not only is the corporation's charter likely to limit permissible corporate activities to that purpose, but the continued maintenance of the corporation's tax-exempt status could depend upon the corporation's restricting its activities to the purpose set forth in its governing documents and as described in its application for recognition of tax-exempt status.[4]

The drafters of the *Nonprofit Guidebook* put this seemingly obvious point as follows:

> It has been said that all organizations exist to maximize *something* for *somebody*: the nonprofit corporation is no exception. Defining the *something* and the *somebody* is a duty of every nonprofit board and every director.[5]

While admittedly a basic point, the consequences of being uninformed or not fully informed regarding the basic mission of, and constraints upon, a nonprofit corporation can be severe. For example, the director of a nonprofit corporation who approves corporate action outside of the express purpose of the corporation may be exposed to liability for allowing the corporation to engage in ultra vires activities, or actually may subject the corporation to taxation or even loss of its tax-exempt status. One commentator has suggested that the director of a nonprofit organization not only should be acutely aware of the corporate purpose, but should strive to ensure that every act of the corporation is calculated exclusively to advance that purpose.[6]

At the risk of stating the obvious, the director of a nonprofit enterprise should understand that the purpose of a *non*profit corporation is not, and should not be, to make a profit, but to advance the specific nonprofit purpose for which the corporation was organized or pursuant to which it has been recognized as tax-exempt. While it undoubtedly is important to assure that a charitable corporation organized to distribute funds for certain purposes has prudently invested its capital to assure a return to distribute in accordance with its charter, the primary purpose of such a corporation is not to maximize the return on its funds but to distribute that return as indicated in its governing documents. This difference, although subtle, is essential to understand. Directors of nonprofit corporations who may have spent their professional lives advancing the interests of for-profit corporations, at first may have some difficulty adapting to this principle. The consequences of conducting the affairs of a nonprofit corporation as though it were a profit-making enterprise can be severe, however, and subject the directors of such an enterprise to criticism or worse.

What Duties Does the Director of the Nonprofit Corporation Owe?

The director of a nonprofit corporation owes all the duties owed by the director of a for-profit corporation, plus the added duty to safeguard the tax-exempt status of the organization. Under Delaware law, the director owes a duty to manage, defined and limited by the duties of care and loyalty.[7] Likewise, the Revised Model Nonprofit Corporation Act ("Model Act") adopts the for-profit standards for the duties of care and loyalty.[8]

In a guidebook prepared by the attorney general of Massachusetts for directors of Massachusetts charitable organizations, the attorney general has suggested that the duty to manage a charitable corporation includes the duty "to oversee your chief executive officer and to see that the charity is faithfully carrying out its purpose without extravagance or waste."[9] The authors agree, and believe that this is the law in virtually every state in the nation.

Although the "duty" to safeguard the tax-exempt status of the corporation often is not set out as such, it is central to the management of most nonprofit organizations. Thus, directors of a tax-exempt, nonprofit corporation will want to ensure that virtually every step the board takes that is even the least bit out of the "ordinary" is taken only after consultation with competent tax advisers.

It also can be said that the director of a charitable corporation has the "special duty" to "advance its charitable goals and protect its assets."[10] The duty to advance the charitable purpose or goals of a charitable corporation and to protect the assets of that corporation has been recognized in virtually every jurisdiction. For example, in a special letter agreement between the Massachusetts attorney general and a major Massachusetts health provider, in which the charitable organization gives certain "assurances" about how it will restructure its corporate governance, oversight, and monitoring practices, the parties agree that:

The fundamental responsibility of the individual corporate trustee is the duty to fulfill the charitable purposes of the corporation in directing the business and affairs of the corporation. In order to fulfill this responsibility, it is the duty of the board of trustees to exercise all corporate powers and to direct the management of the business and affairs of the corporation.[11]

The fact that the director of a nonprofit corporation may not be compensated for service on the board of the corporation,[12] or that the directorship is in the nature of community service, does not alter the existence of the director's duties or ameliorate the director's responsibilities to the corporation and its various constituencies. Every individual who accepts the responsibility of serving on the board of a nonprofit corporation should approach that service with the same level of attention and interest to the welfare of the corporation that he or she would bring to service on the board of a public corporation.

To Whom Does the Director of a Nonprofit Corporation Owe Duties?

The law of nonprofit corporations answers the question "to whom does the director owe duties?" differently, depending upon whether the corporation is organized for religious, educational, or charitable purposes, or is organized as a cooperative or mutual benefit corporation. Broadly speaking, it can be said that the director of a mutual benefit corporation owes his or her duties to the corporation and the members of the corporation.[13]

Directors of a charitable, educational, or religious corporation often may not be able to identify the "members" or beneficiaries of the corporation. Where, for example the corporation is organized to benefit some broad group of people, it may be impossible for the director to know with any specificity on whose behalf he or she acts. Thus, for many years, the law of most states has recognized the standing of the attorney general of the state to act in the interest of the beneficiaries of a charitable, educational, or religious corporation and to call directors of that corporation to account. It is said, therefore, that the directors of such a corporation owe duties to the beneficiaries of the corporation in the person of the attorney general. Where a charitable corporation had both members and beneficiaries, a Delaware court held that the directors' duties ran to the beneficiaries of the charity, not the members of the organization.[14]

While this result may not always be the case, for example where the corporation is organized to benefit its "members" as well as nonmembers, it certainly is true that the directors of a charitable corporation ultimately are held to a duty to manage that corporation for the benefit of the beneficiaries of the charity.

Judicial Review of Directors' Actions

Standard of Judicial Review of Ordinary Decisions

Unlike the case of the business corporation, there is no widely accepted consensus among courts regarding the standard of review by which courts should judge the decisions of directors of nonprofit corporations. Indeed, there is not even a clear consensus whether the courts should treat directors of a nonprofit corporation as trustees of an express trust, or more as directors of a business corporation.

Recently, the Delaware Supreme Court, a court widely respected in matters of corporation law, had occasion to address the standard by which it would judge decisions of directors of a charitable corporation chartered under Delaware law. The court held that, in ordinary circumstances, it would apply a rule akin to the business judgment rule in reviewing the decisions of directors of a nonprofit corporation. The court's formulation of its standard of review differed from the traditional business judgment rule, however, in that it acknowledged a "special duty" of directors of a charitable corporation to advance the charitable goals of the organization and to protect its assets. The court wrote:

> A court cannot second-guess the wisdom of facially valid decisions made by charitable fiduciaries, any more than it can question the business judgment of the directors of a for-profit corporation. However, because the Foundation was created for a limited charitable purpose rather than a generalized business purpose, those who control it have a special duty to advance its charitable goals and protect its assets. Any action that poses a palpable and identifiable threat to those goals, or that jeopardizes its assets, would be contrary to the Certificate and hence *ultra vires.*[15]

This decision clearly signals that, at least in most matters, the courts of Delaware will defer to the informed, disinterested, and good faith decisions of directors of nonprofit Delaware corporations.

Outside of Delaware, the drafters of the *Nonprofit Guidebook*, acknowledging that the cases discussing the business judgment rule are quite limited, nonetheless predict that the rule will become generally applied in the nonprofit context.[16] While the authors agree that the policies that animate the rule in the for-profit context are equally applicable to the nonprofit arena—the judiciary is institutionally no better equipped to second-guess difficult business decisions made by directors of nonprofit corporations than for-profit corporations—it may be difficult to generalize whether and how any particular court outside of Delaware will apply the deferential standard of business judgment review.

Accountability of Directors of a Nonprofit Corporation

As discussed previously, directors of a nonprofit corporation may be accountable to members of the corporation, and, in the case of a religious, educational, or charitable corporation, to the beneficiaries of the corporation in the person of the state attorney general. In most respects, a director's accountability to members of the corporation is no different than a for-profit director's accountability to stockholders. Like their for-profit counterparts, directors of mutual benefit corporations and cooperatives often are elected annually by the membership of the corporation. Although unusual, directors of certain nonprofit corporations are subject to being replaced in a proxy solicitation, just as directors of a for-profit entity.[17]

As noted before, in most states the attorney general is recognized to have standing to call directors of charitable, educational, and religious corporations to account. One court has held that a charitable board's action that resulted in financial harm to the charitable corporation, financial harm to the beneficiaries of the corporation, or personal profit to directors (whether or not at the expense of the corporation) was action that would give the attorney general grounds to seek the removal of directors.[18] The same court held that a charitable director's vote to approve a transaction that was found to be unfair to the corporation, although not dispositive, if proven "would seriously call into question" the "fitness" of the director to remain in office.[19] The court also suggested that in the proper case that director could be held liable for rescissory damages at the option of the attorney general.[20]

As previously mentioned, the attorney general of the Commonwealth of Massachusetts has been particularly active in overseeing the governance of charitable corporations organized there. After conducting an extended investigation into the governance and affairs of one major health-care provider in Massachusetts, the attorney general entered into an extensive agreement providing for a detailed restructuring of the corporate governance of the institution. The agreement provided that the Nominating Committee of the board would adopt certain goals to broaden the trustee selection process and to diversify the boards of the parent company and its subsidiaries. The agreement also imposed term limits on trustees; required modification of the institution's conflict-of-interest policy to require certain quorum and vote requirements in particular situations; mandated that trustees specifically agree to monitor and oversee "material transactions" relating to capital investment, acquisitions, and divestitures and play an active and ongoing role in establishing and overseeing a system of internal controls; and required the formation of standing Audit, Public Affairs, and Executive Compensation Committees, among other things.[21] Thus, not only do directors or trustees of a nonprofit institution face potential liability for a breach of their duty, but in the appropriate circumstance could find themselves and their governance processes under the active direction and control of the relevant state attorney general.

Distinction between Charitable Corporations and Charitable Trusts

The law of many jurisdictions is less than clear regarding whether the courts will treat directors of a charitable corporation differently than trustees of a charitable trust. Under Delaware law the issue now is settled: The directors of a charitable corporation are entitled to many of the protections ordinarily afforded to the directors of a for-profit corporation and the court will not impose trust law principles on corporate directors. The court held that while it would judge the conduct of the trustees of a charitable trust under strict trust law principles, directors of a charitable corporation were entitled to enjoy "the far more flexible and adaptable principles of corporate law."[22] Similarly, while the Model Act expressly states that the director of the nonprofit corporation "shall not be deemed to be a trustee with respect to the corporation,"[23] that view is not yet universally accepted.

This distinction is of critical importance, especially where, as in Delaware, the courts will apply a form of business judgment review to director decisions. The alternative, a far stricter form of review (and potentially of liability) may dissuade competent and experienced directors from serving on the board of worthy charities in the face of unpredictable and uncertain potential liability.

Conflicts of Interest in Nonprofit Corporations

As in the governance of any corporation, directors of a nonprofit corporation may encounter conflicts of interest in the performance of their duties and occasionally may be called upon to evaluate a transaction in which some members of the board—or the entire board—are "interested." As will be seen, the analogue to for-profit corporations is imperfect in this area, and safe-harbor statutes like Delaware's[24] do not readily apply to conflicted nonprofit directors.

The Director's Conflict of Interest

It is likely that if a director serves on a board for long enough, sooner or later he or she will be called upon to make a corporate decision in which the director has a direct or indirect personal interest. In such cases, the paramount duty of the conflicted director is prompt and complete disclosure of the conflict to the board. In most cases, the existence of a disclosed conflict is likely to have very little impact on a board's decision, or the director's liability. It is the *undisclosed* conflict, however, that bears in it the seeds of potential liability for the conflicted director and may call into question the decision taken by the board itself.

To help identify conflicts and potential conflicts, the circulation of an annual conflict-of-interest questionnaire is advisable. The *Nonprofit Guidebook* recommends using such a questionnaire,[25] as do the authors. Any identified conflicts should be shared with the entire board, and carefully reexamined in the event the board is called upon to make a decision that implicates the director's personal interest.

Judicial Treatment of Conflict
Transactions in the Nonprofit Context

In an important case, the Delaware Supreme Court determined how the law of Delaware would treat conflict transactions involving Delaware charitable corporations. The decision in *Oberly v. Kirby* allows the board great flexibility in this regard and provides a much higher degree of certainty than existed previously. The

Oberly court's analysis began with the "basic premise" that interested transactions were not "inherently wrong," even if approved by the board of a charitable, as opposed to for-profit, corporation.[26]

Approval by Disinterested Directors

The court first held that approval of an interested transaction by a truly independent committee of directors of a charitable corporation would have the same protective effect afforded by statute to a for-profit corporation, i.e., it would extend to the transaction the presumptions of regularity inherent in the business judgment rule and shift to the attorney general or other interested party attacking the transaction the burden of demonstrating why the presumptions inherent in the rule should not apply. To be sure, the court made clear that the trial court's review of the work of an independent committee of a charitable corporation in conflict transactions would be "more searching" than its review of the work of an independent committee of for-profit directors, because of the "special duty" of charitable fiduciaries "to protect and advance" the charitable purpose of the corporation.[27] And where the attorney general could show that even completely independent directors approved a transaction that was a "clear threat" to the charitable purpose or the assets of the corporation, that approval would be considered ultra vires and not binding.[28] Nonetheless, independent director approval of such a transaction would shift the burden of proof to the party attacking the transaction, a potentially significant difference.

Judicial Scrutiny

The court also held that, as in the case with for-profit corporations, even an interested transaction not approved by independent directors could be upheld if the corporation were able to demonstrate its fairness. Although the attorney general always has the power (and, under Delaware law, the duty) to challenge any interested transaction not approved by independent directors as detrimental to the charitable corporation, a transaction that was objectively fair to the corporation, and that did no harm to the entity or its beneficiaries, would be upheld even though the directors approving the transaction were otherwise interested in the outcome. Of course, as in the case of for-profit corporation law, in the event the corporation was unable to demonstrate the fairness of the transaction, directors could be held liable in respect of that transaction. In addition, upon a finding of breach of duty, the court has the power to remove directors of a nonprofit charitable corporation.

Cooperatives and Mutual Benefit Corporations

As pointed out previously, nonprofit corporations are not all charitable, religious, or educational in nature. Cooperatives and other mutual benefit societies often are organized in corporate form as nonprofit (and often nonstock) membership corporations. Governance of cooperative corporations often presents special challenges, especially in light of the conflicts of interest often inherent in the fabric of such corporations.

The Cooperative Corporation

Formation of cooperatives may be tax driven[29] or driven instead by a need to pool purchasing or selling power.[30] The leading author on the subject defines a cooperative corporation as a "democratic association of persons organized to furnish themselves an economic service under a plan that eliminates entrepreneur profit and that provides for substantial equality in ownership and control."[31] Cooperatives almost universally limit membership to those who avail themselves of the services offered by the entity. In addition, directors ordinarily are chosen only from among the members of the corporation.[32]

The leading treatise writer lists several principal characteristics of a cooperative:

- control of and ownership by each member is substantially equal;
- members are limited to those who do business with the cooperative;
- transfer of ownership interests is prohibited or limited;
- capital investment receives either no return or a limited return;
- economic benefits pass to the members on a substantially equal basis or on the basis of their patronage of the cooperative;
- members are not personally liable for obligations of the cooperative in the absence of a direct undertaking or authorization by them;
- death, bankruptcy, or withdrawal of one or more members does not terminate the cooperative; and
- services of the cooperative are furnished primarily (and sometimes exclusively) for the use of the members.[33]

No single one of the foregoing list of characteristics is controlling, and a cooperative need not (and normally does not) possess all of the foregoing characteristics.

Duties of Directors of Cooperative Corporations

Directors of an incorporated cooperative owe the members of the cooperative all the duties owed to stockholders of a for-profit organization.[34] In addition, tax law or the charter of the cooperative may impose an additional duty—the duty to declare or defer annual patronage dividends to the members of the organization.[35] Although directors of for-profit corporations often consider whether or not corporate earnings should be distributed as dividends or retained, for at least some classes of cooperatives, the decision whether to allocate or pay patronage dividends must be made formally at least annually.

The director's duty of disclosure to members of the cooperative presents interesting problems in the cooperative context. In the for-profit corporation, for example, Delaware law imposes a duty to disclose in connection with the solicitation of stockholders for action at a meeting. In the case of cooperatives, however, some statutes require annual financial reports and related disclosure. Where a cooperative board is controlled by some, but not all, members of the cooperative, interesting disclosure issues arise. The leading treatise writer on the subject has stated that directors of a cooperative "have the duty of keeping the members informed as to the general activities of the cooperative."[36] Unfortunately, this truism provides little practical guidance regarding whether the director of a cooperative has disclosure obligations that differ from those of the director of a for-profit corporation.

While most state law is in accord that there is no duty of disclosure that arises outside the context where stockholders or members are asked to take some action, an issue that frequently arises in cooperative organizations appears in the context where a disparity of information exists between members with board representation and those without. There is little, if any, law on the issue. One safely could assume that judges called upon to decide such cases would fall back on more familiar disclosure law concepts under state and federal law. Under traditional securities law concepts, for example, it would not be extraordinary for a court to hold that the director of the cooperative doing business with another member of the cooperative could be liable for using inside information the director had to his or her benefit and the detriment of the other cooperative member. Directors of a cooperative should be especially sensitive to making use of information learned as a director to the benefit of the director or his or her employer.

Special Governance Considerations

Although directors of a cooperative, like directors chosen by special constituencies in for-profit corporations, owe a duty to act in the best interests of the entity as a whole and not merely in the interest of the member who caused them to be elected, the ordinary cooperative board may be a body constantly facing the need to make decisions that directly impact each member. Where, as in the case with most cooperatives, the board of directors of the organization is made up largely of member representatives or employees of members, the potential for conflicts of interest in the governance of the cooperative becomes evident.

For example, while the business executive who sits on the board of a for-profit manufacturing corporation has little if any financial interest (except perhaps indirectly as a stockholder) in the board's decision to institute a new pricing policy for the corporation's products, the director of a cooperative organization, if chosen as a representative of a member of the cooperative, may have a significant personal interest in the same pricing decision made by the cooperative board. Because of the nature of cooperatives, many of the decisions made by the board of the organization will have, to one degree or another, a direct impact upon members of the cooperative.

This fundamental interest in so many basic decisions made by the cooperative organization sets governance of such entities apart from most for-profit enterprises. The reality of corporate governance in most cooperatives is that directors are likely to find that they regularly are called upon to make corporate decisions that will impact them directly, or the member organization with which they are associated.

Moreover, while some cooperatives distribute voting power among members of the organization on a per-capita basis, others choose to tie voting rights to patronage in the cooperative. In the later type of organization, larger members will wield disproportionate power on corporate governance issues, notwithstanding the basic notion that all members of a cooperative should receive equal treatment to the extent practicable.

The built-in conflicts of interest apparent in the cooperative structure do not excuse the board from acting in the good faith and disinterested pursuit of the best interests of the organization. As with charitable corporations, although interested transactions are not "inherently wrong," without approval by disinterested directors, the burden will rest with the directors to demonstrate the fairness of a conflicted transaction if challenged, unless the matter is put to a vote of members of the cooperative.[37]

The presence of independent directors on the board of a cooperative often may serve salutary purposes. Although the governance of most such organizations reflects the membership of the organization, the presence of even a few truly independent and active directors may, as a practical matter, help the board of the organization to focus on the well-being of the cooperative as a whole, rather than more parochial interests. In addition, the ability to refer sensitive or particularly controversial decisions to an outsider-dominated committee may provide a layer of protection from liability not present in the absence of truly outside directors. While the authors advocate a cooperative board structure comprised of a substantial number (and, in appropriate cases, even a majority) of outside, nonmember directors, even a small minority of thoughtful and outspoken outsiders may have a material beneficial impact on the governance of many cooperatives.

As in the case with for-profit corporations, the courts have held that a member of a cooperative organization is entitled to bring derivative litigation to enforce the rights of the organization vis-à-vis its directors,[38] and to seek to impose damages upon members of the board of the organization for losses resulting to members because of improper management.[39] Thus, the director of a cooperative organization is well advised to approach his or her responsibilities as director with all of the thoroughness and thoughtfulness he or she would bring to the directorship of a public, for-profit corporation.

Special Tax Considerations in Nonprofit Governance

As noted before, the penalties provided under the IRC for noncompliance with the regulations relating to nonprofit corporations can be quite severe, including the revocation of the organization's tax-exempt status. Recognizing that this is often a draconian step with adverse social consequences, some have advocated the development of alternative, less severe sanctions, such as special fines to be imposed on individual directors.[40] At press time, this idea is receiving serious study, both by the Internal Revenue Service (IRS) and outside lobbies and study groups. So-called "intermediate sanctions" currently being debated would avoid the loss of an organization's tax-exempt status in certain cases of private benefit or inurement, but would visit stiff fines on individual directors. In some of the more recent proposals, the fines levied would not be expressly subject to indemnification.

At the same time, the IRS is conducting a nationally coordinated audit program of major nonprofit hospital corporations across the country, and recently has become active in the review of municipal bond issuers (in many cases such bonds are issued for nonprofit organizations).[41]

In light of greatly increased attention to nonprofit organizations and financings, the director of a nonprofit corporation must pay special heed to tax matters affecting the exempt status of the corporation. Considering recent proposals to levy nonindemnifiable fines on directors of such organizations, it may be that a director's exposure to personal liability could be greater in certain *non*profit organizations than in for-profit organizations. These developments should be closely followed by the directors of all major nonprofit institutions.

Notes

1. *Developments in the Law—Nonprofit Corporations,* 105 HARV. L. REV. 1578, 1581 (May 1992).

2. In 1993, the Nonprofit Corporations Committee of the ABA Section of Business Law published the GUIDEBOOK FOR DIRECTORS OF NONPROFIT CORPORATIONS (George W. Overton, ed. 1993) [hereinafter "NONPROFIT GUIDEBOOK at ___"]. The approach taken in the NONPROFIT GUIDEBOOK is similar to that of the CORPORATE DIRECTOR'S GUIDEBOOK, which was written for directors of for-profit corporations. ABA COMM. ON CORP. LAWS, CORPORATE DIRECTOR'S GUIDEBOOK (Section of Business Law, 2d ed. 1994), *reprinted in* 49 BUS. LAW. 1243 (May 1994). The NONPROFIT GUIDEBOOK is one of the very few modern resources available to directors of and counsel to nonprofit corporations.

3. *See, e.g.,* Internal Revenue Code of 1986, as amended [hereinafter "I.R.C."], 26 U.S.C. § 501(c).

4. *See, e.g.,* I.R.C. Section 501(e), providing for tax exemption for enumerated types of single-purpose corporations. Unlike other Section 501(c) corporations, which simply may be liable to pay a tax on income generated by activities unrelated to the corporation's tax-exempt purpose (the so-called tax on "unrelated business taxable income"), a corporation subject to Section

501(e) may put its entire tax-exempt status at risk by engaging in activities unrelated to its exempt purpose. *See, e.g.,* Florida Hospital Trust Fund v. Commissioner of Internal Revenue, No. 94-3377 (11th Cir. Jan. 2, 1996).

5. Nonprofit Guidebook, *supra* note 2, at 10.

6. Lisa A. Runquist, Responsibilities and Duties of Directors of Nonprofit Corporations: Corporate Issues (unpublished paper, 1992 ABA Annual Meeting).

7. *See* Oberly v. Kirby, 592 A.2d 445, 461–62 (Del. 1991).

8. Subcomm. on the Model Nonprofit Corporation Law of the ABA Business Law Section, Revised Model Nonprofit Corporation Act § 8.31 (1988).

9. Scott Harshbarger, *The Attorney General's Guide for Board Members of Charitable Organizations,* at 1.

10. Oberly v. Kirby, 592 A.2d 445, 462 (Del. 1991).

11. Letter Agreement dated March 23, 1992, between the Attorney General of the Commonwealth of Massachusetts and Berkshire Health Systems, Inc., at 3 [hereinafter "Berkshire Governance Agreement at ___"].

12. Note that some states have passed statutes sheltering *volunteer* directors of nonprofit corporations from certain types of liability. *See, e.g.,* 10 Del. Code Ann. § 8133. Even under these statutes, however, the director who receives any compensation or other benefit for serving on the nonprofit board may not be protected from liability. *See* Lisa A. Runquist, Responsibilities and Duties of Directors of Nonprofit Corporations: Corporate Issues 10 (unpublished paper, 1992 ABA Annual Meeting); *and cf.* Charles Tremper, *Volunteers Vulnerable,* 4 Bus. Law Today 22 (Nov./Dec. 1994); *Developments in the Law — Nonprofit Corporations,* 105 Harv. L. Rev. 1578, 1594 (May 1992). In addition, some statutes, such as Delaware's, do not extend the protection from liability to grossly negligent conduct. *See* 10 Del. Code Ann. § 8113(d).

13. Nonprofit Guidebook, *supra* note 2, at Chapter I (C).

14. Oberly v. Kirby, 592 A.2d at 458.

15. *Id.* at 462.

16. Nonprofit Guidebook, *supra* note 2, at 27.

17. The authors participated in one of these somewhat unusual fights for control of a nonstock membership entity. Needless to say, such a contest poses special problems and challenges.

18. Oberly v. Kirby, 592 A.2d at 462.

19. *Id.* at 469 n.18.

20. *Id.*

21. Berkshire Governance Agreement, *supra* note 11.

22. Oberly v. Kirby, 592 A.2d at 467; *and cf.* Model Business Corporation Act Ann. § 8.30(e) (3d ed. 1994).

23. Model Act § 8.30(e).

24. *See* 8 Del. Code Ann. § 144.

25. Nonprofit Guidebook, *supra* note 2, at 29–30.

26. Oberly v. Kirby, 592 A.2d at 467.

27. *Id.* at 468 n.17.

28. *Id.*

29. *See* I.R.C. Section 501(e), providing tax-exempt status to certain types of single-purpose cooperative organizations.

30. *See generally* ISRAEL PACKEL, THE ORGANIZATION AND OPERATION OF CO-OPERATIVES (4th ed. 1970) [hereinafter "PACKEL at ___"].

31. PACKEL at 2 (footnote omitted).

32. PACKEL at 126–27. To be sure, not every cooperative board is composed entirely of member representatives. Some also include independent outside directors. Because of the special nature of the cooperative, however, such boards are in the minority, and where independent directors serve, they rarely make up a majority of the members of the board.

33. PACKEL at 4, 5.

34. PACKEL at 130.

35. *See, e.g.,* I.R.C. Section 501(e); PACKEL at 130.

36. PACKEL at 130.

37. As noted before, in the case of a charitable organization, it is either impractical or not meaningful to seek a vote of members of the organization in respect of a conflict transaction in light of the strong public interest in such organizations and the interests of the beneficiaries of the organization.

In a cooperative, however, the membership usually is available to vote on such a transaction, exactly as are stockholders of a for-profit corporation. Although not specifically covered in the case law or many state statutes, in light of the widespread recognition of the benefits of a stockholder vote in for-profit conflict transactions, the authors believe there would be no reason why a court would not treat identically the informed vote of members of a cooperative.

38. *See* cases collected by PACKEL at 122 nn.66, *et seq.*

39. PACKEL at 123; *see also* Briggs v. Spaulding, 141 U.S. 132 (1891).

40. *See Developments in the Law—Nonprofit Corporations,* 105 HARV. L. REV. 1578, 1607, *et seq.* (May 1992).

41. *See, e.g.,* John Connor, *Support Grows for IRS Disclosure of Muni Actions,* WALL ST. J., Apr. 11, 1994, at C22: *IRS Studies Naming Munis Deemed to Fail Tax-Exemption Tests,* WALL ST. J., May 6, 1994, at B5D.

CHAPTER 8

Indemnification, Exculpation, and Liability Insurance

Over the past ten or more years, there has been an explosion of litigation against corporate managers, with the result that the exposure of directors to liability has increased significantly. Since the celebrated Trans Union case in 1985,[1] where directors were found personally liable in damages for gross negligence as a result of their haste in approving a merger transaction, multimillion-dollar settlements of class-action lawsuits have become more frequent.[2] The primary areas of exposure include violations of the federal securities laws, corporate takeover litigation, environmental protection laws, and employment discrimination suits.[3]

In response to the Trans Union case, there was a strong demand by directors and persons approached to fill board seats for increased protection from personal liability. State legislatures responded with a variety of remedial legislation. Various forms of protection for directors have evolved, many of which were not available earlier, including statutory indemnification, contractual indemnification, exculpation, and liability insurance, all of which can be combined to protect directors to the fullest extent possible. Each are addressed in this chapter.

Statutory Indemnification

All states have enacted indemnification statutes. The law of the state of incorporation will determine substantive issues relating to indemnification. Almost half of the jurisdictions follow the Delaware model[4] and, accordingly, we focus our discussion on indemnification on that statute.

Statutory Provisions

The Delaware indemnification statute broadly defines the class of persons entitled to indemnification to include any person made, or threatened to be made, a party to a threatened, pending, or completed proceeding (whether a civil, criminal, individual, or derivative proceeding) by reason of the fact that he or she is or was a director, officer, employee, or agent of the corporation.[5] The statute provides for mandatory indemnification in the event the director is successful "on the merits or otherwise."[6] Even if not wholly successful in defending themselves, under Delaware law claimants nevertheless are entitled to partial indemnification if successful on a portion of the action.[7] In comparison, the Model Act requires that a director be "wholly successful, on the merits or otherwise."[8]

Indemnification of directors' litigation defense costs can be made at any time. The obligation of the corporation to indemnify is fixed at the conclusion of litigation when the result is known. Often, however, persons covered under the statute request the corporation to advance monies to pay lawyers' fees and litigation costs as incurred. Prior to advancing litigation expenses to a director, the company is not required to make a determination of eligibility to indemnification under the statute.[9] Indeed, where a corporate bylaw makes expense advancement mandatory, under Delaware law, a director's right to have his or her litigation expenses paid by the corporation in advance of the disposition of the proceeding depends only upon receipt of an undertaking from the director to repay to the corporation the amount advanced if it is ultimately determined that the individual is not entitled to indemnification.[10]

Of importance to directors and other covered individuals is that the Delaware statute includes a nonexclusivity clause providing that the statutory right to indemnification shall not be deemed exclusive of any other right to which those indemnified may be entitled.[11] The statute, therefore, permits an expansion of indemnification rights through agreements, bylaws, charter provisions, or corporate resolutions. The statute also authorizes the corporation to purchase insurance (commonly referred to as directors' and officers' liability [D&O] insurance) against any liability that could be asserted against a director in his or her capacity as director or arising out of his or her status as such whether or not the corporation would have the power to indemnify the director against such liability under the statute.

Prerequisites for Indemnification

Director or Officer Status

The first requirement for indemnification under Delaware law is that the director is sued (or suit is threatened against a director) because of his or her position as a director of the corporation. Indeed, as in most jurisdictions, recovery of expenses by directors or others covered depends upon their being involved in the action by reason of "being or having been a director, [officer, employee or agent]."[12]

"Good Faith"

The second prerequisite to indemnification is that the director must have "acted in good faith and in a manner he reasonably believed to be in or not opposed to the best interests of the corporation. . . ."[13] Although the Delaware legislature did not attempt to define "good faith," the drafters of the Model Act explain that under their indemnification provision, the concept of good faith involves a subjective test, which would include "a mistake in judgment," even if the challenged decision was made unwisely by objective standards.[14] Commentators have suggested that both the "good faith" and "reasonable belief" standards are premised on the concept of the duty of loyalty, not on the duty of care.[15] Thus, directors are entitled to indemnification "unless they fail to meet minimum qualifications touching upon the concept of wrongdoing."[16] Put differently, a director who has demonstrated "a reckless indifference to or a deliberate disregard of the interests of the whole body of stockholders" cannot be said to have acted in "good faith" and is not entitled to indemnification.[17]

"Reasonable Belief"

The third and final prerequisite to indemnification under the Delaware statute is that the director also must have acted in a manner that he or she "reasonably believed" was "in or not opposed to the best interests of the corporation." The element of "reasonable belief" is simply another aspect of examining the bona fides of director action as being genuinely motivated by the best interests of the corporate enterprise rather than the director's own interest.[18] Two commentators on the Delaware statute (both of whom participated in its drafting) have written:

The phrase "or not opposed to" was included to cover the case where a director is engaged in a purely personal transaction, such as a purchase or sale for his own account of stock of the corporation or a purchase of other property, and reasonably believed that the corporation had no interest in the subject matter of his action. Should liability to the corporation be asserted against the director, based on such transaction and the fact that he was a director, he could be indemnified. This would apply, among other situations, where the director is charged with having diverted to himself a corporate opportunity and where he bought and/or sold stock of the corporation.[19]

If a director meets these three prerequisites, he or she has satisfied the threshold requirements of the Delaware statute. Of course, ultimate entitlement to indemnification depends on meeting the statutory requirement of a successful defense. Moreover, additional considerations apply when the claim is based on the federal securities laws, which considerations are discussed in the following section.

Status Suits and Public Policy

Because the federal securities laws constitute one of the primary sources for director and officer liability—particularly the "catchall" antifraud provisions of Section 10(b) of the Securities Exchange Act of 1934 (the "1934 Act") and Rule 10b-5—the question arises whether the Delaware indemnification statute is sufficiently broad to provide protection for violations of such laws. As one commentator has noted:

> Some types of insider trading might be held to be "opposed to the best interest of the corporation"—obviously where the corporation itself is the victim and perhaps where public knowledge of the insider's conduct would tarnish the reputation of the company's management. However, in the circumstances disclosed by most suits under Section 10(b) or 16(b), the insider's conduct would not seem to affect the company one way or another.[20]

Such suits have been called "status suits" because they focus on the indemnitee's corporate office rather than on any acts taken in an official capacity.[21] In *Merritt-Chapman*, an early Delaware case to address the issue, the court ruled that the chairman of the board and president of a subsidiary corporation, who served in those positions because of an employment agreement with the parent corporation, was entitled to indemnification for expenses incurred in successfully defending against charges that he violated Rule 10b-5.[22]

The Delaware statute attempts to resolve ambiguities in favor of the indemnitee by providing that an insider may be indemnified in a suit brought by an outside buyer or seller of stock as long as the insider was acting in good faith and "in a manner . . . *not opposed to* the best interests of the corporation."[23] Thus, the statute is said to confirm the result of an older case[24] that sustained indemnification for expenses incurred by an officer in an SEC investigation of possible criminal violations of the federal securities statutes, where the investigation was "ultimately closed to the satisfaction of" the corporation.[25]

While the Delaware legislature likely intended the Delaware indemnification statute to authorize indemnification for certain violations of the federal securities laws, the necessary question to be answered is whether the protection authorized by the statute is consistent with federal policy. In *Mooney v. Willys-Overland Motors, Inc.*, decided under the nonexclusive section of the original Delaware indemnification statute, the federal appeals court stated that the Delaware statute was limited by public policy and that the nonexclusive clause could not be read to authorize any and all indemnification.[26]

The general rule that has developed is that indemnification is not permitted when the party seeking to be indemnified has acted intentionally or recklessly in violation of the federal securities laws and generally is barred even when a party is merely negligent.[27] Moreover, the public policy that indemnification is unavailable for federal securities laws violations appears inapplicable without an adjudication of willfulness, recklessness, or criminal conduct.[28]

In contrast to the federal securities laws, some federal statutes expressly reflect public policy to permit indemnification. For example, the Comprehensive Environmental Response, Compensation, and Liability Act (CERCLA) of 1980 provides that "[n]othing in this subsection shall bar any agreement to insure, hold harmless, or indemnify a party to such agreement for any liability under this section."[29] Similarly, although the Employee Retirement Income Security Act (ERISA) of 1974 prohibits an agreement relieving a fiduciary from responsibility or liability as against public policy, it does not preclude indemnification by an employer who sponsors a plan subject to that Act.[30] In concert with these statutes, both the Delaware statute and the Model Act authorize indemnification of persons acting with respect to employee benefit plans.[31]

Contractual Indemnification

The Delaware statute contains a nonexclusive provision permitting a corporation to indemnify by contract its directors under circumstances not defined in the statute.[32]

Independent Legal Ground

To obtain indemnification beyond the statutory provisions, "an independent legal ground . . . must be shown in every case."[33] Courts in Delaware and in other jurisdictions have recognized that corporations can grant indemnification rights beyond those expressly provided for in the statute.[34] Indeed, the third circuit, interpreting a predecessor Delaware statute, stated:

> We do not think that public policy requires that the Delaware statute be construed as controlling every conceivable situation which in one aspect may be called indemnification for litigation expenses. . . . Where there exists, as there does here, an independent ground for the payment of litigation expenses, we see no reason to make an overriding reference to the statute.[35]

Similarly, another court has suggested that "there may be an agreement to indemnify for legal expenses which is not founded in, or limited by, the other provisions of the statute."[36] The court went on to qualify that statement, however, when it said "it is generally accepted that an agreement to indemnify . . . to survive into enforceability, must be able to withstand an attack on grounds of policy or basic equity, that is, a defense amounting to illegality. . . ."[37]

Public Policy

Some commentators have expressed concern that the nonexclusive provision of the Delaware indemnification statute (and similar provisions in other statutes) could provide the basis for corporate indemnification practices that go beyond the limits of public policy.[38] The Model Act addresses this issue by precluding indemnification beyond the scope of the statute.[39] Other commentators have suggested that the statute itself can be read to embody the public policy limitations on indemnification.[40] The issue was addressed by the U.S. District Court for the Southern District of New York. In *Waltuch v. Conticommodity Service, Inc.*, the court held that the nonexclusive provision of the Delaware statute "does not permit indemnification without regard to the limitations set forth in the other subsections of Section 145."[41]

Conversely, there is authority for the proposition that rights created under Delaware's nonexclusive provision are not limited by the rest of the statute. One court, construing a bylaw under the Delaware statute that required a corporation to indemnify "to the full extent permitted by law," found that the bylaw made indemnification of the directors "the rule rather than the exception" and declared that the corporate bylaw had supplanted the "backstop" provisions of the statute.[42] The court concluded that the procedures detailed in the statute for determining entitlement to indemnification apply only when a company has elected to indemnify pursuant to those backstop provisions. The court reasoned that because the company had chosen to adopt a bylaw that broadened its ability to indemnify its directors and officers, the company was not required to satisfy the procedures established in the statute "or even to make an evaluation of the directors' and officers' actions."[43] Whether or not a Delaware court would define the outer limits of the authority provided in the nonexclusive provision this broadly, or accept the view set forth by the *Waltuch* court, the statute clearly provides support for wide-ranging agreements or bylaws that broaden or enlarge upon indemnification rights granted in the various other subsections.

Typical Provisions

Regardless of where the limitations on enforceability are drawn, it generally is agreed that the nonexclusive provision provides general authorization for the adoption of various procedures making indemnification more favorable for the indemnitee. For example, indemnification agreements or bylaws could provide for: (1) mandatory indemnification unless prohibited by statute; (2) mandatory advancement of expenses, which the indemnitee can, in many instances, obtain on demand; (3) accelerated procedures for the "determination" required by Section 145(d) to be made "in the specific case"; (4) litigation "appeal" rights of the indemnitee in the event of an unfavorable determination; (5) procedures under which a favorable determination will be deemed to have been made under circumstances where the board fails or refuses to act; (6) reasonable funding mechanisms; and (7) other provisions.[44]

While many of these provisions have not yet been tested in the courts and no guarantee can be given that they will be upheld, there is authority for making mandatory the permissive provisions of the statute when the statutory requirements have been satisfied.[45] Indeed, the mandatory advancement of litigation expenses pursuant to an indemnification agreement was expressly approved by the Delaware Supreme Court in a suit involving alleged violation of Section 16(b) of the 1934 Act.[46]

In making expense advancement mandatory, it is critical to provide an express provision in the contract for this advancement, independent of any right to indemnification. One Delaware court has held that a provision that stated merely that the corporation *"shall indemnify* its directors . . . to the extent permitted by the General Corporation Law of Delaware" could not be read to make mandatory the advancement of litigation expenses, which the court found to be a separate and distinct right.[47] Without an express provision explicitly mandating advancement of expenses, the court determined that the company was free to determine whether, in light of all the circumstances, the advancement of expenses requested would be in the best interests of the corporation.[48] Delaware recently amended its statute to provide that expense advancement issues may be "summarily" determined by the Delaware Court of Chancery, assuring that such disputes are resolved quickly.[49]

Other contractual agreements currently in use include funding mechanisms, such as a trust or letter of credit, thus guaranteeing that funds will be available in the event it is determined that the indemnitee has a clear right under the agreement to be indemnified. Such a contractual funding mechanism was specifically upheld in an Illinois case decided under the Delaware statute.[50]

While contractual indemnification agreements are no substitute for insurance, they do provide an additional measure of protection for directors if insurance is not available.[51] Other benefits of contractual agreements, which could be of particular importance in a change of control situation, include: (1) placing the burden of proving that the applicable statutory standards have not been met on the corporation; (2) creating the right to recover expenses of prosecuting a claim for indemnification; (3) providing for a right to bring suit against the corporation if a claim for indemnification is not paid within a specified time; and (4) providing for indemnification and the advancement of expenses in connection with suits initiated by the director or officer if authorized by the board of directors.[52]

Exculpation

In 1986, the Delaware legislature adopted legislation authorizing charter provisions reducing or eliminating a director's monetary liability for damages in certain circumstances.[53] The purpose of the provision was to enable a corporation to eliminate or limit personal liability for violations of a director's fiduciary duty of care.[54] Most states have adopted similar provisions authorizing the adoption of charter provisions either reducing or eliminating a director's personal liability.[55] All of these statutes contain exceptions in which the director may not be relieved of liability.

Statutory Provisions

The Delaware statute provides that the certificate of incorporation may include "[a] provision eliminating or limiting the personal liability of a director to the corporation or its stockholders for monetary damages for breach of fiduciary duty as a director. . . ."[56] The statute is an enabling provision only and, in the case of an existing corporation, would require a shareholder vote to implement. The statute also provides that any provision so adopted has prospective effect only and applies only to directors, not officers, employees, or agents, and then only to directors acting as directors.

Some corporations have elected to adopt a provision that essentially tracks the statute. Others have couched their provisions in broader language to provide for elimination of director liability to the fullest extent permitted by law. Although the statute offers the option of providing a "cap" on director liability, most corporations utilizing the statute to date have opted for complete elimination of liability.[57]

Statutory Limitations on Exculpation

The Delaware statute provides that no exculpatory provision can eliminate or limit a director's liability for: (1) any breach of the director's duty of loyalty; (2) acts or omissions not in good faith or that involve intentional misconduct or a knowing violation of law;

(3) willful or negligent conduct in paying dividends or repurchasing stock out of other than lawfully available funds; or (4) any transaction from which the director derives an improper personal benefit.[58] Effectively, therefore, the statutory provision provides protection to directors only for breaches of the duty of care.

Moreover, the official commentary to the statute makes it clear that an exculpatory provision may eliminate only the director's personal *liability* and does not eliminate the director's duty of care itself. Such a provision should have no effect on the availability of equitable remedies, such as an injunction or rescission, where a plaintiff is able to demonstrate a breach of the fiduciary duty of care.[59]

Directors' and Officers' Insurance

The Need for Insurance

Directors and officers (D&O) liability insurance has three primary functions: to fill in the gaps where indemnification is legally unavailable; to provide coverage where indemnification is legally permissible but is otherwise unavailable because the corporation either is unable or unwilling to indemnify; and to reimburse the corporation for amounts it pays to indemnify.

Into the first category fall judgments or amounts paid in settlement in a derivative suit, liability for violations of the federal securities laws, and situations in which for one reason or another the director cannot satisfy the statutory standards of "good faith" and "reasonable belief."[60] The second category covers those situations where the corporation is unable to indemnify because of insolvency or where the corporation is unwilling to indemnify because of a change in control.[61] The final category covers contractual obligations of the corporation.

A 1992 survey of practices in the field of D&O liability insurance prepared by The Wyatt Company (the "1992 Survey") found that the projected ultimate average payment to claimants for all claims reported was $3,257,841, with a projected average ultimate legal defense cost of $675,000.[62] If the average payment to claimants is any indication, D&O insurance continues to play an important role in protecting directors and officers from liability. Statutes in every state except Vermont expressly permit a corporation to purchase insurance to protect directors and officers against liability, whether or not the corporation would be entitled to provide indemnification against such liability. In general, the statutes make no effort to define what types of arrangements constitute insurance, nor do they seek to limit the types of activities for which insurance may be obtained.[63]

Typical Policy

Most D&O insurance policies have a two-part structure. The first part of the policy reimburses the corporation for indemnification payments properly and lawfully made; the second part of the policy insures directors and officers in situations where the corporation cannot or will not indemnify them. Most D&O policies are "claims-made" policies that provide protection only for claims made during the time period the policy is in force.

Exclusions

Virtually all D&O policies contain exclusions from coverage. Among the more commonly encountered exclusions are:

1. Deliberate dishonesty
2. Insured v. insured
3. Regulatory agency
4. Personal profit
5. Bodily injury / property damage
6. Violation of Section 16(b) of the Securities Exchange Act of 1934
7. Libel and slander
8. Liability for environmental pollution
9. ERISA liability
10. Pending or prior litigation
11. Failure to maintain insurance
12. Illegal payments or commissions[64]

There are other limitations on coverage that are not included in the "exclusions" section but are set forth in the policy's "definitions" section. Most policies, for example, define "loss" in such a way as to exclude, among other things, civil or criminal fines or penalties imposed by law and matters that may be deemed uninsurable under the law pursuant to which the policy will be construed.[65] The term "wrongful act" generally is defined to apply to breaches of duty by the directors or officers in their respective capacities as such or any matter claimed against them solely by reason of their status as directors or officers. Such a definition has been interpreted to be "broad enough to include litigation under the 1934 Act arising out of an insider's trading for his own benefit."[66] Moreover, although the SEC opposes indemnification for violations of the Securities Act of 1933 as being contrary to public policy, it apparently does not consider insurance for such liabilities to be per se objectionable.[67]

The retrenchment in the D&O insurance market in the 1980s forced some companies to attempt to develop new ways of protecting directors and officers against liability. One such effort was the formation of wholly owned insurance subsidiaries. Some commentators have suggested, however, there is a possibility that such captive insurers will be found to violate the intent of Section 145.[68] The problem is that a "captive" insurance company may not spread the risk and, because risk spreading is a primary characteristic of insurance, such "insurance" may be regarded as indemnification, not insurance. To the extent that coverage is permitted for liability that falls outside the scope of permissible indemnification, such coverage may be deemed to violate the public policy of the statute. Insurance pools, by which a number of companies join together to form an insurance subsidiary that insures the members of the group, are another effort to provide the needed coverage.

As demonstrated previously, applicable law allows for construction of a safety net for directors who face ever-increasingly litigious constituencies. Every individual considering service on any board will want to review carefully the company's indemnification and insurance provisions. Corporate governance practitioners, too, should consider regular reviews of their clients' indemnification and insurance arrangements.

Notes

The authors wish to thank Helen M. Richards, Esq., for her assistance in the preparation of this chapter.

1. Smith v. Van Gorkom, 488 A.2d 858 (Del. 1985).

2. *See, e.g.,* Revlon, Inc. v. MacAndrews & Forbes Holdings, Inc., 506 A.2d 173 (Del. 1985) ($20 million settlement followed ruling by Supreme Court that directors breached their fiduciary duty by issuing a "lockup" option to a "white knight" during hostile takeover bid); PepsiCo, Inc. v. Continental Casualty Co., 640 F. Supp. 656 (S.D.N.Y. 1986) ($22.1 million settlement of shareholders' class action alleging violations of Section 10(b) of Securities Exchange Act of 1934). *See also* DAN A. BAILEY, DIRECTOR AND OFFICER LIABILITY AND INSURANCE: CURRENT DEVELOPMENTS, Second Annual Conference on Directors'

and Officers' Duties and Liabilities, at 1–12 (Nov. 18, 1991) (Institute for International Research) [hereinafter "CURRENT DEVELOPMENTS at ___"] (examples of D&O settlements and judgments ranging from a $9.5 million settlement to a $300 million jury verdict).

3. CURRENT DEVELOPMENTS at 12–29; *see State Farm's $157 Million Settlement Caps Discrimination Suit by 814 Women*, WALL ST. J., Apr. 29, 1992, at A3.

4. MODEL BUSINESS CORPORATION ACT ANN. § 8.50, at 8-309 [hereinafter "MODEL ACT § ___"].

5. 8 DEL. CODE ANN. § 145(d).

6. *Id.* at § 145(c). *See also* Galdi v. Berg, 359 F. Supp. 698 (D. Del. 1973).

7. Merritt-Chapman & Scott Corp. v. Wolfson, 321 A.2d 138 (Del. Super. Ct. 1974).

8. MODEL ACT, *supra* note 4, § 8.52, at 1122.

9. 8 DEL. CODE ANN. § 145(e). *See also* Samuel Arsht, *Indemnification Under Section 145 of the Delaware General Corporation Law*, 3 DEL. J. CORP. L. 176, 177 (1978).

10. The *Model Act* is more stringent and requires a written undertaking to repay the monies advanced and *also* an affirmation of the indemnitee's belief that his or her conduct meets the applicable standard unless the proceeding involves conduct for which liability has been eliminated under the articles of incorporation. MODEL ACT, *supra* note 4, § 8.53(a).

11. 8 DEL. CODE ANN. § 145(f).

12. *Id. See* Hydro-Dynamics, Inc. v. Pope, 708 P.2d 70 (Ariz. 1985) (director and wife who brought derivative action not entitled to indemnification because they sued in their capacity as stockholders); People v. Uran Mining Corp., 206 N.Y.S.2d 455 (N.Y. Sup. Ct. 1960), *aff'd*, 216 N.Y.S.2d 985 (N.Y. App. Div. 1961) (indispensable condition of statute is that defendant must have been made a party to the action by reason of his being or having been a director of the corporation); Sorensen v. Overland Corp., 242 F.2d 70 (3d Cir. 1957) (plaintiff not entitled to indemnification for expenses in defending a lawsuit about a contract between himself and the corporation entered into before plaintiff became a director or officer of the corporation); 13 WILLIAM FLETCHER, CYCLOPEDIA OF THE LAW OF PRIVATE CORPORATIONS § 6045.30 (perm. ed. rev. vol. 1991).

13. 8 DEL. CODE ANN. § 145(a).

14. MODEL ACT, *supra* note 4, § 8.51 official commentary at 1116.

15. WILLIAM E. KNEPPER & DAN A. BAILEY, LIABILITY OF CORPORATE OFFICERS AND DIRECTORS § 20.08, at 662 (4th ed. 1988). It appears, therefore, that even where directors are found to be grossly negligent, they would be eligible for indemnification under the Delaware statute if they acted in good faith. *Id.* The duties of loyalty and care are discussed in detail in Chapter 3.

16. Green v. Westcap Corp., 492 A.2d 260, 264 (Del. Super. Ct. 1985).

17. Allaun v. Consolidated Oil Co., 147 A. 257, 261 (Del. Ch. 1929); *accord* Solash v. Telex Corp., C.A. No. 9518, slip op. at 22–23 (Del. Ch. Jan. 19, 1988). It has been suggested that a corporation facing an indemnification claim should consider whether the director or officer's conduct violated any internal company policy. An interesting issue arises regarding whether conduct violative of

company policy is in "good faith." Robert S. Lavet, *Indemnification of Corporate Directors and Officers in Insider Trading Litigation,* 19 SEC. REG. L. J. 402, 412–13 (1992) [hereinafter *"Insider Trading* at ___"]. Nonetheless, even the most diligent of directors of a large corporation is not likely to know every "corporate policy," and a rule that automatically deprives a director of indemnification for violation of *any* corporate policy may well be unduly harsh in application.

18. *See* Citron v. Fairchild Camera & Instrument Corp., C.A. No. 6085, slip op. at 41 (Del. Ch. May 19, 1988), *aff'd,* 569 A.2d 53 (Del. 1989).

19. Samuel Arsht & Walter Stapleton, Analysis of the 1967 *Amendments to the Delaware Corporation Law, in Corporation* 311, 327 (Prentice-Hall 1967).

20. JOSEPH W. BISHOP, THE LAW OF CORPORATE OFFICERS AND DIRECTORS—INDEMNIFICATION AND INSURANCE § 6.06, at 13–14 (1994 cum. supp.).

21. Section 16(b) of the 1934 Act is designed to prevent the unfair use of information obtained by a director "by reason of his relationship to the issuer." 15 U.S.C. § 78p(b) (1991). The United States Supreme Court held in Chiarella v. United States, 445 U.S. 222 (1980), that liability under Section 10(b) is predicated on the existence of a fiduciary relationship, which gives rise to a disclosure obligation. Under the theory of that decision, when a fiduciary transmits material, nonpublic information that he or she has obtained by virtue of his or her position as a fiduciary to someone who trades in the company's stock on the basis of that information, the fiduciary has breached a fiduciary duty to the uninformed selling shareholders. *Id.* at 235. Thus, a Section 10(b) duty to disclose arises not from mere possession of nonpublic market information but rather from a fiduciary relationship. *Id. See also Insider Trading, supra* note 17, at 404. *But see ALI Principles of Corporate Governance: Analysis and Recommendations,* § 7.19, illustration 4 (1994).

22. 321 A.2d at 142.

23. JOSEPH W. BISHOP, THE LAW OF CORPORATE OFFICERS AND DIRECTORS, *supra* note 20, at § 6.06, at 13. See also 1 MODEL BUSINESS CORP. ACT ANN. § 5, ¶ 2, at 219 (1971) ("phrase 'or not opposed to the best interests of the corporation' was designed to cover proceedings arising out of acts done other than in the capacity of officer or director but arising by reason of status as an officer or director"); Frederic J. Klink, et al., *Liabilities Which Can Be Covered Under State Statutes and Corporate By-Laws,* 27 BUS. LAW. 109, 123 (1972) [hereinafter *"State Statutes* at ___"]; Donald E. Pease, *Indemnification Under Section 145 of the Delaware General Corporation Law,* 3 DEL. J. CORP. L. 167, 170 (1978).

24. Blish v. Thompson Automatic Arms Corp., 64 A.2d 581, 607 (Del. 1948).

25. ERNEST L. FOLK, III, THE DELAWARE GENERAL CORPORATION LAW 99 (1972).

26. 204 F.2d 888, 896 (3d Cir. 1953).

27. Dennis J. Block, et al., *Contribution and Indemnification Under the Federal Securities Laws,* BUS. & SEC. LITIGATOR 3 (Dec. 1990).

28. Cambridge Fund, Inc. v. Abella, 501 F. Supp. 598, 618–19 (S.D.N.Y. 1980). Indeed, the SEC rule governing registration statements filed under the Se-

curities Act of 1933 expressly permits indemnification for expenses incurred in the "successful defense" of a suit brought under the Act. 17 C.F.R. § 229.512(h)(3) (1991). Thus, indemnification for litigation expenses incurred by a former officer and director in defending himself or herself in actions claiming violations of the federal securities acts in connection with an aborted merger, which were settled and dismissed, has been approved by the federal courts. *See* Wisener v. Air Express Int'l Corp., 583 F.2d 579 (2d Cir. 1978); Goldstein v. Alodex Corp., 409 F. Supp. 1201 (E.D. Pa. 1976). Similarly, the New York district court found "public policy" inapplicable to defense costs incurred by directors and officers as a result of an SEC investigation that resulted in charges being brought against the company but not against any of the directors or officers. PepsiCo, Inc. v. Continental Casualty Co., 640 F. Supp. at 660.

29. 42 U.S.C. § 9607(e)(1) (1983). *See also* S. REP. NO. 848, 96th Cong., 2d Sess. at 44 (1980).

30. *See* 29 C.F.R. § 2509.75-4 (1991).

31. 8 DEL. CODE ANN. § 145(i); MODEL ACT, *supra* note 4, § 8.50(2).

32. 8 DEL. CODE ANN. § 145(f); *cf. 1969* MODEL ACT, *supra* note 4, § 5(f).

33. Mooney v. Willys-Overland Motors, Inc., 204 F.2d 888, 896 (3d Cir. 1953) (interpreting a similar predecessor statute).

34. *See, e.g.,* Hibbert v. Hollywood Park, Inc., 457 A.2d 339, 344 (Del. 1983) (former corporate directors were entitled to indemnification for legal fees and related costs with respect to suits filed by them in an unsuccessful bid for reelection under bylaw provision); *Merritt-Chapman*, 321 A.2d at 142 (corporation may pass a bylaw making mandatory the statutory provision for permissive indemnification although the bylaw in question does not do this); *Mooney*, 204 F.2d at 898 (valid termination agreement between director and corporation provided independent ground for indemnification); *PepsiCo*, 640 F. Supp. 656, 661 (relevant bylaw made indemnification of directors and officers the rule rather than the exception, supplanting the "backstop" provisions of Section 145(a) and (b)); Choate, Hall & Stewart v. SCA Servs., Inc., 495 N.E.2d 562, 565 (Mass. App. Ct. 1986) (provision of settlement agreement obliging corporation to indemnify director for his or her legal expenses was authorized under the Delaware statute's nonexclusion provision).

35. 204 F.2d at 896.

36. Choate, Hall, 495 N.E.2d at 565.

37. *Id.* at 566.

38. See BISHOP, LAW OF CORPORATE OFFICERS AND DIRECTORS, *supra* note 20, at § 6.03[1][a]; Joseph F. Johnston, *Corporate Indemnification and Liability Insurance for Directors and Officers*, 33 BUS. LAW. 1993 (1978).

39. MODEL ACT, *supra* note 4, § 8.59. As the official comment points out, this provision would not prevent a corporation from making mandatory what is permissive but would prohibit indemnification for the consequences of bad faith or willful misconduct. *Id.*, official commentary at 1139–40.

40. *See* E. Norman Veasey, et al., *Delaware Supports Directors with a Three-Legged Stool of Limited Liability, Indemnification & Insurance*, 42 BUS. LAW. 399,

414 (Feb. 1987) [hereinafter *Three-Legged Stool*]. *See also State Statutes, supra* note 23, at 127–28 (first five sections of statute are an affirmative statement of the public policy of the State of Delaware and should be so construed).

41. 833 F. Supp. 302, 309 (S.D.N.Y. 1993).

42. *PepsiCo,* 640 F. Supp. at 661.

43. *Id. Cf.* Macmillan, Inc. v. Federal Ins. Co., 741 F. Supp. 1079, 1082–83 and n.2 (S.D.N.Y. 1990) (where bylaw incorporated the standards of conduct set forth in Section 145(a), corporation was required to grant indemnification in accordance with Section 145(d) because bylaw did not supply a procedure that supplanted it).

44. *Three-Legged Stool, supra* note 40, at 415. Such agreements should contain standard severability clauses so that if any provision is declared invalid, the remainder of the agreement will survive.

45. LEWIS BLACK & A. GILCHRIST SPARKS, ANALYSIS OF THE 1986 AMENDMENTS TO THE DELAWARE CORPORATION LAW 313 (Prentice-Hall 1986).

46. Citadel Holding Corp. v. Roven, 603 A.2d 818 (Del. 1992); *see also* Security Am. Corp. v. Walsh, Case, Coale, Brown & Burke, C.A. No. 82-C-2953 (N.D. Ill. Jan. 11, 1985) (applying Delaware statute to mandatory advancement bylaw).

47. Advanced Mining Sys., Inc. v. Fricke, 623 A.2d 82, 84 (Del. Ch. 1992) (citation omitted).

48. *Advanced Mining,* 623 A.2d at 84.

49. 137th Delaware General Assembly, Senate Bill No. 323, *amending* 8 DEL. CODE ANN. § 145(d) and (k).

50. *See* Security Am. Corp. v. Walsh, Case, Coale, Brown & Burke. Particular caution should be exercised in deploying such devices in the face of a threat to control, however, for a court may conclude such action is evidence of entrenchment motive. *See* Tate & Lyle plc v. Staley Continental, Inc., C.A. No. 9813 (Del. Ch. May 9, 1988) (enjoining funding of certain irrevocable trusts).

51. *Three-Legged Stool, supra* note 40, at 416.

52. A. GILCHRIST SPARKS, ET AL., INDEMNIFICATION, DIRECTORS AND OFFICERS LIABILITY INSURANCE AND LIMITATIONS OF DIRECTOR LIABILITY PURSUANT TO STATUTORY AUTHORIZATION: THE LEGAL FRAMEWORK UNDER DELAWARE LAW, 696 PLI/Corp. 941, 959–60 (May 7, 1990) [hereinafter "THE LEGAL FRAMEWORK at ___"].

53. 8 DEL. CODE ANN. § 102(b)(7).

54. Senate Bill No. 533, 133d Legislature, 65 Del. Laws c. 289, official commentary at 2 (1986).

55. MODEL ACT, *supra* note 4, § 8.50, at 8-304 to 8-306.

56. 8 DEL. CODE ANN. § 102(b)(7).

57. "Many Delaware corporations plan to eliminate or limit liability of directors." *American Society of Corporate Secretaries Newsletter,* Nov. 1986, at 1 (reporting results of survey indicating that of 165 companies, only twenty-one indicated an intent to limit liability rather than eliminate it). On the other hand, the ALI Corporate Governance Project provides for a cap on liability for

due-care violations. *ALI Principles, supra* note 21, § 7.19. The ALI Principles would not extend to damages recovered against a director or officer whose conduct involved a knowing and culpable violation of law or enabled the director or his or her associate to derive an improper benefit. *Id.*

58. 8 DEL. CODE ANN. § 102(b)(7).

59. *See* Senate Bill No. 533, 133d Legislature, 65 Del. Laws c. 289, official commentary at 2 (1986). *But cf.* Lennane v. ASK Computer, C.A. No. 11744 (Del. Ch. Oct. 11, 1990), *appeal refused,* 583 A.2d 660 (Del. 1990) (court declines to issue an injunction based on evaluation of the balance of hardships flowing from injunction notwithstanding the preliminary conclusion that plaintiff had demonstrated a breach of the duty of care and a charter provision eliminating director liability for breach of the duty of care).

60. CURRENT DEVELOPMENTS, *supra* note 2, at 50–52.

61. *Three-Legged Stool, supra* note 40, at 419.

62. *ALI Principles, supra* note 21, § 7.20, Reporter's Note 8, at 287. Approximately 65 percent of the claims disclosed in the 1992 survey were closed, of which 20 percent were dropped by the claimant and a majority of those not dropped resulted in no payment to claimants.

63. *ALI Principles, supra* note 21, § 7.20, Reporter's Note 4, at 279–80.

64. *See* CURRENT DEVELOPMENTS, *supra* note 2, at 93–108; and *see ALI Principles, supra* note 21, § 7.20, Reporter's Note 8, at 287–88; THE LEGAL FRAMEWORK, *supra* note 52, at 965–69; JOSEPH F. JOHNSTON, ET AL., CURRENT ISSUES AND PROBLEM AREAS: DIRECTORS' AND OFFICERS' LIABILITY INSURANCE AND INDEMNIFICATION, 3d Tulane Corporate Law Institute 7–9 (Mar. 14–15, 1991).

65. THE LEGAL FRAMEWORK, *supra* note 52, at 966–67.

66. Joseph W. Bishop, *New Problems in Indemnifying and Insuring Directors: Protection Against Liability Under the Federal Securities Laws,* 1972 DUKE L.J. 1153, 1161 (1972).

67. THE LEGAL FRAMEWORK, *supra* note 52, at 970.

68. *Three-Legged Stool, supra* note 40, at 420.

CONCLUSION

Lipton and Lorsch may have been right when they wrote in 1992 that the corporate governance system was not working. On the other hand, they may well have been wrong. The first half of this decade has witnessed tremendous upheaval in corporate governance, as institutional investors finally have come to a working understanding of the enormous influence they can wield on the governance system, and likewise have come to a rough consensus on how they will coordinate action to exert that influence. Counseling directors of large industrial corporations today, one is able to perceive a sense of how pervasive and powerful the institutions have become, as few strategic initiatives are undertaken without giving consideration to how the institutions will view the corporate action.

At the same time, the pervasive judicial and growing regulatory emphasis on structure and process appear to have begun to take hold and bear fruit in the governance arena. For example, the SEC initiatives regarding compensation committees of public corporations, considered radically interventionist in many circles just a few years ago, now have become an accepted part of the governance landscape. Nominating committees, too, have become far more sensitized to director interlocks in selecting candidates for directorship, and many boards have given serious and searching consideration to adoption of the GM Governance Guidelines, or variants of those guidelines. In the transactional arena, directors and their counsel are far more attuned to the importance of process as a critical element of decision making than previously, and the courts have insisted that the process employed in the transactional setting be lively and meaningful and not merely an empty charade.

In our view, the corporate governance system in this country is working, and working better than it has in many years. While we have not conducted rigorous empirical studies to support our conclusion, and such studies are sorely needed in the corporate governance area, as Delaware practitioners in the corporate governance arena, our subjective experience suggests what we believe the empirical evidence would show: Directors are more aware of their responsibilities and more willing to approach those responsibilities with the commitment and sense of duty that sometimes have not been clearly in evidence in the past. In short, the emphasis on better structure and more rigorous process in decision making is beginning to impact positively the substance of the decisions being made leading to tangible results both in the boardroom and the marketplace.

While much of the emphasis in this book has been on process and structure, in our view, the discipline of corporate governance has much to do with both, and both are critical to the qualitatively better decision making demanded of modern boards both by increasingly powerful shareholder groups and an active and assertive Delaware corporate judiciary.

ABOUT THE AUTHORS

Daniel A. Dreisbach practices corporate law at the Wilmington, Delaware, firm of Richards, Layton & Finger, where he is a Director. Mr. Dreisbach has also coauthored *The Board of Directors* (BNA, 1994) and authored articles that have appeared in *INSIGHTS* and the *Corporate Governance Advisor*, among other publications. Mr. Dreisbach holds degrees from the Pennsylvania State University, Lehigh University, and the Temple University School of Law.

Gregory V. Varallo is a member of the Delaware State and American Bar Associations, and is active in the Business Law Section of the ABA. Mr. Varallo practices law in Wilmington, Delaware, at the firm of Richards, Layton & Finger, where he is a Director. Mr. Varallo holds degrees from Temple University School of Law (J.D., 1983) and the University of Pennsylvania (B.A., 1980), and has published numerous articles and contributed to several books, largely in the field of corporate governance and contests for corporate control.